FORBIDDEN PARTNERS

The Incest Taboo in Modern Culture

JAMES B. TWITCHELL

New York   COLUMBIA UNIVERSITY PRESS   1987

Library of Congress Cataloging-in-Publication Data

Twitchell, James B., 1943–
Forbidden partners.

Bibliography: p.
Includes index.
1. Incest—United States   2. Incest in popular
culture—United States.   3. Incest in literature.
4. Incest in art.   I. Title.   II. Title: Incest taboo
in modern culture.
HQ72.U53T85   1986   306.7'77   86-11705
ISBN 0-231-06412-8 (alk. paper)

Book design by Laiying Chong

Columbia University Press
New York   Guildford, Surrey

Copyright © 1987 Columbia University Press

Printed in the United States of America

For
LWT *and* Mary

Contents

Preface

    ALL HUMAN BEINGS are raised in families. Although families can take different structural forms such as the extended family, the stem family, the joint family, or our own nuclear family, which itself is changing into the blended and/or serial family, they are held together by a matrix of rights, expectations, obligations, and role relationships. Some of this cohesion is demanded by biology; however, much is encouraged by culture. Biological factors have to do with the necessities of procreation and are, for the most part, tied to female physiology. All human females have a menstrual, not an estrus cycle and typically have one child at a time, and that child has a nursing period that is relatively intense and time-consuming. Nonbiological factors vary widely but are characterized by one commonality. They are carried from generation to generation by a culture, a communal memory of successful choices, or at least those assumed to be successful. The more important the choice, the more likely it is that the society will explain it as determined by outside forces: by the gods, by fate, by biology.

    No society is exempt. For instance, we in the West have assumed that since the female "must" remove herself from communal activities in order to give birth and to nurse, she "should" remain close to the hearth as a matter of fulfilling her genetic destiny. Since the male has little to do with the reproductive process after insemination, he has no "paternity drive" and should dedicate his energies to extrafamilial endeavors. Don't our bodies reflect these differences? Man is the more muscular and rapid; woman the slower-moving and more precise. Therefore men rule politically (matriarchies flourish in the imaginations of adolescents, not in the societies of humans) and women rule domestically. Such, we say, are the laws of Nature, more specifically of "Mother Nature."

There is great stability in the particular sex roles that have evolved in Western societies. They have made us economically efficient. But we are now realizing that the roles themselves are really a mixture of biological and social factors. In fact, this realization may prove one of the more revolutionary aspects of modern life. True, our patterned transactions do result in part from instinct, drives and reflexes, but they also are the learned preferences of generations. But which conduct is learned, which instinctive, and in what proportions? More perplexing still: if role behavior that we once considered predetermined is really culturally prescribed, how has that behavior been preserved and retaught? And why is it that we want to believe we have no control over certain processes? What is the relationship between license and restraint? What is the nature of inhibition?

Since the rise of the women's movement, social history, and sociobiology, the etiology, let alone efficacy, of habitual behavior has been so often called into question that it is rare to find any student of human life who is willing to invoke biology to explain any but the most obvious differences between the sexes. In fact, many patterned interactions that we have assumed to be instinctual such as territoriality, sexual dominance, jealousy, pecking orders, and the like are now questioned almost as a matter of course. Could these be habits inculcated by generations of repetition? Could these traits be carried by what the sociobiologists call "culturgens?" It has even been suggested that behavior, expectations, and traditions that we assume to have radiated from biological necessity might be considered more appropriately statistical probabilities along an ethnographic curve.

No area of human activity is more interesting to study, and yet more neglected in the humanities, than the codes of reproduction. Here all the unique behavior of the species is focused: kin selection, reciprocal altruism, mate choice, parental

investment, aggression, and social order. We used to think
that these were instinctive transactions. We now know better.
And what of the sex drive itself? How much of it is biological,
how much socialized, how much habit? What does "doing what
comes naturally" mean? Remove a rhesus monkey from his
family, raise him alone through adolescence, and he will not
be able to mate successfully. Would the same also be true of
humans? Is most of what we know about sex learned? If sex
is in the head, how did it get there?

Forbidden Partners focuses on one area of sexual behavior in
one culture for one short period of time. It is my contention
that the unease we feel thinking about, let alone talking about,
incest is to a considerable degree a *learned* behavior, a cultural
conduct, a habit. This does not mean that our anxiety is lessened, or that violations will not be fiercely treated. Just the
opposite is true. As in the case of especially important habitual behavior, incest avoidance is usually presented as instinctual and transgressions are punished as if they were *unnatural*
acts. They are, rather, *uncultural* acts.

I know nothing about the incestuous act in "real life" except
that we hear about it often enough to be profoundly disturbed. Is this because we know more about the hidden family than we did a generation ago? Or are restraints breaking
down? Is the taboo on incest going the way of the taboos on
masturbation and homosexuality? Have we always treated incest with opprobrium? Are we different today than we were a
generation ago? Is there any reason to believe rates of commission are any higher now than in the 1880s? Will knowing
how our great-grandparents responded be of any help in understanding our responses?

In speculating about these and other matters I intend to examine the anxiety of incest as it has been continually refitted
into fictional family structures since the turn of the nineteenth
century. I make no case for our cultural uniqueness or for our
similarity to other cultures, nor do I argue that fiction reveals
fact. I only suggest that if we look at the codified memory of
our recent past—our literature and popular culture—we will
see how our present concern with certain intrafamilial rela-

tions is the predictable, but by no means inevitable, outwork-
ing of bourgeois family dynamics. In other words, the roles
played out in families today are the direct result of romantic
and Victorian concepts of father/mother, sister/brother, and,
most especially, parent/child.

Perhaps I should describe how I came to this topic, as it
may explain my approach and bias. About a decade ago I became interested in why the vampire myth was picked up and
exploited in romantic art as a mythologem for human interactions, and more specifically as an analogy to describe the energy transfer between artist, work of art, and audience. In *The
Living Dead: A Study of the Vampire in Romantic Literature* I attempted to trace the myth in early nineteenth-century literary
culture. The more I thought about the myth, the more I realized that it was not an art myth even in the hands of artists
but rather a popular culture story which had been briefly co-
opted by the poets. The vampire tale was, and still is, essentially a retelling of one of the favorite Western cautionary tales,
"Little Red Riding Hood," with the wolf role fleshed out and
made recognizable not just as human but as paternalistic. The
artistic exploitation was interesting in large measure because
it was so short-lived and because it returned the story to the
folk where it is now endlessly told as the tale of Dracula.

Trying to account for the enduring attraction of the vampire
story led me to write *Dreadful Pleasures: An Anatomy of Modern
Horror*. This study considered not only Dracula but Frankenstein, Dr. Jekyll and Mr. Hyde, the Wolfman, and to a lesser
extent, the Phantom of the Opera and the Hunchback, as well
as all those creatures from black lagoons and outer space. I
argued that certain of these myths have endured because they
teach an important lesson (how to reproduce properly) to an
important audience (the about-to-reproduce adolescents) with
a most powerful stimulus: horror. I contended that horror myths
are primarily incest-forbidding fairy tales instructing the younger
family members whom to avoid sexually in order not to produce monsters. If these myths work no one should wish such
a fate, nor even be willing to contemplate it. In other words,
these stories perform a central biosocial service and we should

be cautious about casting them aside as the sludge of adolescent entertainments. They help instill important habits during a crucial stage of maturation.

In *Forbidden Partners* I am interested in how all media—the gothic and pornographic novel, illustration and painting, the art poem and the folk ballad, the movie, television, the X-rated videocassette, the law, philosophical treatises, advertising, utopian speculations, and in fact all human communication—carry our second most important reproductive message: avoid incest.

The net I've cast is clearly huge and much has slipped through. Often I have been unable to make appropriate comparisons, to label properly, much less to understand what I have caught. But this much seems clear from a culturological perspective. First, if any trait characterizes the human family it is the prohibition of incest. Second, if we want to understand the dynamics of the modern family we will have to study the unfolding of this trait in the nineteenth century as the modern nuclear family takes shape. Other conclusions are less clear: 1) The attraction theories of Freud as well as the aversion theories of Westermarck, while promising simplicity, do not hold up. 2) Parental incest is an act so different in motivation and consequence from sibling incest that it may deserve a separate name and category. 3) The mix-up of the incest taboo, exogamy, and the act itself is symptomatic of our profound ambiguities not just about sex, but about social order. 4) A comparison of nineteenth century English and American expositions will show that even in relatively homogeneous cultures the prohibition can take on different aspects. This is especially true when the treatments attempt to subvert the prohibition, for in so doing the rebel must confront consequences that are often ideologically revealing. 5) Any theory that attempts to be universal will have to find iteration in art and popular culture texts. (As well, I may also show by inadvertent example how much easier it is to have a strong curiosity than a strong thesis.)

Of the many people who have helped me I must single out Vernon Bullough, Judith Lewis Herman, and Marvin Harris for their valuable advice; Peter Thorslev for his provocative study of the continental use of the incest motif as well as his encouragement for my project; Richard Brantley, Anne Dalke, and Melvyn New for pointing out sources I would have otherwise missed; and, most especially, Robin Fox for his unstinting aid. He willingly suffered my ignorance and generously provided many insights, most of which I have eagerly passed off as my own. I am grateful as well to the Division of Sponsored Research at the University of Florida for their financial support.

Forbidden Partners

CHAPTER 1

THE ENIGMA OF INCEST

One very cold night a group of porcupines were huddled together for warmth. However, their spines made proximity uncomfortable, so they moved apart again and got cold. After shuffling repeatedly in and out, they eventually found a distance at which they could still be comfortably warm without getting pricked. This distance they henceforth called decency and good manners.
—the fable of social norms as quoted by Edward O. Wilson, *Sociobiology*

IN APRIL 1977 Victoria Pittorino met the man of her dreams, David Goddu. She was twenty-four, a lab technician trainee with a promising future; he was twenty-two and unemployed, with a troubled past. He had dropped out of high school, fathered a child, run afoul of the law, been wounded in a high-speed police chase, and spent time in jail, but was now struggling to get his life under control. They fell in love. "Love at first sight," said Vicky, and David seemed, if not reformed, at least softened by her presence. It was a physical presence rather like his own: both were about five-foot-five, and stocky, with thick brown hair, slightly down-turned mouths, and similar clefts in their chins. In June they married.

By July Vicky's dream had become a nightmare. Unlike Eve, who awoke to find that her Adam was really wonderful in the flesh, Vicky found out just the opposite. This man's flesh, she was told, was poison. He would have to go. By the end of the summer the state of Massachusetts, home of such fictional trespassers as Hester Prynne and Pierre Glendinning, had annulled the marriage. Incest was charged; they had committed an unspeakable act: they were members of the same family.

David and Vicky knew that somehow their relationship was forbidden, but they didn't know exactly which part was objectionable: love, marriage, or procreation. They had been separated from early childhood by their natural mother. Vicky went to foster parents in Arlington, and David was sent across the state to Holyoke. In 1973 Vicky had gone to the town hall of her birthplace in Lawrence, Massachusetts, and asked to find the name of her natural mother and of her brother whom she vaguely remembered. In the 1970s, with the growing liberalization of adoption procedures, this was not an unusual request. She told the local official that she was tracing her family tree, "like in *Roots*," and was given all the information she wanted, and more. Vicky started to put back together the family her mother had been forced to separate almost two decades earlier. She met her natural mother and later her natural brother, David. They were delighted that Vicky had brought them back together. Her actions promised a fairy tale ending for a separation-from-birth tragedy. What motif in our culture is more powerful than the family reunion? But David and Vicky slowly realized they wanted more than reunion. They wanted to explore what they were experiencing—the physical attraction of lovers. As the *National Enquirer* (July 19, 1979) was to report:

> Every night during the next week, they spoke on the phone for five hours. And when the weekend came, David went to her house for a visit. On Tuesday, April 10, as they both sat watching TV, David nervously turned toward her. That was the magic and frightening moment he kissed her for the very first time. But their happiness was soon dealt a terrible blow. (p. 26)

Their parents, natural as well as adoptive, were not just embarrassed, they were horrified at what they saw happening. Vicky and David were dumbfounded by the response: they had just found their family, and were now losing it again. In fact, it was Vicky's adoptive mother who went down to the courthouse to sign the complaint charging the couple with incest. Why should they be singled out, Vicky and David wanted to know; exactly what had they done that was so wrong?

Their parents' lawyer told them. If they were married they would have children and the children would be "imbeciles." All of the families were Catholic and abortion was out of the question. David said they would not have children; he would have a vasectomy, and subsequently he did. Their lawyer entered with a different concern: David and Vicky had committed a crime and nothing they could do now could change that. The violation did not lie in having children; it was in being married in the first place. They were criminals and the courts would treat them as such. David and Vicky argued that legally they were not siblings. They had been separated by law, raised by legally appointed parents, and legally belonged to different families. The lawyer was proven correct. The court did indeed rule that they were siblings, a ruling based on biology, not on family. Nothing, it seems, is thicker than blood. Referring to laws dating back to 1695, which could have been used to incarcerate them both for up to twenty years, the marriage was annulled by Judge Frances Lappin. Victoria was upset: "You know it's weird, because they want to put you in jail for being in love. Like love is against the law." David was distraught. Not only had he lost his new wife, but once again he had been arrested and booked. They were put on probation but permitted to live together so long as they did not "commit incest." But what that meant was unclear. Were they incestuous if they had sex but did not marry, and nonincestuous if they married, but abstained? David and Vicky went back to where they were residing (in David's six-year old Mercury Capri, as the tabloids reported with Puritanical glee) no longer as husband and wife but as outcasts "living in sin." They spent the rest of the year being besieged by reporters from the local newspapers, *Time*, *Newsweek*, and the *New York Times* before finally selling their story to the *National Enquirer* for $1,000 and reportedly to a Hollywood studio for $75,000.[1]

One hundred and fifty years before David and Victoria

learned the social and legal consequences of violating the "oldest taboo," George Gordon Byron and his half-sister, Augusta, were finding out for themselves. As a teenager away at school George Byron was melancholy and lonely, but at least it was better than life at home. His mother had been a strict, domineering woman who in hysterical fits verbally and physically abused him. George was a pretty boy, almost effeminate, and subject to bouts of depression in which he withdrew and ate compulsively. By his mid-teens he carried over two hundred pounds on his smallish five-foot eight-inch frame. He was also afflicted with a club foot that caused him acute embarrassment, which did not go unobserved by his mother who, when annoyed, referred to him as "the lame brat."

During adolescence, George located his half-sister, from whom he had been separated since early childhood. They started corresponding; as his relationship with his mother became more strained, they became more intimate. Augusta and George shared the same father, now dead, and their letters show that they considered themselves orphans in a hostile world. George even asked Augusta to consider him "not only as *a Brother* but as your warmest and most affectionate *Friend* . . . you are *the nearest relation* I have in *the world both by the ties of Blood and affection*."[2] From all accounts she considered him exactly that. However, the next year she was courted by, and finally married to, her cousin Colonel George Leigh. It would be five years and three daughters later that Augusta would meet her brother again, but when they did meet they became almost inseparable—going to parties, to the theater, and possibly to bed. The Colonel had proved an irresponsible wastrel and George, having grown in stature and maturity, was now a dashing and intense young man of twenty-three. Augusta often came to London from her home near Cambridge and sought solace and comfort from her brother. This was reciprocated: "My sister is in town, which is a great comfort—for, never having been much together, we are naturally more attached to each other."[3]

Like Victoria and David, Augusta and George looked remarkably alike: both were limpid-eyed and fleshy, with pale, almost pallid complexions, full Grecian lips and frowns that could suddenly cloud their full faces. They were also, rather like David and Victoria, aliens in a world that seemed to be passing them by. Maybe it was this sense of adolescent isolation that led to their deepening intimacy, or maybe it was their rebellion against the strictures of religion and society. However it happened, by the end of the summer of 1813 even their few friends knew that their attraction was becoming physical. The circumstantial evidence, especially from George's letters, was almost conclusive proof, if any was called for, that their relationship was crossing the boundaries of decency. Whether or not such proof would ever have held up in court was debatable then, and still is.

Such liaisons between brother and sister have probably occurred since the first separation and later reunion of siblings, but this tabooed affair at the beginning of the nineteenth century was to prove by far the most important in modern Western culture. For George Gordon was in the process of becoming an important personage in the early nineteenth century; he was becoming the first great cultural hero, as well-known and recognized and imitated as any movie star of today. His name was already on the lips of the aristocracy and literati, and would soon be known to all. Lord Byron—to the Europeans simply "The English Lord"—was at that time quite possibly the most famous English author, second only to Shakespeare. George had inherited the title and the peerage at nine years of age and was rapidly creating, both consciously and unconsciously, the persona of the rogue noble, the melancholy outcast who has sinned but is unrepentant. Still, had matters progressed differently in the next year, we might well not have had one of the most prominent eidolons of romanticism, a figure that even Bertrand Russell considered the most important development in Western nineteenth-century culture: the Byronic Hero.

Later that year, in the midst of his reportedly torrid affair with Augusta, Byron considered marriage to Annabella Milbanke, a prim aristocrat who was the antithesis of Augusta in both looks and demeanor. Did Byron pursue this relationship as a smokescreen, as genuine affection, or as a way to force his life into a more conventional mold? We will never know, but we do know that about nine months after he expressed interest in Annabella, Augusta gave birth to a daughter, Elizabeth Medora. Elizabeth always believed Byron to be her father, although he never acknowledged paternity. In September he proposed to Annabella and she dallied, postponing her answer, which strangely seemed not to bother Byron. "Never was a lover less in haste," wrote John Cam Hobhouse of his best friend's dilatory courtship, but by the next year she had accepted and they were wed.[4]

By 1815 Byron was rapidly becoming a respected and popular poet, thanks primarily to the reception of the first two cantos of Childe Harold. This discursive but resonant outpouring of post-Napoleonic anxiety made Byron the angry young man of his day. As he was being introduced to fame, he was also being introduced to home life with Annabella, and was growing restive. Byron continued to see Augusta even while Annabella was pregnant, and started working on Parisina, a blood-and-thunder tragedy of incest that parallels his own situation; the young protagonist is guiltless, even noble, in his behavior. While writing, he was occasionally plunged into periods of intense depression which were so extreme that his wife consulted two different doctors who both suggested the same diagnosis: her husband was insane. In one of these fits, perhaps to infuriate his wife, Byron seems to have revealed his past sexual relationships with members of both sexes, as well as his ongoing relationship with Augusta to his wife.[5]

The revelation proved catastrophic. In February the Byrons separated: Annabella divulged the "facts," as she called them, to her mother and soon all London knew. Any chance for exculpation, let alone explanation, had passed. The publication of Parisina was interpreted as a confession. Lord Byron, who had been lionized by London society and was literally an overnight celebrity, now became the arch cad, the social incubus. He was spat upon in the streets. On April fourteenth he said farewell to Augusta, on the twenty-first he signed the formal deed of separation from Annabella, and on the twenty-fifth he set sail for Europe, never to return home.

What David and Victoria, Byron and Augusta had done is something our culture has had a hard time understanding, much less forgiving. They had *knowingly* committed incestuous acts.[6] Or at least they said they did, which is almost, if not more, important. What exactly are these "acts," and why should they be so repulsive that we exile the participants almost as if jail is too good for them? In fact, even in jail where felons look down on robbers who look down on murderers who look down on kidnappers, no group of malfeasors is more despised than family molesters. Is incest always molestation? Is it family rape? Does it happen often? Where does the taboo come from? Has it always been so detested, and do all societies abominate it equally? How do we know who is a forbidden partner, and are forbidden partners always the same? How different is sibling incest from the parent-child dyad? How often do child victims make incest stories up? Do they unconsciously "ask" for attention and even violation by seductive behavior? What will happen to partners in incest: will they go insane, have defective offspring, become antisocial? And, as if these questions are not perplexing enough, why do we so rarely talk about something that, when we learn about it, fills most of us with dread and horror? What is the relationship between speaking about (writing about) it and doing it?

The questions are easy to remember. We asked many of them in early adolescence and learned that they usually provoked embarrassment rather than answers, or even discussion. Many of these questions simply cannot be answered definitely, or, for that matter, even vaguely. They are genuine enigmas. However, I would like briefly to survey what little we do know before examining the dynamics of the incest taboo/ inhibition/ prohibition in popular culture and modern literature.

In our culture incest essentially denotes a sexual relationship with a someone who is so closely related that marriage would be forbidden. This rather circular definition is currently being challenged in America, England, and Europe.[7] In France

and Belgium, for instance, there is no "crime" unless there
has been an abuse of authority or, more appropriately, a violation of trust. In the United States and England the parameters are established by blood ties, not by social bonds. In most
of the United States the legal prohibition extends to first cousins, but a more general rule is that if you can name the family
relationship, a sexual relationship is forbidden. Since our sense
of family rarely extends beyond second cousins on either side,
the prohibition stops with first cousins. Here, for instance, is
Abigail Van Buren (May 16, 1983) responding to what has become an almost monthly query:

> *Dear Abby*: I'm 21 and have always considered myself to be a
> healthy, normal, red-blooded American man, but I'm begin-
> ning to wonder how healthy and normal I am. Here's the prob-
> lem:
> At a family reunion last July, I saw my first cousin, who lives
> in another state, for the first time in five years. She's 19 and
> I've always liked her, but when I saw her at the reunion I saw
> her in an entirely different way. I mean, I really couldn't be-
> lieve she was the same little girl I knew. I also didn't feel toward
> her like a man should feel toward his cousin.
> Ever since then, I've been having these romantic dreams about
> her. Last weekend I had a date with another girl, and while I
> was kissing her, I kept thinking about my cousin. Now I'm
> wondering how to make my dreams come true.
> I'm told that first cousins aren't allowed to marry in some
> states. Why not? Who made up that dumb rule? —*Dreamer*

And Abby's reply:

> *Dear Dreamer*: That "dumb" rule isn't so dumb. If there are
> any genetic weaknesses or tendencies toward hereditary dis-
> eases in your common ancestors, your children risk severe health
> problems, so if you're not already kissing cousins, better keep
> it that way.

Abby's knowledge of biology is informed by folklore as is
her location of "cousin" as too close for social comfort; "kissing cousin" is in the popular lexicon of *our* culture but not of

many others. Other societies that measure family with different gauges, such as descent through the maternal or avuncular lines, prohibit different partners. It is not the genetic risk that is worrisome; it is the social one. The naming function of language by which we assert the father/mother/sister/brother/uncle/aunt/cousin placement may well be one of the strongest announcers and enforcers of the taboo.[8] The process of naming is the process of categorizing, which is the unconscious establishment of limits, in this case sexual limits.[9] Marry your cousin in our society and you risk unbalancing your family, not your progeny. In other words, the semiotics of incest—a social code—may be far more potent than the biology of inbreeding—a genetic code.

What makes these sexual limits currently so important to consider is that the blending of families has removed much of the psycholinguistic potency of the names. Almost half of American families are now "rem" (remarried) families in which the social and spatial ties have been expanded, and hence barriers have become less distinct. "Father" may really mean "stepfather" or even "second stepfather." Add to this the sibling confusion caused by the fact that 60 percent of American children are now being raised with brothers and sisters who are not full blood relatives, and the problem is still more magnified. A recent study by Diana Russell of 930 randomly selected San Francisco women showed an astonishing 17 percent of the respondents molested by stepfathers. (This study was presented to the Second International Conference on Family Violence and is the highest figure I have seen for stepparent-child violation.) In fact, this family jumbling has become so common that clinical psychologists even have a newly coined term, the "Phaedra Complex," to describe it, and a course of treatment to reestablish the "natural" (i.e. repressed) family constellation.[10] Here again is the doyenne of American morals, Miss Van Buren, who saw fit to publish the following without comment (November 3, 1982):

> *Dear Abby*: The letter from "Crushed," whose 16-year-old daughter became pregnant by her 15-year-old adopted son, made

a point that few people are willing to acknowledge. We are born with the instinct to function sexually, so why all the denial? How can people in this society be so technically advanced and so socially primitive? Why don't we teach our children the truth about sex? Sex between siblings is taboo. It usually (but not always) occurs when the older person exploits the younger one out of curiosity or in search of sexual gratification. When children are sufficiently mature physically to reproduce—and the sperm meets the fertile egg—pregnancy occurs. The egg doesn't know (or care) if the sperm is a relative.

Incest is far more common than most think. I know. It happened in our family. I was a 15-year-old boy (young man, actually) when my 9-year-old precocious sister came into my bed one night while we were home alone. Our parents were respectable, church-going, middle-class people. They never told us anything about sex. All we knew is what we'd picked up from the other kids. What went on between my sister and me didn't last long, fortunately. But it did happen. The guilt and shame lasted a lifetime, although we never talked about it. I am 72, and my kid sister died last year at 66.

Why am I writing this? Because I hope some "respectable" parents who are too shy to tell their kids about sex will see this. Most parents assume that their kids will "naturally" abstain from having sex with a sister or brother because they will "know" it's wrong. Not true. Kids will naturally explore and experiment unless they are taught not to. And even then, the opportunities for it should be minimized and all temptations removed.

I know this is much too long for your column, so go ahead and cut it to suit yourself, but please get the message across.
—*Anonymous in Minnesota*

This situation is not just occurring with more frequency in blended families; increased sexual activity is happening more often at the margin of the traditional family. As the nuclear family becomes less stable and as life spans increase, in-law sexual encounters become more and more common. We usually read about this in news stories from New England or from Appalachia because their law books still carry legal prohibitions dating from the seventeenth century. In the most recently publicized case, a 26-year-old woman and her father-in-law were finally allowed to marry in Massachusetts, but only after a protracted court case. And in Vermont a special plea was made to allow an 83-year-old uncle to marry his 65-year-old niece only because both of them were well past child bearing years.

Of course, the incest prohibition has always been breached, for prohibitions *depend* on violations. But how should we account for the fact that this is done sometimes flagrantly, and even aggressively? In world history we have such blatant line-breeding "violations" as the Incan empire, the native Hawaiian royalty, the ancient Persian rulers, the Ptolemaic dynasty in Egypt. None of these aristocratic societies made any secret out of doing in public exactly what was forbidden to commoners in private. Was sexual transgression a prerogative of royalty or was it simply a means to consolidate power and possessions? Cleopatra, for instance, was the issue of at least eleven generations of incest and was herself a sibling partner. In the popular imagination it was just this inbreeding that resulted in the appearance of hemophiliacs in late nineteenth-century European royalty, as well as the slack-jawed mountaineers of Appalachia. Are these and other biological aberrations the direct result of incest per se? Most modern geneticists suspect not. If inbreeding occurs in a small and homogeneous population and lasts for generations, it exaggerates all genetic propensities, both good and bad. In most populations, be they racehorse, beefcattle, or human, the risk of disgenic abnormalities is counterbalanced, in the short run, by "hybrid vigor."[11]

The incest taboo is enforced in societies that have no knowledge of reproductive causality, let alone of genetic complexity. Anthropologists have studied societies that have much less severe sexual restrictions than our own; some that rearrange the forbidden partners in ways almost totally unrecognizable to us. A dozen or so societies have been found that even countenance intrafamilial sex; the most recent discovery was in Malaysia in 1982. Here was a small nomadic tribe of ten families that had repopulated itself through very close incestuous breeding when it did not appear to be necessary (*New York Times*, November 11, 1982, p. 15). However, none of these exceptions—either the conscious assertion of royal preroga-tive, or the unconscious family mix in relatively primitive tribes—detracts from the general principle that in almost all societies certain designated members are forbidden to have sexual relations with certain other members. The existence of some sort of incest taboo is universal.

Another phenomenon to be accounted for is that within a society's history there is often much variance in incest occur-rence—or perhaps in incest awareness. In our Anglo-American culture, there have been two periods of intense popular con-cern. The first occurred at the turn of the nineteenth century, and was in large measure the result of Byron's actual, and the romantic poets' literary, interest in brother-sister incest. The second period is the present, especially since the 1970s, as the "last taboo" has become a subject of some study and consid-erable passionate, often acrimonious, debate. The current sit-uation is worth examining because it illustrates both the com-plexity and the force of sexual prohibition in general and of incest in particular.

Buried within the pioneering Kinsey Report were some start-ling unassimilated data. The incidence of forbidden intrafam-ilial sex seemed to have been reported by about 4 percent of all respondents. Wardell Pomeroy, one of the original collab-orators, suggested that the real figure was closer to 10 per-cent. In the original report no particular mention was made of this fact because Kinsey and his associates at Indiana were more interested in accounting for general sexual traits than in isolating particulars. When the databases of this first unbiased study (at least unbiased with regard to incest) were made pub-lic a decade ago, they corroborated the studies being made by the National Center for Child Abuse, which had specifically targeted incest as a subject of concern.

Other studies soon followed in the 1970s, many of them involving surveys of the sexual experiences of middle class college students in "Introduction to Psychology" courses. The numbers started to rise as did the sense of concern because these were not the children of the deprived poor. These were *our* children, *our* siblings. But the proportions really skyrocketed when such groups as prostitutes were studied (90 percent) or runaways (50 percent) or drug addicts (40 percent). Relationships were becoming clear. By the end of the '70s it was thought that between 4 and 7 percent of the female population had been abused or involved in intrafamilial sex. These earlier speculations have since been supported by figures from the American Humane Society as well as from local child abuse centers in Minnesota, California, Texas, and Florida.[12] The incidence of incest is simply too common to be ignored any longer. It is approaching the status of epidemic. Or, at least, that is the way our culture is classifying it.

These percentages do translate into huge numbers; millions of women have experienced what was thought to be rare. Not only do we know that incest is omnipresent, but we now have a sense of who the victims are. Father-daughter or surrogate father-figure incest is the most prevalent (approximately 70 percent), then brother-sister, including adopted or "rem" siblings (20 percent), and the remainder is uncle-niece or in-law activity, and finally in much smaller numbers mother-son (which has not been explained by the Freudians, who made oedipal dynamics so important). Incidents of father-son and, especially, mother-daughter incest were supposedly unheard of, but these homosexual liaisons do occur and if their symbolic forms, which we see in sports and advertisements, are any indication, the percentages may be higher than anyone expects.

The ramifications of these numbers are not clear to all who have studied them, but incest in America is almost plaguelike in our collective imaginations. In the popular press we have been assured that these numbers reflect only the tip of the iceberg of home violence. It is now thought that only about one in twenty instances of incest is reported, and it is known that only one in four ever ends up in court where the situation becomes public knowledge. Public knowledge and opinion, which everyone agrees is crucial if anything is to be done about child abuse, is rapidly shifting from benign neglect to active concern. A Lou Harris poll in 1976 showed that only 10 percent of the population polled considered child abuse a national problem, while in 1983 the figure had risen to 90 per cent. Regardless of the definition of incest, from actual penetration to sexual arousal to betrayal of trust, the figures simply by themselves are staggering. In September 1983 Attorney General William French Smith announced the formation of the Task Force on Family Violence, which will at least provide national figures on this complex and stormy side of modern family life. It is hoped that the study will also show what connection, if any, exists between spouse abuse, child abuse, incest, rape, and mistreatment of the elderly. Additionally, the Task Force will investigate whether a propensity for such violence is carried like a contagious disease, not only within a society and between societies, but also between generations. If such family violence is a learned trait, then we may well expect a geometric burst of such activity.

But are matters bad, getting worse? Witnessing what the numbers on incest may be made to mean is an instructive lesson both in statistics and human behavior. To the sexologists who were left in the mid–1970s with no taboos to debunk after adultery, homosexuality, and masturbation had been accepted as, if not natural, then at least not unnatural, incest became the last vestige of socially repressed sexual behavior. "Open marriage," "gay rights," and "self-knowledge," were joined by a new phrase: "consensual incest," or by the more extreme "positive incest." The logic of this condoning argument is that, if the statistics are correct, then there must be millions (the figure suggested is over six million) of women who have been willing, or unwilling, participants in incest and, if incest is so destructive to one's self-image and psychic stability, there should be millions of neurotic victims all around us. Where are they? If incest is so bad, why are there not more observable signs of troubled behavior? If incest is so heinous, how can so many victims lead supposedly normal lives? After all, say these sexologists, we are now realizing that about 8 percent of all current populations are homosexual, and that this has always been the case. Homosexuality has not been "bred-out" of the human species. Homosexuality must therefore in some sense be "natural." Yet, a generation ago homosexuality was tabooed with fearsome energy, as we believed that the participants were terribly sick, even insane. Could not the same situation obtain with incest?

Modern sexologists such as Seymour Parker of the University of Utah's anthropology department and James Ramey of Bowman Gray (Wake Forest University) Medical School have not only concluded that incest may not be as horrible as we had been led to believe, but have suggested that it may not really be harmful at all. And, whatever the statistics may reflect, incestuous acts may have been occurring at roughly the same percentage throughout our recent past. Human sexual behavior does not change as rapidly as the Sunday supplements would have us believe. Ramey's "Dealing with the Last Taboo," in the *Sex Information and Education Council of the United States Report* (SIECUS), which elaborated on the figures as they were known by the late 1970s, was sufficient to stir national interest, most of it condemnatory. A little later, in 1979, Joan Nelson startled the American Psychiatric Association by contending that there is "a significant amount of consensual incest activity reported as beneficial," and listed her own case as an example. Soon after that Professor Le Roy G. Schultz of the School of Social Work at West Virginia University told an assembly of doctors and nurses at the national conference on Sexual Victimization of Children: Trauma, Trial and Treatment, that some "incest may be either a positive, healthy experience or at worst, neutral and dull."[13] Professor Vern Bullough, Dean of Natural and Social Sciences at the State University College in Buffalo, succinctly stated the case in a letter to the *New York Times* (April 17, 1984):

> As an expert in the field of sexuality, I can only condemn the sexual abuse of children. But as a historical expert, I also have to challenge the statements . . . that child sexual abuse is increasing.
>
> I know of no evidence to indicate that this is the case. I would agree, however, that today child sexual abuse is more likely to

be reported than in the past. One has to remember that not too long ago "respectable" newspapers like *The Times* would not publish stories dealing with child sexual abuse. That there is publicity, a healthy thing, does not mean that the incidence has increased.

What is dire, according to this interpretation of modern incest, is the social guilt and stigma that our society imposes on the innocent victims in the act. Incest has its victims all right: they are the ones who are exposed. The shame they suffer is not natural guilt, but rather the effects of social banishment. In studies that have followed the Vaillant Harvard study, such as the Chess and Thomas New York Longitudinal Study, it seems that childhood trauma is most often washed out by the mid-30s. Even the Freudians, who emphasized early trauma, have had to admit, as Anna Freud did, that "the people we see in treatment are those whose earlier difficulties continued. We don't see those who adapt to trauma."[14]

Unfortunately, this view, which may have some merit, has been inadvertently caricatured by those on the fringe of sexology who make their mark by finding all sexual prohibitions to be stultifying to "self-fulfillment." It may simply be that in the world of academic sexology, the only way to make a reputation is to argue against taboos regardless of social consequences. In any case, what had been intimated in the SIECUS report found an audience not in academic journals but in men's magazines. Here is Philip Nobile, writing in *Penthouse* ("Incest: The Last Taboo"), introducing his subject: "Few things are as powerful as a deviation whose time has come. Homosexuality, wife swapping, open marriage, bisexuality, S&M, and kiddie porn have already had their seasons. Just as we seemed to be running low on marketable taboos, the unspeakable predictably popped up." Incest is a game, Mr. Nobile continues, "every family can play" (p. 117). Nobile assures us that when Warren Farrell, author of *Beyond Masculinity*, finally finishes his definitive *The Last Taboo: The Three Faces of Incest* and finds a publisher (only Bantam bid on the original project and they backed out when they learned of the thesis), we will see that "positive incest" is no contradiction. What makes this point of view especially provocative and even hazardous is that "positive incest" has been taken up by such groups as the North American Man-Boy Love Association (NAMBLA) to argue by analogy that there should be no taboo on pedophilia. After all, didn't the ancient Greeks do it and didn't they have a magnificent culture?

The pro-incest arguments have not gone uncontested. The upholders of the taboo have for the most part been located in child abuse centers and in the women's movement. For these groups and their constituencies, there is no such actuality as "positive incest"—to assert such simply contradicts what they take to be the underlying dynamics. The female participant is never partner, always victim. Incest is child abuse. Incest is rape.

First to defend the social importance of the incest taboo was Amherst College English professor Benjamin DeMott. In "The Pro Incest Lobby," he attacked Pomeroy, Parker, Ramey, and the rest for their "strident, village atheist postures, for their sneering at 'defenders of morality' as though defending a moral standard instantly stamped one a criminal, and for their half-baked conclusions" (p. 15). Yet DeMott, for all his protestations, was unable to counter the arguments that, if the current statistics are correct, the knot did seem to be unraveling, that victims did suffer guilt perhaps more from social stigma than from personal anxiety, and that incestuous acts may be less destructive than seductive or intimidating behavior that stops short of the physical. Still, DeMott sounded the opening salvo of what has proved to be a boisterous campaign.

If *Penthouse* has been the voice of the pro-incest lobby, *Ms.* has articulated the conservative viewpoint. These mass-circulation, primarily single-sex-directed magazines have debated the subject with a vigor approaching fury. A year after De-Mott's piece appeared, Elizabeth Janeway, whose *Man's World, Woman's Place* (1971) and *The Powers of the Weak* (1980) have become cornerstones of the women's movement, proffered a more comprehensive view. Janeway made the crucial distinction between types of incestuous encounters: coeval step-relations, cousin, uncle-niece, brother-sister and finally the disturbing dyad of father-daughter. Although we use the same word for all types and often inflict the same penalty, the degree of violation is markedly different. Incest has no analogy with homosexuality, infidelity, abortion, or masturbation because incest—especially parent-child incest—involves a fundamental betrayal of trust, literally a trespass. In "Incest: A Rational Look at the Oldest Taboo," Janeway isolated the trauma of parent-child incest, not only as sexual violation, but as a social failure to nurture offspring.

Janeway also articulated an updated explanation for incest prohibition that recently has had an attentive audience, thanks to the broader social concerns of the women's movement. In a patriarchy, especially in one that attributes value to the accumulation of property, women are valuable primarily as the means of reproduction, and secondarily as tangible property. The taboo on incest not only guarantees the male that "his" female is reproducing only his own genetic progeny, at least initially, but it also stabilizes society by controlling the supply of mating partners. In other words, women's rights to their bodies are not just subsumed by the patriarchy, they are transformed into units of trade. This is an extension of an interpretation of incest that has had currency since Lévi-Strauss and the French structuralists isolated incest avoidance as the primary step in the transition from animal to human culture. The exchange of women, far more than any other human interchange, links families and provides the basis for producing surplus and social harmony. Hence the connection between incest and virginity, for what is traded must be of equal value or there will be strife. Elizabeth Janeway extended the mercantile metaphor, arguing its implications from the feminist view:

> The . . . argument against incest is both simple and practical. If girls are not virgins, they are much less valuable as barterable merchandise between families or clans. Past marriage patterns were controlled by ongoing political and economic needs of families, male-headed families. Marry a virgin off well and

you could gain powerful allies, or a chance at inheriting valuable property, or a friend at court.

Once this kind of value was placed on chastity, it extended
to the sexual activity of older women: mothers had to be controlled so that no questions could be raised about the legitimacy of their offspring, and thus about property or rights or
titles within or between families. The incest ban guaranteed
that daughters would be delivered to their husbands in a condition of virginity that would prevent occasions for disturbing
the peace, and that mothers would not be exposed to intrafam-
ily encounters that could raise doubts about the legitimacy of
heirs. (p. 64)

It is no doubt because of the heightened awareness of male-
female interaction encouraged by women seeking an explanation for their role in modern life that incest has become a subject so much discussed in the popular press. It is now acknowledged and even explained in magazines bought both over
and under the counter. Those pioneers of human sexual response, Masters and Johnson, presented an initial overview
in *Redbook* in 1976; Louise Armstrong discussed "The Crime
Nobody Talks About" in the quintessential check-out magazine, *Woman's Day*, in 1978, and Lorna and Philip Sarrel, sex
counselors at Yale University, explained the beginning of the
current controversy in "Incest: Why It Is Our Last Taboo" in
Redbook. Susan Sawyer examined the ramifications of the reports of the Sex Information and Education Council of the
United States for *Family Health*, and *Glamour* published a piece
for teenagers on "The Ultimate Family Secret" in November
1981, as *Teen* had done a year earlier. Even *Reader's Digest*, the
vade mecum of the socially and sexually conservative, admitted in "Incest: Facing the Ultimate Taboo" that, abhorrent as
it was to discuss such matters, incest was a pressing problem
that could no longer be ignored.

Perhaps the most important recent development in incest
awareness is not what is being said, as much as who is saying
it and where it is being said. The study of incest is no longer
the province of the academy but is being discussed openly in
any number of forums. It is surely important that only twenty

years ago when Professor Norman Farberlow, together with his colleague Gordon Allport, assembled a text for the Atherton Press Behavioral Science Series called *Taboo Topics*, there was no mention at all of incest. And Dr. David Reuben in 1969 did not think incest was part of *Everything You Always Wanted to Know About Sex But Were Afraid to Ask*. In the 1980s this neglect, or purposeful exclusion, would be unthinkable. So there have been book-length reminiscences of actual events (Katherine Brady, *Father's Days*, 1979; Louise Armstrong, *Kiss Daddy Goodnight*, 1978; Charlotte Allen, *Daddy's Girl*, 1980; William Woolfolk, *Daddy's Little Girl*, 1982); Elizabeth Ward, *Father-Daughter Rape*, 1985, and popular sociological explanations (David Finkelhor, *Sexually Victimized Children*, 1979; Robert Geiser, *Hidden Victims*, 1979; Susan Forward and Craig Buck, *Betrayal of Innocence: Incest and Its Devastation*, 1978; Sandra Butler, *Conspiracy of Silence: The Trauma of Incest*, 1978), anthropological explanations (Emile Durkheim, *Incest: The Nature and Origin of the Taboo*, first edition 1897; Helen Fisher, *The Sex Contract*, 1982), biosocial explanations (Robin Fox, *The Red Lamp of Incest*, 1980), marital guides for "blended families" (Davidyne Mayleas, *Rewedded Bliss: Love, Alimony, Incest, Ex-Spouses, and Other Domestic Blessings*, 1977), feminist studies (Florence Rush, *The Best Kept Secret*, 1980; Judith Lewis Herman, *Father-Daughter Incest*, 1981), and sociobiological interpretations (Charles J. Lumsden and Edward O. Wilson, *Promethean Fire: Reflections on the Origin of Man*, 1983). It is even more significant that books are now being directed to the audience of possible victims—children themselves. Since more than two-thirds of molesters are from within the family, telling a child to talk it over with his parents is like referring the proverbial chicken to the fox. In Colao and Hosansky's *Your Children Should Know*, Bass and Thornton's *I Never Told Anyone*, and, for younger children, Oralee Wachter's *No More Secrets for Me*, sexual abuse is explained in terms a youngster can understand. These works all share an implied realization of the high incidence, dramatic effects, and interdigitating social, medical and moral ramifications of incest.

There have been full-length articles on incest in popular

newsmagazines such as *Newsweek, People,* and *Time,* as well as extended reports in the *New York Times, Washington Post,* and *Los Angeles Times.* Violations of the "last taboo" have also been detailed in such television "newsmagazines" as NBC's *Weekend* and ABC's *20/20,* where it was not sensationalized, but was presented as part of dysfunctional family dynamics. However, when television fictionalizes incest the results are not so mixed: the treatments are uniformly less restrained. After *That Certain Summer* and *Love, Sidney* had shown how daring the networks could be on the subject of homosexuality, incest was destined to be next. After all, television taboos are made to be broken. In 1983 NBC had the questionable idea that a novel more notable for its hebetude than for its titillation would prove profitable television fare when they adapted the best selling novel *Princess Daisy* in which a sour-faced Englishman molests his fresh-faced American half-sister. This production appeared on two consecutive nights; relatively few viewers bothered to tune in the second night. The violation of family taboos has been played out for full effect on *Quincy* and is found as well in the none too subtle subplots of *Dynasty, Falcon Crest,* and *Dallas.* For such interactions to be exploited on the evening soaps one can be sure they have been first tried out in the afternoon. They have been, again and again.

The startling exception to such standard fare was ABC's *Something About Amelia* (1984) in which charming Ted Danson, who plays good guy Sam on *Cheers,* was a believable, even likable, molester of his teenage daughter. Stereotypes were not invoked; no drinking, no leering, no happy-ever-after ending. The cliché "forbidden love" was shown to be just that. There were no bedroom scenes, which was predictable considering the audience; nor, fortunately, were there the typical shots of the father going into the daughter's bedroom with the door ominously closing behind him. Instead, the drama focused on confession, guilt, denial, and finally counseling. Although the demands of the network, as well as the demands of drama itself, left the conclusion somewhat idealized, the demystification of incest was socially important. And if *Amelia* had ended realistically with the father going scot-free, the family broken, and Amelia in foster care, the youthful audience that could have been prodded into activity would only have remained the more silent. Although the network publicists touted the "therapeutic approach" and the critics claimed "trivialization," the fact that *Something About Amelia* was carefully made, viewed by a large audience, and awarded three Emmys may be a portent of deepening sensitivities and awareness.

Certainly popular culture has never tired of consuming either the myth or the reality of incest. Like a lightning rod of popular interest, the subject itself very often conducts stories out of actuality and recharges them into fiction, especially when the perpetrator is rich and famous. The Pulitzer divorce of 1983, for instance, was transformed into a media event not only because of our fascination with the purposeless, but because Roxanne Pulitzer finally claimed that her husband had told her that on more than one occasion he "had sexual relations" with his daughter. Mrs. Pulitzer told the court: "They'd lay on the bed together, drinking champagne. She'd sit on his lap hugging and kissing him for hours. She'd sunbathe without a top and then they'd lie together when she was naked from the waist up." He, of course, countered that she was a lesbian. There was no such prurient detail when the press reported that the heir to the Upjohn fortunes molested his fourteen-year-old stepdaughter. The judge first sentenced Roger A. Gauntlett to five years' probation and chemical castration with the Upjohn drug Depo-Provera which suppresses the male hormone testosterone. After a public outcry against the leniency of the sentence, Gauntlett was resentenced to five to fifteen years. And there is no doubt that the most shocking disclosure in George Simenon's biography, *Intimate Memoirs*, 1984, was not his sexual fixation on his troubled daughter, Marie-Jo, but rather his bizarre attempt to divert us from the conclusion that it was literally incestuous. The emotional distress that Jerry Falwell suffered from a *Hustler* magazine parody of a Campari ad in which Mr. Falwell was depicted as losing his virginity to his mother in an outhouse was sufficient to cause a jury to award $100,000 to compensate for emotional distress and another $100,000 as punishment. It seems that some labels are so offensive that they cannot be shielded by the First Amendment. The fact that "not to be taken seriously" appeared at the margin was overwhelmed by the jury's sense that nothing could mitigate Mr. Falwell's distress at such an implication.

Incest has also been the ostensible subject of both pulp novels (Carolyn Slaughter, *Relations*; Barbi Wood and Jack Geasland, *Twins*; Mary Stewart, *The Wicked Day*) as well as serious ones (Vladimir Nabokov, *Lolita* and *Ada*; Pete Hamill, *Flesh and Blood*; Gore Vidal, *Two Sisters*; Anthony Burgess, *M/F*; John Irving, *The Hotel New Hampshire*). Brother-sister incest has even been the subject of an erotically vulgar song by the teen idol Prince ("Sister" on the *Dirty Mind* album).

Ultimately, however, it has not been the real world, the art or pulp reconstructions, or even the fanzine attention to the taboo that has allowed us to speak of the unspeakable. It has been the cinema. As has been the case with each new socially explosive issue in the modern world, the cinema, with its privacy and darkness, its broad range and low censorious control, its willingness, even eagerness, to explore the edges of modern life, and especially its audience conditioned to expect the new and different, that has proved to be the most important medium of exposition. In fact, the making and breaking of taboos has always been a central function of popular culture industries. "Seeing it at the movies" has been the basis of so much that is known and believed in the twentieth century, and our reaction to incest is no exception.

It is not happenstance that one can record in the shift from imaging women in the mold of Ingrid Bergman or Katherine Hepburn in the 1950s, to Brigitte Bardot or Audrey Hepburn in the 1960s, to the current image of the child Lolita as with, say, Nastassia Kinski, Tatum O'Neal, Brooke Shields, or Jodie Foster, that our views of the attainable (and the socially permissible) are changing. Pubescent sex has become the implied, if not stated, subject of our shifting sexual interests, if not obsessions. How much this new sensual and childlike eidolon implies sublimated daughter or sister is not yet clear, but the surface plots of recent films are not difficult to fathom.

In the last few years brother-sister incest has been the theme, not implied but stated, of films like *Obsession*, *Scarface* (as in the original), and *Cat People*, while father-daughter violations surfaced in *Chinatown*, *Just a Game*, and *Stay as You Are*; uncle-niece incest was shown in *Ecstasy*, and mother-son incest in *Luna*. *Variety* (May 20, 1981) thought the surge in family violation was a sign of the changing times and reported this statistic: while there were only a handful of films dealing with incest from the 1920s to the '50s, from the 1960s to 1981 there were more than a hundred, and much more importantly, these films have proved profoundly influential. These were not midnight movies or peek-a-boo cheapies, but box office successes. Films such as Bergman's *Through a Glass Darkly*, Sjoman's *Night Games*, and Visconti's *The Damned* were more than intellectual European films; they were popular worldwide. More important still, they moved the cinematic treatment out of the art house into the main street theater without ending up at the drive-in. This is not to overlook the fact that many treatments of incest were simply awful and belonged at the perpetual drive-in, for example, *Candy*, *Pretty Baby*, and *Caligula*; but even sexploitation from Hollywood tells much about the changing interests and fixations of a paying, and hence serious, audience. The simple fact of the matter is that from the 1960s on, incest was no longer a blacklisted subject but was becoming first shocking, then interesting, and by the 1980s, almost ordinary.[15]

Typical of recent films such as *Paper Moon*, *Class*, *Firstborn*, and *Reckless*, in which family relations border on the overtly sexual, is *Blame It on Rio*. In what is intended to be a rollicking romantic comedy, a 43-year-old father played by Michael Caine is essentially seduced by a prematurely buxom and almost perpetually bare-breasted daughter surrogate who takes her orthodontic retainer out only long enough to demand, "Make love to me." Thus, we all soon know what the "it" is that we are to "blame on Rio." What are we supposed to expect at Carnival time; what are Saturnalias for? As Pauline Kael noted in her 1984 *New Yorker* review, this film is not good fun:

(Twentieth Century-Fox)

Blame it on Rio, 1984

"Blame It on Rio" is about father-daughter incest, in a disguised form . . . it's understandable that the moviemakers thought they were on to something, because they are, but it's not something they can handle in this touristy manner—and it may be that these particular moviemakers couldn't handle it in

any manner. Most of "Blame It on Rio" is an attempt to squirm
out from under its subject . . . [but it degenerates] into a smarmy
sitcom. (p. 115)

Blame It on Rio continually invokes a kind of "love boat" ethos—
anything is acceptable on the high seas—yet it also radiates
prurience by ironizing the familial roles. Clearly, the American public was attracted to this combination for, while the film
was not a box office hit, it has been one of the best selling
video films in 1985.

What is perplexing about incest, especially the father-daughter
dyad, in contemporary popular culture is that it has little direct appeal if it is presented openly as such. In fact it may
simply be that nubile females are attracted to older men and
vice versa, and the only incest is that inferred by those looking for it. If you look, for instance, at any of the descriptive
catalogs of pornographic video movies where this forbidden
scenario should be played out for an eager audience if there
were any demand for it, you will find that only ten or so of
the literally hundreds of titles center on either sibling or parental incest. Even more curious is that in studies of sexual
fantasies incest is an almost nonexistent subject. When we show
our own pornographic videos in the imagination, which we
seem to do on an average of seven or eight times a day, we
do not want to imagine this family configuration. Sadomasochism, homosexuality, rape, group sex, yes; but incest, no.[16]

If most of us do not wish to fantasize about incest, regardless of what the Freudians say, then how do we account for
its currency in popular culture? Clearly, this is at the center of
the incest enigma; it may not be the act, but the shock, the
frisson, that appeals. And to witness that shudder we need
only to glimpse the exploitation of incest in an industry that
by its own admission is more concerned with the sizzle than
with the steak—advertising.

One of the first advertisements to specifically associate a
product with the implications of the women's movement (the
You've Come a Long Way motif) was a 1976 ad for Old Grand-
Dad bourbon. Here at last in dad's sanctum sanctorum, the

"Equal pay, equal recognition
and the first woman admitted
to The Club...
What more could you ask for?"   "Old Grand-Dad."

Old Grand-Dad
When you ask a lot more from life.

Head of the Bourbon Family.

(Old Grand-Dad Distillery Co.)

Old Grand-Dad, 1976

sexually and economically independent young woman is asked
what more she could want. She is in the tabernacle of powerful males where secret business decisions are made, she can
read the *Wall Street Journal*, and she has an equal "chair." Yet,
she is not relaxed. One can tell from her posture that she is
still tense. That she should ultimately only want "Old Grand-

Dad" is pun intended; that we should be told elsewhere in the copy that Old Grand-Dad is head of the family and is what you ask for "when you ask a lot more from life" is less clear, but no less powerful. "A lot more" than what? The subtle conflict of signs, the merging of images, the invocation of the forbidden, is a not too subtle appeal to both the traditional purchasers of this usually masculine product as well as to a new market in which equal pay and equal recognition go along with equal and open sexuality. Or, so the older masculine audience may be tempted into believing.

Here are two recent advertisements from upper-class family magazines, *Psychology Today* (March 1982, p. 9) and the *New Yorker* (August 6, 1984, p. 47). The message in the Metropolitan Insurance Company ad is not clear until one realizes that the intended audience is the middle-aged male, the primary purchaser of life insurance. But the picture, which purports to be an image of the man's wife at the time of marriage, say, fifteen years ago, is, in fact, more the image of his budding daughter. The buried text of the bold-face copy—"The longer you're married, the more your wife has to lose"—seems to refer to the wife's sexual competition in the form of the next generation. Simply put, the daughter is displacing her in the husband's eyes. The Lolita-like invitation to what is associated with the bridal night, the slightly tilted pelvic area, the come-hither eyes all imply sex, to be sure, but not sex between co-evals, but sex between father and daughter. Whom, one might ask, do we buy insurance to protect: aging wife or the captivating girl-child? The ad implies the answer.

The Braemar sweater ad, however, bypasses implication for statement. If Mommy, who is the more likely reader of the ad than Eunice, wants to make sure she keeps Daddy for herself and far from Eunice (even though Eunice will clearly get the job and stay by Daddy's side), she had best buy *the* sweater.

Probably the most extraordinary of all these advertisements in this genre is a recent Pepsi commercial which shows two teenage girls in their bedroom preparing themselves to meet their dates. They behave almost like sisters, moving in front

(*Metropolitan Insurance Companies*)

Metropolitan Life Insurance, **1982**

of each other for mirror space. They are clearly competing to
see who is prettier, who can be sexier, and this girl rivalry has
been prefigured in a string of Pepsi spots, done in the European style, in which the camera has lovingly focused on bodily parts while the Pepsi can passes slowly by. The doorbell

(*Braemar International*)

Braemar Sweater, 1984

rings and the sisters put down their brushes, powders, lip-
sticks, and Pepsi and run downstairs to greet their date. It is
an archetypal scene in television from the first family show.
The door opens, they ooh and aah, Daddy's home!

This exploitation in advertising culture doesn't help us to

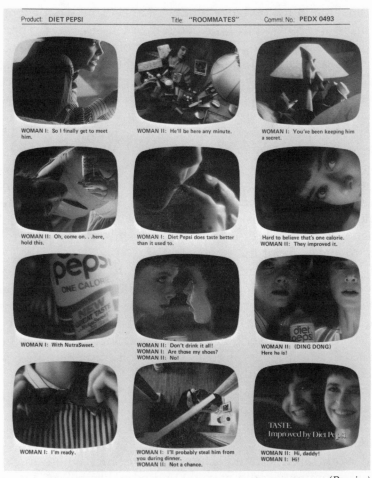

Product: **DIET PEPSI** Title: "ROOMMATES" Comml. No.: **PEDX 0493**

WOMAN I: So I finally get to meet him.

WOMAN II: He'll be here any minute.

WOMAN I: You've been keeping him a secret.

WOMAN II: Oh, come on. . .here, hold this.

WOMAN I: Diet Pepsi does taste better than it used to.

Hard to believe that's one calorie. WOMAN II: They improved it.

WOMAN I: With NutraSweet.

WOMAN II: Don't drink it all! WOMAN I: Are those my shoes? WOMAN II: No!

WOMAN II: (DING DONG) Here he is!

WOMAN I: I'm ready.

WOMAN I: I'll probably steal him from you during dinner. WOMAN II: Not a chance.

WOMAN II: Hi, daddy! WOMAN I: Hi!

(Pepsico)

Diet Pepsi, **1984**

understand the act, or the aversion, or the taboo, but it does point to our preoccupation with what we earlier, especially in the late nineteenth century, refused to openly admit: we are drawn to contemplate, for reasons ranging from titillation to revulsion, sexual acts in fiction which we would abhor, or at least avoid, or profess to avoid, in reality. Ultimately, however, the figurative and the real are not separate worlds. What we imagine in fiction has a tendency to become what we must confront in reality. But knowledge works both ways. The impact of simply hearing a terrible secret often enough makes it first less terrible, and then less of a secret. As long as incest is hidden by the mantle of secrecy, as long as it is an unspeakable subject, it will continue to have a potency far in excess of what may be necessary for the general welfare. R. D. Laing speaks of "potentration," or the way avoidance of a subject reinvests it with power. And Michael P. Weissberg argues in *Dangerous Secrets* that the power of silence, together with collusion, denial, and guilt, imbues maladaptive acts like child abuse, alcoholism, suicide, and incest with a power that is almost destined to dislocate first the self, and then the family, when it is revealed. But, even knowing this, do we *want* to be able to speak about the unspeakable?

It would be comforting now to turn to the scientists and have the veil of silence lifted. Until quite recently this would have proved disappointing. For what has characterized the academic study of incest is that in almost every discipline in which it has been seriously considered, incest has become a locus of crucial, but almost totally self-contained theories. Theories of incest, either as taboo, act, desire, or impetus for some other activity, have flourished independently, only rarely crossing the margins of allied disciplines. In part this may be an ironic testament to the vigor of our anxiety that even in academia incest was excluded from general discussion, and field work rarely funded. Here is an instance where the academic community could have influenced public policy, but until the 1970s this influence was nil. Now the impetus for further study is coming not only from social scientists but also from feminists, victims, and even from the government and insurance companies who are realizing the costs, both human and financial, of abusive families. Additionally, there is now the promise of unified theories thanks to the ability and willingness of scientists to entertain often contradictory information from such far-flung disciplines as demography, primate research, and even nutrition.

To give just a smattering of what was developing in the

sciences during the same time frame as this study of Anglo-American culture, I have grouped the most important theories under the general rubrics of biology, psychology and sociology. Although I will try to be more discursive in a brief Appendix, let me outline the general arguments here more to illustrate how far-reaching the study has been than to argue any specific validity. These theories are of considerable interest to the cultural historian as they illustrate how for the last century and a half we have been almost obsessed with establishing an ideology, a concept, or, if you will, a myth, to explain and hence control an enigma.

In biology the explanation of incest avoidance was first couched in terms of instinct and then in terms of genetic preference. It seemed logical to Victorian scientists that we had been instructed by Nature (God) to avoid incest. It was well known that linebreeding caused deformities. The prohibition did not always work just as the Bible had warned, but still it was logical to assume that instinct must somehow operate because by the time most genetic deformities could be observed in human offspring and the causality determined, the parents would be long since dead. Yet, matters were complicated by the discovery made at the end of the eighteenth century that linebreeding also produces the opposite of genetic deformities—it produces hybrid vigor. Additionally, it was clear that certain aristocratic societies, such as the Egyptian, Incan, and European ruling classes, were doing just what this instinct should be forbidding. So instinct was not operating all the time, which detractors said should make us rethink what *instinct* really is. In fact, until recently these ambiguities had made the most articulate proponent of this theory, Edward Westermarck, the butt of a misunderstanding. Why should we have an incest taboo, claimed the skeptics, if the aversion to incest was "natural"? We don't taboo what we don't do.

The biological explanation was not the only theory hounded by contradiction. Paradox abounds in psychological explanations as well—especially in the psychoanalytic theories of Freud. Matters are topsy-turvy as here instinctive incest avoidance is inverted to be instinctive incest desire. Freud contended that we have learned that sexual repression in the service of social stability is worth the price of civilization and its discontents. We have learned this lesson the hard way, from the bloodshed and guilt of the primal horde. The taboo on incest is the necessary restraint that got us out of the jungle even if it did mean going to the couch. The price of culture is individual neurosis. Here, as well, skeptics have never been lacking. "If incest taboos represent repressed incest wishes, do laws against homicide mean that we *want* to murder?" The oedipal configuration, which has always been a cornerstone of psychoanalysis, has been shaken not only by logic and empirical studies, but by the recent unfolding of Freud's own considerable doubt about the "seduction theory" when applied to individual reality and/or fantasy.

Not all was lost. There was promise elsewhere in the social sciences. Contradictions were thought to be resolved in the sociological arguments of the twentieth century as the taboo per se became quite beside the point. What was more important was the institution of exogamy—the rule that one must "marry out or be kicked out." In other words, sex is redirected into the service of social alliance. The taboo is not so much on sexual desire as it is on the centripetal concentration of the family.

These core explanations are still being expanded. The biological view has received affirmation from the demographers and sociobiologists who essentially claim that if left unhampered, the selfish gene would find an equilibrium between the deleterious extremes of inbreeding and outbreeding. The psychoanalytic view has found new vigor in Lacanian theories that essentially resolve ambiguities by asserting that the oedipal configuration doesn't have to be taken literally in order to be provocative. And the socialization theories have been carried forward by Lévi-Strauss' exchange theories, as well as by the feminists, who explore the ramifications of the incest taboo in patriarchies in order to explain the socioeconomic role of women.

Clearly, what is happening in the social and biological sciences is that the boundaries of disciplines are being blurred.

It is a characteristic of all approaches, however, be they biological, psychological, or sociological, to assert the importance
of cultural reinforcement. It is in this context that I mention
the theories of Robin Fox, for it seems clear that, although
certain ramifications of his conclusions may be questioned, his
eclectic approach is a harbinger of how future studies will be
conducted.

In *The Red Lamp of Incest* (1980) Fox attempts to juggle as
many of the past theories and speculations as possible while
adding a few of his own. His previous expertise has been in
kinship studies (he authored *Kinship and Marriage*, co-authored
The Imperial Animal), but for the last two decades he has attempted to articulate a field theory that could account for what
we know about evolution, primatology, alliances, brain function, and psychoanalysis. The remarkable aspect of his present work is not that he occasionally drops a ball, as detractors
have been quick to point out, but that he keeps so many in
the air at once. Joseph Shepher, in the most recent survey of
the subject, *Incest: A Biosocial View*, calls *The Red Lamp* the "most
important book on incest in the last hundred years." This is
not because Shepher agrees with Fox (he often doesn't), but
rather because Fox's approach is so inclusive and synthesiz-
ing. It is not just cross-cultural; it is cross-disciplinary.

The most important schism Fox attempts to bridge is the
seeming impasse between the strict biological view (incest
abhorrence) and the psychoanalytic view (incest desire). He
makes allies of Westermarck and Freud by supposing that
Freud's primal horde did indeed occur and that we have taken
that lesson to heart, or rather to our genes. Over millions of
years and thousands of generations we have evolved kinship
and mating patterns that have rewarded those who have formed
social alliances and have been able to "equilibrate" individual
desire in favor of cooperation. Those who could defer aggression and sexual impulse protected descent patterns and pre-
vailed. As a result the social system that has evolved in most
human societies is divided into three parts: dominant males
who monopolize the sexuality of females, females who have
not yet gotten into the breeding system, and satellite males

who must struggle by various means to be included. The willingness to avoid incest by all parties—not by the stern prohibition on incest but by the pragmatism of exogamy—is one of many mechanisms holding this tripartite system together. The organization succeeds as all parties stabilize, not getting all they want but at least not running the risk of getting nothing.

Incest avoidance has not been hard for us to achieve. After all, if we go back to the most fundamental level, the question of why we reproduce sexually in the first place, we will see that incest avoidance is an a priori concern. As the German psychologist Norbert Bischof first made clear, the primary advantage of sexual reproduction is genetic variation. Hence, incest that would cause genetic concentration defeats the "purpose" of the sexual process. If cloning were the operative principle, incest would make sense. All sexually reproducing species have therefore what might be considered a natural tendency to steer clear of linebreeding. What separates our species is that we have developed an elaborate ideology to boost, as it were, our own proclivities. This does not mean that if we are forced to choose between inbreeding and extinction we will choose extinction. Not in the least, for under pressure, especially social pressure such as we see in the breeding patterns of certain aristocracies and endangered groups, we will indeed breed closely. It is not an infallible system. Iron laws do not exist in nature. She governs by "rules of thumb."[17]

What makes us exceptional is that we have a communal response. We have a developed language. Culture helps us remember what nature intends. (It also encourages us to subvert, for manifold reasons, the very norms it establishes.) While there are natural set-mechanisms to avoid incest—proximity, third party identification (you don't mate with organisms around your mother), smell, color, and perhaps even sucking aversions—all human societies have a second line of defense. This is the defense of language, for clearly taboos are functions of linguistic organization. As we have seen, much dovetails into the incest taboo—matters such as kinship, exogamy, power configurations, and alliances—but what is of interest to me is that while there may be a kind of collective inhibition, the controls on the individual are fragile. And here the individual artist is especially interesting to study because since the French Revolution and the budding concept of the avant garde, he has often been rewarded for refusing to support the accepted norms. Or, at least, for pretending to do so.

There is another reason why modern culture has focused on incest and this is almost too simple and too close at hand to have been observed earlier. For over 90 percent of human history intergenerational incest would have been statistically improbable. Until very recently the human lifespan was approximately thirty-five years, and infant mortality over 80 percent. Father-daughter incest just did not have much of a chance to occur. Sibling incest as well was avoided by birth spacing as well as by the basic proximity aversions. Since the act was improbable, so too was the concept—so too was the taboo. Ideology was unnecessary. Incest was a myth only for the gods. For millions of years hominid breeding patterns followed the simplest dictates of economy—namely, availability. Until relatively recently family members simply were not available.

The modern world has undergone a profound and, in evolutionary terms, a hyper-rapid transformation. It takes no sophisticated demographic study to realize that we live longer, remain together in the family longer, and have concentrated with increasing tension on the nuclear family. As family historians like Lawrence Stone (*The Family, Sex and Marriage in England*) and Edward Shorter (*The Making of the Modern Family*) have demonstrated, we stay sexual longer within a smaller radius and this implosion inevitably has had profound effects.[18] Along the way we have broken down and reassembled patterns of social authority, class structures, and hereditary descent patterns, all the time effacing the natural avoidance inhibitions. Just on the basis of statistical probabilities, one would expect the incidence of all intrafamilial sexual activities to increase.[19] Add to this our adulation of youth, our views of teenage romance and courtship, and one can see that there may be a connection between our growing interest in pedophilia and an increase in intergenerational incest.

In such a situation, a situation which essentially characterizes all modern industrial societies, one would expect that the incest taboo would be invoked with progressively greater concern. We should be prepared to expect that the dropping of the age of menses, the advances in contraception, the realignment of sex roles, and especially the sexualization of youth would call forth both a weakening of inhibition as well as increasing concentration on the taboo. It has even been suggested that we are the first to use the term "sexual molestation" in part because we are the first to have the possibility. The paradox of greater intrafamilial sexual activity appearing at the same time the taboo is fiercest is not to be unappreciated. There is usually a correlation between the levels of interdiction and incidence of forbidden activity; it takes the existence of speeding cars before there is the posting of a speed limit.

However, I am not really going to comment in *Forbidden Partners* on the contemporary Anglo-American situation other than to say that it does not seem unpredictable. I am instead going to concentrate on the early modern world where the genesis of our present concern first evolves, where the subject of incest, as well as its prohibition, seems to become a central communal concern.

Moving from the macro-observations of an evolutionary anthropologist like Fox to the traumas of everyday life is like parachuting onto concrete. The trip down is interesting enough; it's the landing that shocks. Let me reiterate that I never mean to imply that individual violations of the prohibition are not traumatic and often life-threatening. Indeed, they often are. I do think, however, that we are now at a point where academic theories, social studies, legal cases, and popular concern are all coming together. This may be not just a propitious time to look at our recent cultural history; it may be one of the first times we *could* look. It is difficult to predict what the results of popular awareness will be, but one fact is certain. Incest will never again be so "unspeakable." Awareness without understanding may prove a mixed blessing. With other taboos like homosexuality, masturbation, abortion, and adultery, there has been a relationship between censure and silence. As long as we don't discuss it, we can forbid and punish it. Incest may not be analogous, let alone even similar. As I will try to make clear in the next chapter, we have not even been sure what the word means. Although most human beings have felt sexual ambivalence, have masturbated, and have been unfaithful in varying degrees, only at certain times and in certain cultures have we admitted it. When we do the sanctions seem to lessen. Incest is different. We have not all violated the privacy of a family member's body. Nor do most of us know a child molester, even though "he" may be living right next door. Nor do most of have such desires—even in our fantasies.

One of the most frightening aspects of our new interest in, and knowledge of, intrafamilial sex is that the incidence of incest *seems* to be increasing exponentially as information becomes available. This is happening at the same time we are interested in maintaining *and* subverting the taboo. Is this because our methods of discovery are revealing what has always been present? Or is it because once we start to learn about such behavior, we start to accept it while denying it? Could increased incidence be both the cause and the effect of curiosity? In this particular area, not only might ignorance be bliss; ignorance might be the only solution. For if incestuous behavior is a learned process, a communicable disease, as some social scientists now assert with reference to the undeniable explosion in statistics, then this may well turn out to be a major public health problem for which the only cure may be, ironically, its return to obscurity and silence.

It may be, however, and this is the practical aspect of my study, that from time to time in modern history incest has been singled out and made the subject of intense popular interest and then, like so many other subjects, evaporated leaving only an abandoned trail for the cultural historian to follow. The current eruption does not seem so ephemeral. To understand it I intend to trace the trail of the incest prohibition as it has passed through verbal and visual artifacts of the last two hundred years: from the milieu of George Gordon, Lord Byron to the culture of Victoria Pittorino and David

Goddu. I start at the end of the eighteenth century just as the folk ballads are being collected and made part of print culture, because here the modern interest becomes part of the modern record. We have the first stable "texts." Then I continue through the art literature of romanticism and the popular literature of the gothic, through seeming neglect in Victorian polite prose but obvious relish in pornography and horror myths, and finally end where we started in the current wash since the publication of *Lolita*, the genesis of the women's movement, and the rise of concern about the modern family. Along the way I briefly survey the more censorious treatment in American nineteenth-century culture. I neglect most of the twentieth century because the prohibition/titillation seems to be carried primarily in nonprint media: the movies, television and advertising. But as I hope I have already shown in this chapter, the American approach to the subject of incest has been anything but restrained. Of all Western cultures in the twentieth century, Americans have become progressively emboldened in their treatment, both condemnatory and condoning, of incest.

Whether or not there is a correlation between what we do and what we say we do, whether we really prohibit what we claim to prohibit, remains to be discovered. A few generations ago many Western societies punished adultery and violations of celibacy with death, secure in their belief that otherwise their society would fall apart. As it does from time to time, the popular press predicts that the "nuclear family" is heading for a meltdown, but the experience of the past may make us wonder. The "end of the family as we know it" has been, after all, one of the favorite journalistic subjects since the eighteenth century. This much, however, is clear: incest, whether actual or figurative, has been one of the most enigmatic and far-reaching concerns of humankind especially in the modern world. How we ultimately come to understand it, if we ever can, both determines and is determined by the most fundamental concepts of nature, family, sex roles, society, and self.

CHAPTER 2

THE HORROR OF INCEST

The horror of incest is an almost universal characteristic of mankind, the cases which seem to indicate a perfect absence of this feeling being so exceedingly rare that they must be regarded nearly as anomalous aberrations from a general rule.
—E. A. Westermarck, *The History of Human Marriage*

AS BEFITS ANY interpretation of the transmission of a social code, the appropriate place to start discussion is with its popular terminology. For what we choose to name is only slightly more important than the name we choose for it. There are two words that have travelled together for the last few generations which express with appropriate concision our communal response to intrafamilial sex: we call it the "horror of incest." Although these words are linked like Siamese twins in popular lexicon, it was the translators of Sigmund Freud who, during this century, conjoined them into the current cliché. Freud's term *Insestscheu*, which literally means "incest avoidance" or "shy of incest," has been translated first as "dread of incest" (A. A. Brill) and then more forcefully as "horror of incest" (James Strachey). We can see our intensifying response to this act in the darkening amber of linguistic consciousness. And we are not alone. In French, German, Italian, Spanish, and English, "horror" has become the prefix of "incest," conveying not just opprobrium, but revulsion as well.

While we think we know what "incest" means and where

it came from etymologically—probably derived from the Latin "castus," meaning pure, and later transformed with the negative to "incestus" which means lewd and impure—it is more interesting to note what happens to the definition when Latin is not at the root. In many non-Romance languages the term for incest often implies blood contamination, thereby specifying a more particular "impurity." For instance, the German *blutschande*, Danish and Swedish *blodskam*, Czech *Krvesmilstvo* (krv = blood), and Hungarian *vérfertözés* (contamination of blood) all do what English politely overlooks. They name corruption as an ineluctable result of an illicit act, and they locate that corruption literally in the blood.[1] But what of the word that often accompanies the blood-befouling? What is the meaning of "horror?" To understand that meaning we are initially taken back to the Latin *horrēre*, which means "to bristle" and describes the way in which the hair on the nape of the neck stands on end during moments of shivering terror. In fact, the shiver we associate with horror is the result of the constriction of the skin that stiffens the subcutaneous hair follicles and thus accounts for the rippling sensation, almost as if a tremor were fluttering down our backs. From this comes the most appropriate trope for horror—creeping flesh or, more simply, the "creeps." This physiological phenomenon clearly has self-defense as its biological purpose, for we pause momentarily in horror, frozen between fight and flight, ironically at our most attentive and yet most vulnerable. Medical science is now exploring the biochemical substance corticotropin which triggers this response by signaling the pituitary gland to produce hormones; but it is enough to realize that physiologically, at least, there is an involuntary frisson involved with incest. Is this shudder, often triggered by the mere contemplation of incest, the result of biology or of social conditioning? Do we abhor incest or abhor our inability to subvert desire? Or is it a combination of both?

As is often the case with words used to outlaw certain kinds of human behavior or desire, the vocabulary of intrafamilial sexual activity is full of internal contradiction. Freud correctly pointed out that "taboo" really meant not only "forbidden" but also "holy" and it is even true that "incest" not only means "impure sex" but also implies, through the ancillary meaning of "cestus" or girdle (usually of Venus; by folk extension, the occluding vaginal membrane), that which should arouse passion. The "losing of the girdle" in Greek tradition is a common trope expressing sexual activity, quite specifically linked with the god of marriage, Hymen. This view of incest as an act denied to men but permitted to the gods is a staple of ancient mythology where the heavens are populated by precisely the kind of breeding forbidden to man.[2] So too, the concept of horror is resolutely paradoxical. Although horror is a moment of dread, a second of full-passioned fixity, of panic, it is in this same moment that theologians like Rudolf Otto located the sense of awe that leads to the evolution of spiritual consciousness. Dumbfoundedness leads in both directions: to flight as well as to pursuit. In fact, in *The Idea of the Holy* (1917), Otto even argued that it is from this shiver ("daemonic dread") that the visionary and mystical experience (*mysterium tremendum*) emanates.

That the experience of horror is first physiological and only later, perhaps, numinous, seems encoded in all its hybrid and mutant linguistic forms. The word "horripilation," for instance, is still used in zoology to describe the condition commonly known as gooseflesh. And this shivering sensation, so prominent as the effect of horror, found a pathway into medical terminology where through the nineteenth century "horror" described the sudden tremors associated with the plummeting of body temperature as a fever receded. So a patient experiencing the "horrors" was just at that moment of transition between the sensations of a boiling fever and the chill, caused by the evaporation of sweat, that follows. This same sense of static turbulence migrated even into nautical jargon where "horror" was a graphic term used by sailors to catalog the cresting of a wave in a rough sea; it describes the topmost oscillation of surging water—the foam.

I mention the oxymoronic qualities of all these words that

surround forbidden acts, not only because the concept of incest is so amorphous and vague that words are really all we
have to decode, but because the act/taboo/aversion itself finally defies complete and precise explanation. How ironic that
when the culture is codifying what it supposedly most abhors
it should be linguistically the most imprecise, even the most
ambivalent. Maybe that irony is purposeful—an index of sorts.
Maybe the "horror of incest" is a sensation that, on one level
at least, is the fascination of the dangerous; the attraction of
the moth for the flame. On the other hand, it is an undeniable
magnet of human curiosity. Is it a coincidence that incest, this
most unclean act, has been interpreted by psychoanalysts as
representing universal desire and frustration, and by at least
some anthropologists as meaning just the opposite: acts of
universal dread and abhorrence?

One can witness the violent yoking of contrary states by
looking closely at images we have consciously constructed to
produce horror, for they often betray our embedded and unconscious sexual anxieties. Here are some examples of what
was chosen in 1977 to be included in an exhibition at the Bronx
Museum of the Arts entitled "Images of Horror and Fantasy."
There was no attempt in the exhibition to be chronological or
complete, just an attempt to show what has horrified since the
mid-nineteenth century. So I, too, picked these examples almost at random to give a sample, because one finds that if a
modern artist is attempting to horrify *without* being political
(as with, say, Grosz, Blake, Picasso, Dali, Dix, Gillespie), he
or she will almost inevitably be drawn to unresolved sexual
confusions in which implied and/or stated incest will often be
present.

What we see again and again in these modern paintings is
the reconstruction of the imagery of sexual chaos that started
finding expression in the gothic at the turn of the nineteenth
century and has continued in the current forms of romanticism. Doubtless we have experienced this anxiety for centuries, but only in modern horror art have we displayed it quite
so publicly. In Klee's *Outbreak of Fear* (1939) we see the explo-

(Museum of Fine Arts, Bern)

Paul Klee, ***Outbreak of Fear,*** **1939**

sion of bodily parts that need to be reordered and made whole. Now there is nothing incestuous about this, but we may see in it what seems to stimulate sexual unease. For what is the part most imaged, the part off to the side that needs to be centered? It is the phallus. Let that organ be out of line, either literally or figuratively, and we feel discomfort. We feel more discomfort looking at Sibylle Ruppert's *The Last Ride* (1976), where we see a compressed human upper form that has been mated (the toes are human) with some foul reptile, while another hybrid, this time an owl with scorpion legs and another bird head, hovers above. To understand how these atrocities

(Collection of artist; photo, Serge Alban)

Sibylle Ruppert, *The Last Ride*, 1976

were created we need only look at Alfred Kubin's *The Ape* (1906). Somehow the bestial part, the simian part, has linked with the human, and the results are indeed horrible. Again nothing incestuous here, but we are finding the general visual field in which our reactions become more precise, more acute. What if the beast in the jungle is not really an animal, but rather a projection of some feral aspect of the self, or, worse yet, of the family?

We may only come to realize the displaced partner in these images by comparing them to versions in which the family romance is no longer metaphoric, but is made actual. Here,

(Albertina Museum, Vienna)

Alfred Kubin, *The Ape,* **1903–6**

for instance, is Sibylle Ruppert's *My Sister, My Wife*, where much of the ambiguity about the nature of the monstrous act is resolved. The iconography tells the story of a man obsessed and guilt-ridden. The horror is that the transformation be-tween desire and suppression of desire is here held in limbo, fixed in what Jean Cocteau called "la zone." Thus the man is Janus-faced, one part asleep, the other in acute pain. His body is hermaphroditic: one part male, about to be brutally castrated, the other part full-breasted and sensuous. And what need be said of his hideous partner, presumably the transfixed creature caused by the mix alluded to in the title: my sister [is] my wife? She is no longer female, no sister, no wife, but a demon, a beast which, as with the creature of *The Last Ride*, is really a mix of devouring mutants.

Clearly, a new category is being formed here, a category so between terms of recognition that it is almost literally and figuratively a third sex—the sex of/in/about incest. And so here is exactly that situation reiterated appropriately in *The Third Sex*.

Once again we see Ruppert's power to horrify coming directly from her displacing categories via fantastic transformations, all of which have sexual relations as their point of spewing forth. In *The Third Sex*, however, we simply can no longer tell which is which—all is compressed into one organic demonic mass of protoplasm. It is homosexual, yes, but it is even

(Collection of artist)

Sibylle Ruppert, *My Sister, My Wife,* **1975**

(Collection of artist)

Sibylle Ruppert, *The Third Sex,* **1977**

more sexually implosive; not just members of the same sex in
the acts of excitement, but members of the same sex made
into a different sex. Yet, even here, ambivalence is again characteristic. Death seems almost loosed from the loins of life,
which, in turn, is devoured by the bestial. Who violates whom?
All is mixed up, horribly so.

(*Museum of Fine Arts, Boston, Bequest of William P. Babcock*)

Francisco Goya, *The Sleep of Reason Produces Monsters,* **1796–98**

One could argue that much of what we see in the horrific imagery of the twentieth century was first envisioned in the nineteenth by the master of the modern macabre, Francisco Goya. Here is one example of Goya's veritable catalog of family perversions known as *Los Caprichos*: This collection of what Goya bitterly called his "caprices" is usually passed off as the work of a madman, but clearly they maintain their hold over our imaginations by portraying scenes of bizarre family romance which still endure. "The sleep of reason produces monsters," said Goya, and, once out of the submerged land of fantasy, what these monsters do is to violate the sleep of those who should be most protected. Only censorious Reason, the superego, the communal agreement on what is right and proper, keeps the forces of perversity subdued.

Had Goya entitled his masterpiece of horror "Saturn Devouring Man" instead of "Saturn Devouring his Children" (1819-23) the shock might have been mitigated, but once we see the image we realize that the forms are not a god and a man, but a man and a child. Had not the act of a father eating his child had obvious sexual overtones, the horror would not have resonated with such intensity.

So while it is rare to see a modern artist paint scenes of actual incest, just as it is rare that a modern writer will literally describe it in words, when we account for the archetypes that inspire horror we often find incest implied underneath other relationships.[3] Perhaps the artist who sets off these vibrations more compulsively and resonantly than any other modern master of horror is Edvard Munch. His series of lamias, female vampires, whose bodies literally enwrap and twine around their male victims while their mouths hungrily suck the life-force from the victim, are on the surface a conscious reiteration of the "la belle dame sans merci" theme of romanticism. Lurking under this theme is a displacement of forbidden sexual passion, often familial sexual passion. As William S. Lieberman has written of these vampire paintings, the young man "is trapped and enveloped by woman, the witch, who like a mother . . . smothers by her embrace."[4] As we shall see, the myth of the vampire, more usually told about the older patriarch who seduces the virginal maiden rather than about the older woman/younger male, owes much to our recurring fear of, and fascination with, incest.

We need not look at the visualization of horror to see how potent the act of incest is in our culture, nor do we need to overemphasize the coupling of "horror" and "incest." We need

(Prado, Madrid)

Francisco Goya, *Saturn Devouring his Children,* **1819–23**

(Kommunes Kunstsamlinger, Oslo)

Edvard Munch, *Vampire*, 1875

only be aware of how the tabooed act is embedded in the organizing systems of language with more odium than is expressed toward any other forbidden behavior. We have obvious unconscious linguistic triggers in such phrases as "he's
old enough to be her father," which seems bland enough until
you realize that the phrase is invariably pejorative, implying a
relationship that violates social expectations. But still the tone
is not vituperative. The phrase refers, after all, to father-
daughter incest which culturally we are more likely to countenance. We have a multitude of folk, popular, and country and
western songs addressed to "baby" or "daddy" that play off
the emotional spark of displaced fathers and daughters. And
we have jokes such as: *Mountain Mother*: My, Billy, your prick
is bigger than Dad's! *Billy*: Yes, that's what sister always says.
Or, *Mountain definition of a virgin*: A girl who can run faster
than her brother; or, a girl who has no brother. G. Legman
points out in *Rationale of the Dirty Joke* that these are some of
the oldest jokes we seem interested in telling. We move them

into rural locales as if to say they do not describe where *we* live. They are not cruel jokes, but rather ones that pass censure together with forgiveness, or at least with understanding.[5] After all, it is only a song; it is only a joke; it only happens in Appalachia.

We reserve our lingusitic wrath for the most abhorrent act: mother-son incest. The most obscene and ferocious curse in the English language, and in almost all other languages for that matter, is "mother-fucker," which with gnomic concision expresses both social and familial outrage at a fever pitch. It is of more than passing import that not only is this one of the first curses learned, so potent that its occurrence can change any movie to an "X" rating, so ferocious that no artist has ever softened it in art, and yet, as with so many other words in this area of human behavior, it is also profoundly paradoxical. The word "mother-fucker," as any current dictionary of contemporary slang will report, is also starting to mean, especially in black patois, a best friend. At this level we are also able to romanticize the usually dreaded mother-son dyad in such tunes as "I Want a Girl Just Like the Girl Who Married Dear Old Dad." Still, this configuration is rarely a subject of jokes, and even less often a subject of exposition however, subtle or sympathetic.

Such censorious concerns and prescriptive codings are prominent in popular culture, while usually hidden in the symbolic grammar of artistic recreations. Witness the number of folk stories, especially fairy tales, that warn their pubescent audience away from dangerous liaisons within the family, and you will see that our dread of incest has been with us at least since the beginning of mythmaking.[6] Our culture is no exception. Not only do we share motifs, we share entire sagas. Here, for instance, are two of the most famous stories we choose to tell our children: "Little Red Riding Hood" and "Beauty and the Beast." True to our concerns about the dominant forbidden relationship, they address not mother-son but father-daughter incest.

The trials and tribulations of Little Red Riding Hood have been many, but here is the way we now relate them.[7] One morning Little Red Riding Hood sets off from her mother's house to take her grandmother some cakes and wine. When she gets to the woods, she meets a wolf who asks where she's going and she tells him. She is not frightened by the wolf, in fact, at most she is maybe a little uncomfortable. The wolf tells her to linger a while and pick some flowers for grandmother and, even though she had been told earlier by her mother not to dally, she does. Meanwhile the wolf goes to the grandmother's, swallows her whole, and waits between the sheets for the next morsel—the granddaughter. She comes; they perform the famous litany about large ears, eyes, hands, and mouth, and Little Red Riding Hood is soon gobbled up. Just happening by is the good woodsman; he finds the wolf in a postprandial snooze, breaches the wolf's intumescent stomach, and safely delivers both Little Red Riding Hood and her grandmother. The connections with giving birth are clear and reinforce the sexual allegory. They then fill the wolf's stomach with stones, and when he awakens he falls over and dies.

Bruno Bettelheim in *The Uses of Enchantment* (1975) argued that this tale has lasted through generations because it addresses the problems of a young girl's sexual initiation. The fact that the girl-child must travel from mother's house (there is no mention of father) past a wolf to whom she is attracted (surely his questions belabor the obvious, for he knows the way to grandmother's house, and if he had only wanted to eat Little Red Riding Hood he could have consumed her then) until she comes to her destination ("grand" mother's bed, complete with that wolf). Note, says Bettelheim, that the wolf is not the seducer; true, he eats Little Red Riding Hood, but she is profoundly implicated. Remember, she gives the wolf directions, then dallies sufficiently for him to be abed before she arrives, and certainly she can't be that ingenuous about grandmother's lupine appearance. The implied moral, unknown even to the teller of the tale, is that Little Red Riding Hood had best be careful not to lose her "little red cap," her "girdle," her "cestus," to the first man she meets, because we all know who that *first* man will be. She should work together with her (grand) mother to make sure this particular wolf is kept from the door, or, more appropriately, from the bed.

In the fairy tale, however, mother and daughter don't work

Gustave Doré, *Little Red Riding Hood*

together. In fact, it is important that the wolf dispatch the surrogate mother before the (grand)daughter can be his. All parties unconsciously collude, and so it is left for a fourth party,
the woodsman, the "good" father, as it were, who has hitherto been missing from the family, to intercede. Rife with as-
sociations of pregnancy and birth, the wolf's stomach is cut
open and mother and child are reborn.

Then, as if to make sure the wolf will not stir again, the
woodsman fills the belly with rocks. In some renditions, especially those "collected" (i.e., sanitized) by Perrault in the
seventeenth century for the court of Versailles, the story ends
without this return to normalcy. There is no good woodsman.
The little girl has been bad and she must be punished. But the
good woodsman belongs in the tale, for he reminds us what
Little Red Riding Hood has done may be wrong, yes, but not
immoral or even unexpected. Little Red Riding Hood has fol-

lowed bad advice; her trust has been violated; she has not been vigilant. She will not let such careless seduction happen again.[8]

Now here is the unfolding of a corollary to Little Red Riding Hood—the tale of Beauty and the Beast. A rich man with many children, usually three boys and three girls, has fallen on hard times. The girls are like Cinderella's stepsisters, whining about their need for jewels and dresses, except for the youngest, called "the little Beauty," who is sympathetic with her father's plight. As he prepares to go off to find another fortune, he asks what he may bring home as gifts and the older girls ask for expensive dresses and baubles, but Beauty asks only for a rose. Months pass and the disappointed father prepares to return empty handed. A short distance from home he happens on a palace in the deep woods, and when he enters he finds everything seemingly prepared for his arrival. There is food set out and a bed freshly made. He spends the night and the next morning he spies a rose. Remembering his promise, he picks it for his Beauty. Quick as the proverbial wink of folklore, this act calls forth a hideous Beast (he is never described in the fairy tale) who, after a little intimidating banter, agrees to let the father go in exchange for one of his daughters three months hence. The Beast even gives the old man a chest full of gold to seal the bargain.

The father never intends to sacrifice a daughter; instead he plans to return to the Beast himself after providing for his family with the gold. But when he tells his children of his plans, his boys want to search out and destroy the Beast, while his girls tell him to quit worrying and spend the gold—that is, all except one, and we all know who she is, and we all know what she does. Beauty goes to the Beast of her own free will as an act of selfless love for her father. The Beast accepts her. He does not molest her; rather he tends her and only occasionally asks that she be his wife. She politely refuses and, again, he seems to understand and accept. All he wants is that she stay near him, and this she promises to do.

Soon Beauty learns that her father is ill, and asks the Beast if she may go to visit him. "Promise you will come back to me in a week," the Beast says. "I will," she promises, and she would have, had her jealous sisters not detained her. On the tenth night Beauty dreams of her Beast; she misses him, remembers his tenderness, and she now realizes his happiness is more important to her than his looks. Once again, quick as a wink, she is magically transported to his side where she tells him of her newly understood affection, and how she now realizes she wants to marry him. At this very moment she looks into his ugly face only to see that he is no longer a beast but a handsome prince. The sick father rapidly recovers and comes to live with them, as do the rest of the family. The evil sisters, however, are turned into statues and will remain this way until they do penance for their hatefulness.

Again, Bettelheim points out in *The Uses of Enchantment* that the barely concealed symbolism tells another tale. The father's love is symbolized by the immaculate rose; yet, beastliness would occur if that image were violated. The father must love his daughter in a special way; hence they must separate during a crucial part of her maturation. The Beast takes over with tenderness and distance until the father weakens. When the girl's willingness to leave her father and to transfer that love to the Beast show that she is strong enough, her father returns to her side. Only when both parties are stable and secure, when the father is old and the daughter mature, can the Beast finally transform into the prince. Only then is the sexual danger over. At last there is reunion and joy. As Bettelheim remarks, "Beauty and the Beast" communicates a

> view that sex must be experienced by the child as disgusting as long as sexual longings are attached to the parent, because only through such a negative attitude toward sex can the incest taboo, and with it the stability of the human family, remain secure. But once detached from the parent and directed to a partner of more suitable age, in normal development, sexual longings no longer seem beastly—to the contrary, they are experienced as beautiful. (p. 308)

Indeed, I think this is the case; but note two important aspects of this tale: it is told from Beauty's point of view, and there is absolutely no attempt to make the Beast horrible. This fairy tale illustrates the positive aspect of displaced sexual attachment; it is not a horror story because at this point in the young audience's maturation there is no need to prohibit what is neither desired nor threatened. There is only a need to prepare for this if, and when, it happens. All through the story Beauty moves of her own free will, and when she finally reaches the point where she can appreciate the Beast for what he is, namely, a character she *can* love, she is at last ready for mature sexuality. In other words, she is now ready for some real horror myths. At the end Beauty need not choose between her father and the Beast. She needs only choose particular kinds of affection—both are loving, but one is platonic, the other sexual.

How does this fable ever become a horror tale? As we might suspect, the monstrous sexual love imaged through the Beast has to intrude on the devotional love of the father. If this happens, the fairy-tale ending is impossible; there can be no "happily ever after." Allow Beauty to yield to the Beast too soon, or let the Beast become too aggressive, especially while the father is foremost in her life, and the imagery of horror will intrude. The Beast will become, as we shall see, a vampire.

These are by no means the only incest-oriented folk tales with continuing currency. Feminist interpreters of the incest taboo can point to a number of tales which, as opposed to "Beauty and the Beast" and "Little Red Riding Hood," are not just cautionary but implicitly exploitative. For instance, Florence Rush in *The Best Kept Secret: Sexual Abuse of Children* draws our attention to a folk tale retold by both Boccaccio in *The Decameron* and Chaucer in *The Canterbury Tales*: the popular story of "Patient Griselda." Although we are not sure what the story originally addressed, we do know two important things about it. First, the folk soon lost interest in it after it was commandeered by the art culture. Second, thanks to Boccaccio and Chaucer, this story was picked up again and again by artists so that it now has become almost the prototype of the Petruchio-Katherina saga, which lingers still in the sitcoms of television culture.

Griselda, a peasant girl, married a rich marquis. Although she was a good wife, the Marquis thought it best to test her devotion as well as his domination. So he told her that he had killed all their children. Griselda forgave him. She passed the first test. He continued to test her and she continued to "pass," continued to accede to his mindless domination. In his last test the Marquis brought home a twelve-year-old girl, a girl of just his daughter's age, and explained to Griselda that she would have to step aside—he wanted to marry this young girl. There is some indication that this girl is really his daughter, and some reason to believe that Griselda recognizes her as such, but the good wife says nothing. If that is what the Marquis wants, then so be it. All Griselda asks is that he treat the child kindly. With this act of complete self-effacement, she passed the final exam with honors. Now that the Marquis has established his rights to the family (he can destroy it at will), and his rights to sex with whomever he pleases (with his own daughter if he wants), he confesses to Griselda that it was all just a test; she has proved a "good wife." He will keep her. They can live happily ever after. The moral, if such a story needs a moral, is clear: A wife should accept her subservient role even if it means tolerating sexual outrages.

In *Father-Daughter Incest*, Judith Lewis Herman retells a variant of the perennial preteen favorite of girls—the magical story of Cinderella. In the bowdlerized story we now have, thanks to Walt Disney and the makers of Barbie dolls, Cinderella is cruelly exploited by her stepmother and stepsisters, is transformed by her fairy godmother, goes to the ball in a wondrous gown, dances with the prince, and is, at the end, rewarded for long suffering, good looks, and polite behavior, with a prince. She does what all girls and their patriarchial families desire—she marries "above her station." Men are the salvation, the route to riches and security; woman's role is to trust and be patient. If she waits long enough, she will get one of her own. Marxist and feminist critics may assure us of the political and social improbabilities of this tale, but that has never detracted from its commercial appeal. This distaff Horatio Alger has never been more popular with merchandisers, and less popular with concerned women.

But Herman mentions another version, probably more popular with the folk, in which the good mother dies, leaving her
daughter alone with a distraught and then lustful father. The
girl is devoted to her mother's memory and, as her father becomes more oppressive, finds peace only at her mother's
graveside. There the daughter plants a thornbush, which she
waters with her tears and cares for with her sighs. Meanwhile
her father becomes still more demanding, and his desires become more obviously incestuous. In despair the daughter leaves
home rather than have to fend off the advances of one who
should be her protector. This is surely not the "bachelor father" of popular culture and television fame, but he is probably closer to the reality of generations of desperate children.[9]

In a syncretistic layering with Christian mythology this Cinderella also becomes Saint Dympna, whose mother dies, who
is sexually approached by her father, the king, and who has
to flee "across the seas" and into the forest near Antwerp. There
she hides out with the peasants. Rather than allow her a life
of her own, the evil king tracks her down, furious that she
would have left him, and beheads her. What had she done to
deserve this? She had spurned his advances. She was fifteen
years old.[10] Dympna was subsequently sanctified by the Church
and is still remembered because, although her story is bizarre,
it is not uncommon. Could there be a more ironic retelling of
what we now think is *the* Cinderella story? Or one more appropriate?

Since my concerns are with incest in the literature and popular culture of the modern Anglo-American tradition, I will
examine one of the few relatively untainted sources of our
communal mythology—the orally transmitted ballad, more
particularly the folk ballads collected by antiquarians at the turn
of the eighteenth century. In these relatively uncensored and
certainly unaffected tales of often destructive family romance,
we will see what many of the romantic artists on both sides of
the Atlantic were to take as one of their favorite themes—the
maintenance of sexual order within the family.

Near the end of the eighteenth century Bishop Percy and
others, including Sir Walter Scott, collected and transcribed
songs that were then being sung or remembered by untutored

English folk. They collected these songs at the last possible moment, for the growth of print was having a dramatic censorial effect on ballad content. In many cases only vestiges of the original song have survived. These songs in turn were collated in the twentieth century by Francis Child, who made the first scholarly effort to categorize them and their variants, and to give a brief account of how they were gathered. We have no idea how many songs Percy, Scott, and other collectors heard but did not transcribe, or, how many, for reasons of propriety (Percy was a bishop; Scott a country gentleman), they transcribed with deletions and "corrections."

But we do know two important things. First, the process of oral transmission is one of the most censorship-free means of expression. We will sing songs we are frightened to say and we will say things we are frightened to write. Second, the ballad was one of the few means the folk had to communicate important information to their progeny. It was their living will, their legacy, their memory. They depended on oral transmission to carry their teachings, from how to hunt, plow, and sew to how to act in the family and in society. John Spiers, one of the first scholars to study the ballad as a repository of social instruction, noted that the ballad dealt with all the important aspects of life: "with birth, instinctive action, death and the decay of the body."[11]

It is of more than passing import that Spiers should consider that "instinctive action" required a separate category. Human behavior should need no instruction about instinctive behavior—most of the time. Yet, as we have seen, certain acts seem to fall on the border between instinct and instruction, and it is here that we often find the subject of incest. There is one kind of ballad in this category that is clearly important in both number and passion, and that is usually called the "domestic tragedy" ballad. In this ballad the family unit is thrown into chaos because of something one member has done to another member. More often than not, what has occurred is some form of "instinctive behavior," and more often than not this "instinctive behavior" is incest. It is an incest so cataclysmic to the folk community that the lex talionis, or revenge plot, is called

into action, and death to one, if not to both, of the participants results.

As we might expect from what we now know of the statistics of incest, there are very few mother-son violations in the
English ballad; in fact, none that I have been able to find. As
well, there is little father-daughter incest. The English ballad
community seems to respond most especially to sibling incest.[12] So in "Lizzie Wan" (Child Collection #51), the weeping
Lizzie is asked by her father why she is so sad, and she confesses it is because she is pregnant. Lizzie is next asked by her
brother why she is so sad, and she tells the same story. He
asks whether she has told their parents who got her pregnant.
She says no. He cuts off her head and trisects her body. He
then goes to his mother who asks why he is so wet with blood,
and he says he has killed his greyhound. No, his mother says,
hound's blood is not so red, and he confesses to the grisly deed.
The mother's classic question, "O what wilt thou do when thy
father comes hame?" (stanza 11), prompts the son to say that
he'll drown himself. No emotion is expressed: mother does not
wail; son does not cry; father does not beat his breast. The
singers of this song have expressed the tabooed act, the consequences have been meted out, and the ballad is over. It is
surely interesting that the father first asks the daughter and
that the mother is first consulted by the son, but the real center of interest is in the sibling incest and its necessary punishment. It is almost as if the folk have learned the consequences
of certain acts and will now brook no further discussion.

Sibling incest is also obvious in such ballads as "The King's
Dochter Lady Jean" (Child Collection #52), in which the pregnant girl—depending on the version—either commits suicide
or is killed by the brother. And the same is true in "Bonny
Hind" (Child Collection #50), where the pregnant sister kills
herself and her unborn child after she realizes that her mysterious lover is none other than her brother. In each of these
ballads there is a very delicately implied ambivalence. The ballad community sympathizes with the adolescents but recognizes the need for punishment—hence the *lex talionis*. So the
sister must die and the brother must mourn, or vice versa, *not*

because of their illicit love, but because of the family's revulsion and the group stigma imposed by breaking the code. True, more often than not the female partner suffers more than the male, but the folk seem to have made no editorial decision about who is to be blamed.

There are a number of other sibling incest ballads in which the theme is better disguised, but the paradoxical "emotional core" is left intact. Here is one of the few instances where the ballad community is willing to employ symbolic language and incidents. Usually the folk avoid any sophistication which inhibits immediate understanding. After all, only art cultures think that how you say it is as important as what you say. To the people who compose and transmit the ballad, the form is not a means of amusement as much as it is a medium for group expression of group concern. In an oral culture what you sing is what you remember, and so song is not to be wasted. It was only with the proliferation of the print medium in the eighteenth century that the ballad became primarily amusement or propaganda. When this transformation happened incest prohibitions migrated into other forms of popular culture where its message was the same (don't do it, don't even think about it), but its immediacy was lessened.

When we do find symbols in the ballad, however, it is more usually the result of the group's growing self-consciousness than of artistic design. For instance, in most versions of "The Cruel Brother" (Child Collection #11) the incest theme seems to be displaced, even suppressed. This is the story: the youngest sister is courted by a knight who must have the consent of each member of her family before marriage. The knight dutifully asks all members except Brother John. After the marriage, John appears, walks up to his sister, stabs her with his knife and walks away. Now why did he stab her is the question that the audience and the singers must have asked, but in the extant versions we are never told. Was it because his consent was not asked? Because he was not involved in the ceremony? Because somehow she had disturbed inheritance lines? Or was it because the folk who made the story were giving vent to deep desires that they could express only through symbolic song, but never through experience? I suspect it is only when we infer from what we see happening in other ballads that we might deduce that the stabbing of the sister is a metaphor for the incestuous act that cannot even be articulated without calling forth the code of punishment.

One finds the same projection of sibling incest in "Babylon" (Child Collection #14). Here the brother, Babylon, returning home through the woods, meets three women and demands from each that she give up either her maidenhood (especially in variant #14D) or her life. The first says no and so he "kills" her with his "wee pen knife." The same fate befalls the second. But while he is attacking (raping) the third, she says, "Stop! I'll call my brother who is in the woods." He asks, "What is thy brother's name?" and she responds, "Babylon." He realizes what he has done, he knows the penalty, and straightaway kills himself. No emotion is expressed, no regret, only a flat affect. He wanted to "sin," he sinned, and he paid the penalty.

The same theme, in different guises, is repeated in "Sheath and Knife" (Child Collection #16), where incest is actually admitted in one of the variants (II, 16). In this ballad the pregnant sister asks to be killed by having the brother shoot her in the stomach with a silver arrow. He does, and returns to court. Asked why he is so sad, he replies that he has lost his "sheath and knife." Here the symbol may work on two levels. First, the sheath and knife refer to the mother and child; and second, considering the phallic importance of the knife in the other incest ballads, the sheath and knife may well symbolize the incestuous intercourse.

Thus, the overt mention of sibling incest in the domestic tragedy ballad is quite common, as is its symbolic treatment. But there is no such mention of maternal incest, and only displaced mention of father-daughter incest. Only by the farthest stretch of the imagination could one conjecture oedipal relations beneath such ballads as "Sir Hugh or the Jew's Daughter" (Child Collection #155) or in "Little Musgrave and Lady Barnard" (Child Collection #81). It may be that the only oedipal incest ballad in the whole of the Child collection is the Percy version of "Edward" (Child Collection #13B). In this ballad the son has killed the father, apparently in collusion with the mother. But the Percy version has been shown by a number of twentieth century scholars to be ersatz. It was more probably written by an individual and inserted into the Percy collection.[13] There are no such suspicions, however, with the sibling incest ballads. To find parent-child incest we need look to other folklore.

The ballad has always conveyed huge quantities of social, especially sexual, information. Witness that today preteens are still profoundly influenced by the jungle drums of popular music while learning the rhythms and routines of courtship and mating behavior. There is even a video genre that couples popular music with corresponding images, and a television channel (MTV: Music Television) that presents these pantomimes, often both violent and sexual in nature, to an eager audience. The orally transmitted folk ballad, however, for all its vitality, was no match for print media. The codes that had been transmitted for ages from mouth to ear were literally conscripted in a never-ending line of print. From the eighteenth century until quite recently, the primary print form that carried these socializing instructions was the novel, and the subset of the novel that dedicated itself to the specific subject of intrafamilial sexual behavior was the genre that we still associate with horror—the gothic novel.

The introduction of movable type, the developments in recasting fonts, the steam-driven presses, as well as expanding educational systems for the middle and lower classes made literacy increasingly prevalent and audiences progressively younger. Literacy became synonymous with education, with indoctrination. For with literacy comes contrived self-consciousness and with this circumspection comes the necessity both to instruct and to subvert. Certain subjects must be hidden to protect certain audiences and just as predictably they must be uncovered. Censorship is a modern dilemma. Tribes don't make books, individuals do, but literate tribes establish audiences by inclusion and especially by exclusion. By Queen Victoria's time, sexual taboos were no longer primarily transmitted to all by the ear, but only to some through the eye. The ballad had become the broadside, and the broadside had become the penny dreadful. Stories that had been told or sung were now finding their way into repeatable print, and that print was held in the hands of particular audiences. The fingerprints of those audiences can still be seen around the edges of pages that carried what the group needed to preserve. In many cases we still return to these texts because we too need to be reminded. In the next chapters I will examine the specific genres that were the primary carriers of these social instructions—the sentimental and the gothic. For the present, however, I would like to follow one tale of incest horror that has continually migrated between folk and art media, because it shows how the frisson of incest finds incorporation into various media. This saga has found its way to the ears, eyes, hands, and minds of a particular and needful audience—the young—for generations.

The story of the vampire is probably one of the most common tales in our culture. More movies, and perhaps more comics, costumes, and televison programs, have been made from this one tale than from all others; in fact, an entire vampire soap opera appeared a few years ago—*Dark Shadows*. Literally tons of other schlock has been produced, most of which is so vulgar that it even gives popular culture a bad name. So, on the assumption that what we dispose of is almost as important as what we keep, I should like to examine the flotsam of this myth in the hope that we may understand why it has endured through countless lifetimes.

Clearly, the vampire myth has been a prime carrier of horror; that it is also one of the more powerful caveats against incest is not so clear. Let me briefly reiterate the story because, rather like the automatic refrains of the ballad, we know it too well to think about it. Any twelve-year-old schoolchild can describe the vampire and his horrid habits and that, of course, is precisely why the story is so important; it is a cultural scenario learned early and repeated again and again throughout the pre-teenage years.

The vampire, aka Dracula, the Count, etc., is an older man

who both terrorizes and seduces younger women. He is handsome, tall, powerful, rich, has a strange middle-European ac-
cent (this the influence of Bela Lugosi—Stoker's literary Dracula spoke perfect English), and strange appetites. His actions
are divided into two parts. The first part of the story describes
how the vampire sates his horrid appetites, and the second tells
how he can be controlled and eventually destroyed.

In the first half of the story we learn that the vampire is
cursed; he must have blood, and this blood invariably must be
from a young lady. So he *must* attack her. His attack is notable
for its total lack of violence. I cannot think of any other mon-
ster-molester in our culture who does such terrible things to
young victims in such a gentlemanly manner. He is always
polite and deferential, and his victim is almost always passive
in return. In folklore, the young female may even subtly initiate
the affair by granting the demon access to her bedroom, or by
helping him to cross a blessed threshold, or by unlatching a
window, or even by looking at him as if she were willing to
be his victim. The attack, if it really can be called such, is so
well known in our contemporary cinematic folklore as to be
boringly prescripted. The female victim is most often preparing for bed, dressed in a negligee, usually white and inviting.
The vampire mysteriously appears; she may somehow encourage the rapprochement; he captivates her (literally "en-
thralls" her), kisses her, then bites her on the neck, sucks her
blood (this is often excised to concentrate on her sensual reaction), and leaves her swooning. She visibly weakens; he
continues to return night after night until she seems to die,
but is actually transformed into the very type of demon who
has "attacked" her. In what seems a most intriguing instance
of the *Doppelgänger* motif, the victim now becomes corrupt and
seeks new victims of her own. The price she has paid for being
susceptible, for not being cautious, is eternal damnation. Like
the ballad, this myth dispenses its punishment with heartless
regularity. Make this mistake, it says, and you will suffer—even
the priest can't help you now.

Here the second part of the story unfolds: this is the "modern" part, influenced by literature and especially by the cinema. The young female, corrupted into sin, must seek victims of her own. She has become a "lamia," a female vampire. Obviously, the story could descend into tedium unless the proto-vampire, the older male violator, is destroyed, and so, of course, he must be. In *Dracula*, which is the first story to emphasize vampire destruction, Dr. Van Helsing, a wise father figure from across the sea, leads a horde of young men (who were all in love with the young victim, appropriately named Lucy) in spirited pursuit of Dracula. Much academic criticism has it that Dracula represents the evil father: he is older than the "boys," has his own home in Transylvania, and is savvy in the nefarious ways of the world. Van Helsing, on the other hand, is the "good" father, having wisdom and love to offer in place of self-aggrandizement and worldly goods.[14] This is clearly stated in the myth. Hence, the end of the story has the good boys under the tutelage of the wise father chasing the bad patriarch until they destroy him. They kill him, incidentally, not by staking but by decapitation; female vampires, in a scene full of phallic overtones, are staked.[15] This chase scene is often enacted in our modern renditions with the Van Helsing figure played by a doctor—a hematologist, or in some cases even a psychiatrist.

The English anthropologist Maurice Richardson first described the correlation between this chase-to-the-death and Freud's thesis, developed in *Totem and Taboo*, of the primal horde. This interpretation makes considerable sense, for Dracula is indeed the evil father out to violate what the boys want (namely the young, innocent women), and so patricide must be committed. The boys may suffer guilt, but at least they get what they want, and the price seems worth it. Very often in the modern movie versions, Dracula is happy to die, to be freed from his hideous habits. In a sense his death relieves the boys of unnecessary guilt, while allowing their sociobiological needs to be met. Still, it is clear that the sin of Dracula is not that he violates women, but that he chooses this particularly susceptible victim, and that his relationship with her mimics forbidden sexual activity within the nuclear family. For what does he promise her but that she will be his wife, his queen. Yet, what is she to him but his child, his ward . . . his daughter.

The end of the story, Dracula's pursuit and destruction, seems simple enough; as a matter of fact, the primal horde explanation is standard now in both literary criticism and psychology. What is perplexing is the sexual excitement that the first part of the myth seems to arouse. So let us reexamine it, keeping in mind the puerile nature of the audience, both male and female. The most startling aspect of the folkloric vampire is that he must first attack members of his own family. This prerequisite has been lost in our modern versions, but it is clear in almost every early story in almost every culture. We may have neglected this because we find it too dull and predictable, but it may also be, as I hope to illustrate, because this familial tie makes all too clear the vampire's specific sexual design.

We should recall that the only act the vampire commits is that of sucking. He does not rip bodies apart like the werewolf or a Mr. Hyde; he dismembers no one. His only physical deformity is slightly protruding incisors, and this aberration does have a rather utilitarian purpose. His sucking, however, produces catastrophic results. A case could be made that here the latent, or not so latent, oral desires of the preadolescent audience are being projected in order to be suppressed. Sucking is fun, yes, but you should not do it. Dracula himself is, in a sense, "oral cannibalistic," and that will not do. It is wrong; it violates a prohibition. But if you look at the psychodynamics of the sucking within the myth, you will discover that the woman apparently enjoys it; as a matter of fact, it is highly sexual for both partners. You will also observe that the sucking is a displacement of other more overtly sexual acts.

This scene is still more complex because as the vampire takes blood, he is also inseminating his victim with evil. In this myth a rape scene is played out through the gauze of fantasy, and you only need remember how this is enacted in the cinema to recall the eroticism of this violence. He wants her, she may even want him; yet something is terribly wrong. Something evil is happening for which he will have to be destroyed and she will have to be punished. It might be suggested that their activity is overlapped as well with a recreation of the "primal scene." In particular, the young male audience witnesses the older man defile the virgin (to this audience, at least, the mother is virginal), while at the same time imagining themselves to be that powerful man. Hence this audience response to the vampire is paradoxical. On one hand, the vampire is bad, evil, sucking what he should not be sucking, being sexual where he should not be; yet, it is all somehow very alluring. Remember, the vampire has everything a young man could want. He is powerful, he has all the night to himself, he has all the women he wants, and, especially, he has this particular one. The ambivalence is played out in the affective response in which the audience seems to say: "The vampire, if he would play by the rules and not attack my woman/mother/sister/daughter, is wonderful, but if he makes mistakes and overreaches his limits, I'll have to fight with him."

Not all is weighted on the vampire's side. He is terrified of church icons, holy water and the rest; he is photophobic; and he has other inexplicable fears—garlic, wolfsbane (here, I suppose, lycanthropic overtones of the myth do make sense), running water; many of these phobias are clearly regional in nature, such as the Transylvanian fear of blue eyes or red hair. He is not invincible, although he may posture otherwise, and the audience knows it. Young ladies wear crosses for more reasons than reminders of faith; they were literally thought to be anathema to fiends. The power to persuade his victim to remove her cross voluntarily is one of the vampire's most accomplished and important feats. It is the father's ultimate statement of power. He can cause her not only to fall under his sway, but also in the process to renounce a more powerful Father.

For a myth so loaded with sexual excitement there is no mention of sexuality. It is sex without genitalia, sex without confusion, sex without responsibility, sex without guilt, sex without love—better yet, sex without mention. The only time sexuality ever surfaces is in the rare cases when the male is victim to the female vampire, the lamia. Here, the pattern of attack is vaguely similar, but the results are dramatically different. The female vampire is older than her male victim, knowledgeable in the ways of the world, and inducts her novitiate not into evil but into manhood. Whereas the young female victim of the older male attack is socially exiled, the young male victim is strengthened through sex. Ernest Jones, one of the few psychologists to have studied this myth, explains this aspect of it in the context of the audience. In *On the Nightmare*, he writes:

> The explanation of these phantasies is surely not hard. A nightly visit from a beautiful or frightful being, who first exhausts the sleeper with passionate embraces and then withdraws from him a vital fluid: all this can point only to a natural and common process, namely to nocturnal emissions accompanied with dreams of a more or less erotic nature. In the unconscious mind blood is commonly an equivalent for semen. (p. 119)

When we look into literature, Jones' thesis is reinforced. For instance, when Jonathan Harker, the young protagonist in *Dracula*, is approached by three lamias, the description is full of barely sublimated sexuality. It is indeed dreamlike:

> In the moonlight opposite me were three young women, ladies by their dress and manner. I thought at the time that I must be dreaming when I saw them, for, though the moonlight was behind them, they threw no shadow on the floor. They came close to me, and looked at me for some time, and then whispered together. All three had brilliant white teeth that shone like pearls against the ruby of their voluptuous lips. There was something about them that made me uneasy, some longing and at the same time some deadly fear. I felt in my heart a wicked, burning desire that they would kiss me with those red lips. It is not good to note this down, lest some day it should meet Mina's [Jonathan's wife] eyes and cause her pain; but it is the truth. They whispered together, and then they all three laughed—such a silvery, musical laugh, but as hard as though the sound never could have come through the softness of human lips. The fair girl advanced and bent over me till I could feel the movement of her breath upon me. . . .

I was afraid to raise my eyelids, but looked out and saw perfectly under the lashes. The girl went on her knees, and bent
over me, simply gloating. There was a deliberate voluptuous-
ness which was both thrilling and repulsive, and as she arched
her neck she actually licked her lips like an animal, till I could
see in the moonlight the moisture shining on the scarlet lips
and on the red tongue as it lapped the white sharp teeth. (pp.
47-48)

This masturbatory excitement is maintained in the cinema:
the seductress takes the young male across puberty into manhood. A price must be paid, of course, but the price is very
often that he will destroy her, or at least come to terms with
her. But the young female victim will *never* take charge of her
male attacker. Clearly, the social stereotypes of male dominance and female passivity are being reinforced here at an early
age. And just as clearly we see that the horror is generated
not from this variant of the myth but from the older male-
younger female version.

If the myth seems many things to the male adolescent, how
can one explain its fascination for the adult audience? As recent filmic renditions such as Frank Langella's *Dracula* (1982)
and novels such as Anne Rice's *Interview with the Vampire* (1980)
and *The Vampire Lestat* (1985) show, the audience for this myth
dissipates with age, but does not disappear. Is this the re-
working of unresolved sexual tensions, a wish fulfillment, the
return of the repressed, or could it be as well a recapitulation
and condensation of mature sexuality? Why, in short, is the
myth interesting to people who should "know better"? Why
does the audience extend past adolescence, and why does the
myth continue to carry horror? A thesis developed by Freud
in "On the Universal Tendency to Debasement in the Sphere
of Love" may be of some help. Simply put, Freud conjectured
that:

Since we must recognize that all the relevant factors known to
us—the strong childhood fixation, the incest-barrier and the
frustration in the years of development after puberty—are to
be found in practically all civilized human beings, we should
be justified in expecting psychical impotence to be a universal

affliction under civilization and not a disorder confined to some individuals. [The result to the male is that] this is the source of his need for a debased sexual object, a woman who is ethically inferior, to whom he need attribute no aesthetic scruples, who does not know him in his other social relations and cannot judge him in them. It is to such a woman that he prefers to devote his sexual potency, even when the whole of his affection belongs to a woman of a higher kind. [However] in the case of women there is little sign of a need to debase their sexual object. This is no doubt connected with the absence in them as a rule of anything similar to the sexual overvaluation found in men. (pp. 185-186)

Hence, the vampire myth reinforces not only a social paradigm but a psychological one as well. There is considerable sexual hostility and horror in the myth, although it often seems rather muted. The male vampire debases the female victim; he destroys her virginity, makes her an outcast; but the female vampire does no such thing to the male—in fact, she has less interest in him than he has in her. On both sides of the vampire myth the incestuous behavior seems primarily motivated by the male.

Then why should the myth appeal to the adolescent female? When she is the aggressor, the femme fatale, she does indeed live out a fantasy of power, a fantasy that flows through folklore from Lilith, the first man-destroyer to, I suppose, Theda Bara, the most famous of the Hollywood "vamps." Clearly, it may be important to be the preserver and destroyer of male power, but why should the female audience respond to the role of victim? Is it because she is the one least likely to have "natural" inhibitions? Does her passive, even conspiratorial, role support a now outdated and erroneous view of rape, in which the victim secretly encourages the rapist? Or does "rape" here beg the question? Although this Reichean view has been repeatedly debunked by feminists, most notably in Susan Brownmiller's *Against Our Will*, it may ironically be supported and maintained by myths like these.[16] This may be a male story meant to be "overheard" by females, for it recapitulates the view of father-daughter incest in which the child secretly conspires.

A more probable explanation of why the vampire appeals to the pubescent female is offered in another work by Freud in the series "Contributions to the Psychology of Love." Whereas in "The Universal Tendency to Debasement" Freud attempted to explain male impotency, in his next paper, "The Taboo on Virginity," he discusses female frigidity. His thesis, simply put, is that the adolescent female, denied her primary love object (father/brother), must settle for a husband who can at best imitate her original choice. Furthermore, her defloration is an initiation of considerable complexity and some inevitable disappointment. What is supposed to be pleasurable is discomforting. How to resolve these paradoxes is one of the functions of myth and ritual, and in many "primitive" cultures the rupturing of the hymen is performed by a surrogate father in a highly stylized ceremony. Again, in Freud's words:

> The customs of primitive peoples seem to take account of this *motif* of early sexual wish by handing over the task of defloration to an elder, priest or holy man, that is, to a substitute for the father. There seems to me to be a direct path leading from this custom to the highly vexed question of the *jus primae noctis* of the medieval lord of the manor. (p. 204)

It is tempting to extend this *droit du seigneur* not only to the medieval lord, but also to Count Dracula.

Could this displaced family romance not also account for the curious ambivalence of the female in the vampire myth? When the male audience interprets the action, the female represents his own forbidden mother, virginal to him, who is being violated by his father, an ironic projection of himself in the guise of the vampire. When the adolescent female views the myth, she is the victim, virginal again, but now being swept through her "initiation" by a gentle lord—a father who must then disappear into the darkness, leaving her to other men and other experiences.

We have few other myths in our culture so supple yet so complete as this. It endures through mindless repetition because it not only covers the stages of sexual growth, it does so from both male and female points of view. Little wonder, then, that the lead singer with "KISS," a popular singing group whose appeal is primarily to teenagers, is decked out as a vampire; that there is a vampire puppet on Sesame Street, "Count Count," who teaches numbers to our children; that vampire comics are one of the most popular genres in that febrile medium; that children should want to eat a "vitamin enriched" breakfast cereal named "Count Chocula"; that vampires are almost omnipresent on Saturday morning cartoons; that so many vampire movies and television shows have been especially crafted for early adolescents ("Abbott and Costello meet Dracula," "Billy the Kid and Dracula," "The Munsters," "The Groovie Goolies," etc.); that wax teeth complete with incisors are a popular Halloween mask . . . the list goes on and on. I doubt that there is another image of such cultural vitality. Superman, Tarzan, Wonder Woman, the cowboy, and Batman (perhaps a mutation of Dracula himself complete with the bat transformation, but this time in the service of goodness, not the Prince of Darkness) all pale in comparison. The vampire is a most complete condensation of the problems and the resolutions of family romance. That is why adolescents return to it again and again until they learn not what the story means, but what will happen to them should they allow fantasy, or even "real life," to involve them in behavior that can only lead to "a fate worse than death."

To see how variations of this family concussion were transformed with equal ambiguity, although greater concentration, into art culture, we need return to the transformation of sensibilities that ushered in the modern world. We need return to romanticism. For there at the bridge of classic and modern is the first conscious articulation of our anxiety about incest. Although this anxiety is often couched in bravado and flamboyance, we will see that what characterizes the romantic temper is not a desire to subvert the family, but rather an often awkward and embarrassing need to reinforce it.

CHAPTER 3

"STRANGE FITS OF PASSION": INCEST IN ROMANTIC ART

Strange fits of passion have I known:
And I will dare to tell,
But in the lover's ear alone,
What once to me befell.
    —William Wordsworth

NO MATTER HOW one interprets incest, it is axio-
matic that the reproductive codes of the human race
are carried both by biology and by culture. That "we must
reproduce" is the a priori mandate of the genes. But with
whom, when, and where are obviously also the concerns of
society. How a society remembers what sexual behaviors have
proved the most efficient, and how this information is coded
into preservable texts, is the subject of this and the following
chapters.

How reproductive codes are embedded in a culture is a huge
subject. In fact, it is the major concern of sociobiology, and
the minor concern of all the social sciences. Clearly strict limits
are needed if one is to attempt any in-depth study of even a
minor aspect of the question. I intend to examine only literary
and subliterary treatments of incest in Anglo-American culture and only those "memories" primarily recorded in the early
nineteenth century. One might well ask, since these memories
stretch back to the beginning of culture and extend forward

into the immediate present, why concentrate on the nine-teenth century? For two reasons: for the first time a self-con-scious art movement, romanticism, exploited the frisson of in-cest for various purposes; and for the first time a Western culture was able and willing to preserve not only the "best that has been thought and said," but also what *really* was being thought and said. In the early nineteenth century we find that an art culture, which historically has controlled the media of memory, namely print, as well as a popular culture, the mem-ory previously carried by individuals and primarily commu-nicated by "word of mouth," were preserved.

That the nineteenth century is such a full attic of our past perceptions and attitudes is not because our great-grandpar-ents were any more candid about family matters than their forefathers (although it sometimes seems that way), but rather because so much of what they thought and said *could* be re-corded. Knowing Byron's every thought makes him seem much more disobedient and rebellious than someone like Collins or Cowper who could commit relatively little private and per-sonal knowledge to print. As "getting into print" became eas-ier, authorial caution slackened and tabooed subjects were broached. With new methods of paper production, the intro-duction of nonbleeding permanent inks, printing plate cast-ing, and especially the sophisticated production of the mas-sive steam-driven presses, the range of recordable information and thoughts was vastly expanded. Not only could a greater variety of human experience be recorded, but, more impor-tant, for the first time there was a reading audience curious to learn about themselves as perceived by others and motivated to read as earlier they had been eager to listen. By the first quarter of the nineteenth century this newly literate audience had swelled tenfold. Thanks to the establishment of schools they could read, and thanks to the rise of capitalism they could purchase what a generation before had been the privileged "texts" of aristocracy. The broadside and the newspaper re-placed fireside instruction and doorstep gossip; Gutenberg changed not just what we knew, but also how we found out about it.

For the purposes of examining the incest taboo I am going to treat both popular and art culture as if they were independent memories of behavior. If only for heuristic purposes, it may be instructive to see the difference between what we say we ought to believe and what we do, in fact, believe. Very often, although we imagine the avant garde to be taking risks, the art culture really reinforces the status quo while popular culture, which seems to uphold tradition, is far more experimental. I don't mean this as Marxist rhetoric—there is certainly no predestined dialectic operating with regard to procreative behavior—but I do mean to assert that romanticism is far less revolutionary in sexual mores than has often been claimed both by the poets and the critics.

I intend to trace the incest taboo as it unfolds both consciously and unconsciously in the work of individual artists on both sides of the Atlantic. In this chapter I will concentrate on central poetic works by English poets, primarily Shelley, Byron, and Wordsworth, and in the penultimate chapter I will study particular prose works by American writers, notably Poe, Hawthorne, and Melville. Here in art culture the texts are stable, well studied, and, I will contend, not as radical in approach and treatment as popular culture texts. In between I want to put forward what was simultaneously happening in popular culture, where the circumspect demands of genre, decorum, and diction were put aside in favor of mass production and consumption. The conduction of the taboo in mass media allows us to see for the first time in the West what the majority of people *wanted* to know, not what they had been told they *should* know. Whereas the art culture depended on intermediaries, namely priests and then critics, to explain and preserve sacred texts, popular culture usually protects its texts by copying them in multitude. So if such information is preserved, it is not because a sacerdotal caste locks it away, but because there is too much of it around for it to disappear. Under the aegis of popular culture I will examine two veritable conduits of social information that are still brimful: the pornographic and the gothic novel.

That the general subject of family life, and the more specific topic of incest, would be a major concern of romanticism was predictable. After all, Western artists from Euripides to Chateaubriand had addressed this subject, and all the major preromantic English artists—Chaucer, Spenser, Shakespeare, Milton, and Dryden—had, with varying degrees of candor and insight, explained the social ramifications of mismanaged family sexual relations.[1] Almost without exception, the preromantic treatment of incest is reflexively condemnatory. Think only of the sibling incest in Ford's *'Tis Pity She's a Whore* or Dryden's *Don Sebastian* or his *Love Triumphant*; recall Chaucer's retelling of Patient Griselda in *The Canterbury Tales*, where the father's supposed act of incest is shocking, but finally revealed to be a ruse. Or what of the recurrent theme of displaced intrafamilial sexual tension that partially causes the ultimate tragedies of *Hamlet*, *Othello*, and *King Lear*? As Mark Taylor has recently argued in *Shakespeare's Darker Purpose: A Question of Incest*, these are central works not just in Elizabethan culture but are prescient allegories of family life in Jacobean, Restoration and Neoclassic times.[2]

Perhaps the most important preromantic scenario of incest, both because it is so visual as well as so deeply embedded in Christianity, is the Miltonic configuration of Sin and Death in *Paradise Lost*.[3] As Satan rises up from Pandemonium en route to the earthly world, he is stopped at Hell's Gate by a hideous swarm of monsters. There are two large beasts: one is a fearsome figure of wrath and the other is a female who is reptilian below the waist. All around squirm snakey and deformed vermin oozing from the lower part of her body.

Satan would have slashed his way past the first misshapen creature, seized the key to Hell's Gate from this woman, and been on his way upward, had she not cried out, "O father, what intends thy hand . . . against thy only son?" (2.726–727). Satan is dumbfounded and so she explains the ungodly mess Satan sees before him. She is Sin—born, like Athena from Zeus, from the head of Satan who, once he saw what his mind had labored forth, became enamored with seeing himself in her. So enamored in fact with his own mirror self that he inseminated her, his daughter, as an act more of narcissism than of eroticism or violation. (We can already see in Satan's motivation what the romantic poets found so alluring in this perversion of the creation scene.) With the fall of Satan after the battle in Heaven, Sin is made the keeper of the keys to Hell and there she gestates the issue of Satan's self-love. Sin continues the story,

> Pensive here I sat
> Alone, but long I say not, till my womb
> Pregnant by thee, and now excessive grown,
> Prodigious motion felt and rueful throes.
> At last the odious offspring whom thou seest,
> Thine own begotten, breaking violent way,
> Tore through my entrails, that, with fear and pain
> Distorted, all my nether shape thus grew
> Transformed; but he, my inbred enemy,
> Forth issued, brandishing his fatal dart,
> Made to destroy. I fled, and cried out *Death*;
> Hell trembl'd at the hideous Name, and sigh'd
> From all her Caves, and back resounded *Death*. (2.777–788)

Now it is Death's turn to molest his sister/mother, which he does, and it is the issue of that violent rape that is, even as Sin speaks, still flowing out hourly and clustering about their feet. Sin explains how this came to pass.

> [Death] me overtook, his mother, all dismayed,
> And in embraces forcible and foul
> Engendering with me, of that rape begot
> These yelling monsters, that with ceaseless cry
> Surround me, as thou sawest, hourly conceived
> And hourly born, with sorrow infinite
> To me; for when they list, into the womb
> That bred them they return, and howl, and gnaw
> My bowels, their repast; then, bursting forth
> Afresh with conscious terrors vex me round,
> That rest or intermission none I find. (2.792–802)

Such a scene was too pictorial, too visually expressive, not to be transformed into literal illustration. And indeed it was.

Here, in an art text, was an image to be repeatedly visualized, not only by the illustrators of Milton, but also by a new generation of artists who were scouring popular and esoteric texts to find images of gothic sublimity—images that would horrify. This scene was, in fact, the most commonly illustrated episode from all of *Paradise Lost* in the eighteenth century.[4]

Here are three of those numerous illustrations that presented this scene to the eyes and imaginations of the young romantic poets. First, in the blasphemous trinity as viewed by Hogarth, sin clearly has captured the focus of our attention, trapped like a sentimental heroine between snarling father and hideous brother/son. Beneath her are those writhing beasts that hourly issue forth and betray her involvement, if not her culpability. However, there can be no doubting her allegiance— she looks helplessly to her father (who looks suspiciously like

(Tate Gallery, London)

William Hogarth, *Satan, Sin and Death*, 1764

(Ashmolean Museum, Oxford)

J. H. Fuseli, *Satan, Sin and Death*, 1776

a Roman warrior) while holding her brother/son at bay. This is such a grandiose scene that Fuseli, himself master of the nightmare vision, drew nine variations of it before he realized it was so hideous a scene that it almost invited parody. Before he was done, he simplified the forms, emphasizing Satan and Death as almost gladiators battling for the prize: the woman (daughter/mother/sister) between them.

It was Fuseli's version of Hogarth's illustration that Blake took as inspiration for his depiction of the same scene. We can see at once how Hogarth's vision has become stylized, allegorical and intellectual, almost as if Blake, who could create some of the most horrible images when he wanted, was instead trying to understand the dynamics of the family group. All we need do to see how sensitivities were changing is to compare it to the sculpted, almost classical, version by James Barry. In comparison to Barry's Death, Blake's is no longer skeletonic, but positively transparent. Sin's no longer full-breasted torso is carefully superimposed onto snaky coils, the allegorical key is still front and center, but the background has

(British Museum)

James Barry, *Satan, Sin and Death,* **1775**

been reticulated as if the image is set in bas relief. Blake's vision is so symmetrical, so studied. Not only are the combat-
ants Greek warriors, but even Sin has become a stylized Me-
dusa in what might be an attempt to explain her role as guilty
partner, a role not to be found in Milton. Where Hogarth had

(Huntington Library)

William Blake, *Satan Sin and Death*, c. 1808

created the image to shock and unsettle the emotions, Blake seems to invite us to ponder the frozen relationship of family dynamics.

What makes the romantic attraction not only to this image, but to eccentric family romance in general, different from what had been the tradition in English culture? What makes it something we recognize as modern? As opposed to Chaucer, Spenser, Shakespeare, and Dryden who used the violation of sexual taboo to entertain, to titillate or more likely, to instruct, the romantic artist is initially attracted by the taboo as it seems to promise what Milton inadvertently implies with Satan—self-knowledge. Samuel Johnson in his *Life of Milton* severely criticized Milton's allegory of Satan, Sin, and Death because it implied narcissism, not the more acceptable lust, as Satanic motivation. However, this same impulse toward self-love was one of the primary inspirations of concentric romanticism, and it clearly comes from more than rereading and revising Milton.

Romantic curiosity about the self was sanctioned in part by the rise of natural philosophy, popularized by Rousseau, which had as its epistemological goal the understanding of how we would behave without external taboos. Aligned with this interest in solipsism, the English were especially interested in natural states of consciousness. Inspired by Locke and Hume, traditional notions of states of being, of subconscious and superconscious, of order and disorder, were coming into question. In aesthetics the new category of the sublime, championed by Burke, is testament to a more generalized discontent with categories circumscribed by the beautiful, the picturesque, the pleasing. For what about the attraction of the grotesque, the abrupt, the irregular? Often what was later mistaken by the high Victorians as the romantic's rage for disorder, their delight in the eccentric, was really an attempt to reexamine the boundaries of natural behavior. In this context it was to be expected that sooner rather than later the artist would turn his attention beyond the self to the domestic triangle of father/mother/child as well as to the dyad of brother/sister and attempt to test the balance.

As we shall see, the first effects of this curiosity appeared in popular culture—in the gothic novel and the gothic melodrama—in large part as a result of the surging influence of the German *Schauerroman*. As J. M. S. Tompkins has observed, the romantic poets were not the first to reintroduce incest configurations to culture. "They found [the incest theme] in the first place, in the novels they devoured as boys . . . . The theme has been so closely associated with romantic and revolutionary poets that its wide dispersion in the 'seventies and 'eighties, a generation before the master utterances of romantic poetry, is worthy of note."[5] Thanks to the gothic, upsetting family sexual balance had already become a major concern, and the poets simply applied increasing pressure on the nuclear family until it completely fell apart. As opposed to the gothic conventions, however, the romantic treatment was followed not by reassembling the family, but by heroic resignation or visionary escape—the ultimate resolution via narcissism.

Clearly, in art culture Byron and Shelley were the most conspicuous articulators of the new willingness to play out the results of family imbalance. These two poets form a compelling condensation of romantic viewpoints. Byron's interest is pragmatic, actual, and calculated, while Shelley's is idealistic, fantastic, and ultimately allegorical. It is usually thought that these poets were revolutionary in their willingness not just to countenance violations of the taboo, but in their sympathetic treatment of the participants. I hope to show that quite the opposite may also be true. Certainly, they were enthusiastic about exploding family liaisons into new constellations, but they were uniformly skeptical, even censorious, about the actual practice. As far as results were concerned, they seemed uninterested. Ironically, it was popular culture, not art culture, that played out the forbidden scenarios without recourse to deus ex machina conclusions, abrupt shifts in theme, or expedient tragedies.

Although I have earlier mentioned Byron's affair with his half-sister, Augusta Leigh, it may be instructive to view the self-conscious transformation of this major social event into its artistic reconstruction. For whatever else Byron's *Manfred* is, it still remains one of the most conservative statements of the risks and ravages of family romance. We realize this from the first because Manfred is not an ordinary mortal; he is rather an extraordinary poet/theurgist whose power to manipulate reality involves access to the very operations of Nature. As the drama opens, Manfred is bemoaning some past act that has caused him such pain that he has exiled himself from others, and now wishes to exile himself from his own self. Although we don't know what this act was, his only desire now is not forgiveness but forgetfulness. He adamantly refuses to admit guilt; he quite simply wants to be relieved of all consciousness. Like a budding romanticist he implores the forces of Nature to provide the balm. After all, Wordsworth had promised the resurrection of the self through Nature, and if anyone ever needed a rebirth it is Manfred. So Manfred conjures the palliative spirits from the clouds, the mountains, the water, the winds, and the night, but they are unable to provide the forgetfulness he desires. Suddenly, aware that "oblivion, self-oblivion" cannot be achieved through Nature, a despondent Manfred next attempts suicide, but is rescued literally at the edge of the Jungfrau by a passing mountaineer. This good but ignorant man of the mountains leads the powerful but melancholy Manfred back to his Alpine cottage and there attempts to revive his spirits. He offers wine. A hallucinating Manfred refuses it, saying:

> Away, away! there's blood upon the brim!
> Will it then never—never sink in the earth?
>
>   . . .
>
> I say 'tis blood—my blood! the pure warm stream
> Which ran in the veins of my fathers, and in ours
> When we were in our youth, and had one heart,
> And loved each other as we should not love,
> And this was shed: but still it rises up,
> Coloring the clouds, that shut me out from heaven,
> Where thou are not—and I shall never be. (2.1.21–30)

The metaphor of wine and blood may have eluded the simple mountain man, but it was eagerly and easily decoded by the then contemporary reader. This Byronic hero, this unrepentant sinner, this exile blighted by too much experience, is none other than the archviolator of family taboo—Lord Byron himself.

Lest we happen to pass this by too quickly, Byron makes certain the point is taken. In the next scene his moody libertine reports the one event he has been unable to overcome:

> From my youth upwards
> My Spirit walked not with the souls of men,
> Nor looked upon the earth with human eyes;
> The thirst of their ambition was not mine,
> The aim of their existence was not mine;
> My joys, my griefs, my passions, and my powers,
> Made me a stranger; though I wore the form
> I had no sympathy with breathing flesh,
> Nor midst the creatures of clay that girded me
> Was there but one who—but of her anon. (2.2.50–59)

We need not wait long to learn more of the one who was able to so perplex Manfred, for he now appears all too willing to confess. In fact, he seems determined to:

> She was like me in lineaments; her eyes,
> Her hair, her features, all, to the very tone
> Even of her voice, they said were like to mine;
> But softened all, and tempered into beauty:
> She had the same lone thoughts and wanderings,
> The quest of hidden knowledge, and a mind
> To comprehend the universe: not these
> Alone, but with them gentler powers than mine,
> Pity, and smiles, and tears—which I had not;
> And tenderness—but that I had for her;
> Humility—and that I never had.
> Her faults were mine—her virtues were her own—
> I loved her, and destroyed her! (2.3.106–118)

Hearing this, the mountaineer asks if Manfred is to be taken literally: did he really "destroy" her? No, Manfred replies with characteristic hyperbole, he did not literally kill her, but rather "her heart . . . gazed on mine, and withered. I have shed/Blood, but not hers—and yet her blood was shed; I saw and could not stanch it" (2.3.120–121). Neither could she. Manfred's love, it seems, has destroyed his still nameless inamorata; his love has broken her heart and her plight now somehow threatens to destroy him. What he has done has made him feel so abject (but *not* guilty) that there can be no relief. What exactly could he have done?

The Witch of the Alps, a Venus Genetrix figure, now promises Manfred some relief if he will only submit to her will, but,
as we earlier learned, Nature can be no help for such pain.
She may be nurse to Wordsworth and an inspiration to Keats,
but Byron needs more intensive care. So his protagonist goes
to the throne of Arimanes, the spirit of the Demonic powers
in the universe, where he is commanded to be humble and
submit. Manfred refuses and the forces of Chaos are so startled by his confidence that they allow him to view the spirit
of his victim. Were it not already clear, it certainly is by now:
the Phantom of Astarte is none other than the displaced Augusta Leigh.

Manfred's invasion of Astarte's privacy has traumatized her
forever; she can be invoked but not made to speak, much less
to forgive. Manfred implores:

> Astarte! my beloved! speak to me:
> I have so much endured—so much endure—
> Look on me! the grave hath not changed thee more
> Than I am changed for thee. Thou lovedst me
> Too much, as I loved thee: we were not made
> To torture thus each other, though it were
> The deadliest sin to love as we have loved. (2.4.118–124)

He begs forgiveness but it is not forthcoming: to "love as [they]
have loved" is clearly beyond the pale even for this most mighty
of men. An utterly despondent Manfred is convulsed with pain
while the assembled spirits of anarchy marvel: "Had he been
one of us, he would have made/An awful spirit" (2.4.163–164).
Only such a spirit, it is implied, could have committed the
sins of Manfred and endured.

Byron's Manfred is not such a spirit. He is one of us—he is
a mortal who has transgressed laws feared even by demons.
If such a man as he cannot endure the distress of this act, how
could we imagine, let alone even dream, that we could? It is
now time for the angels to offer if not forgiveness, then at
least understanding, for such heinous acts. In the guise of the
abbot of St. Maurice the cleansing forces of Christian purga-

tion are brought to bear on the stain of incest. But Manfred will have none of it; the mark of his sin cannot be so easily cleansed.

> Look on me! there is an order
> Of mortals on the earth, who do become
> Old in their youth, and die ere middle age,
> Without the violence of warlike death;
> Some perishing of pleasure, some of study,
> Some worn with toil, some of mere weariness,
> Some of disease, and some insanity,
> And some of withered or of broken hearts;
> For this last is a malady which slays
> More than are numbered in the lists of fate,
> Taking all shapes, and bearing many names. (3.1.138–148)

Presumably, Manfred is to be counted among the last group. All this puffery only makes the seriousness of Manfred's sexual transgression the more awesome. If a man of such dominance and force could not withstand the torment of incest, how could others survive? Manfred has found no help in solitude, in nature, in society, in demonism, or in religion because the subtext of this drama argues that there is no help for *this* sin. The only way to forget, let alone be forgiven, is to die.

At the end of the play Manfred faces death with heroic stoicism. The abbot and Manfred see an awesome figure rising up in the mist, and the abbot is convinced it has come to collect Manfred's damned soul. Manfred knows better. He is no Faust (regardless of what the nineteenth century commentators said) and he has not sold his soul for forbidden experience. In fact, just the opposite. He has had a forbidden experience *without* bargaining, and that is the problem. Nothing has mediated his knowledge of what should not be known. He has done it all on his own. The abbot, thinking that this misty figure is from hell, begs Manfred to receive the last rites, but Manfred knows the "dusky and awful figure" will never take him below. The spirit bellows: "Mortal! thine hour is come—Away! I say." To which Manfred replies, sounding self-consciously like Milton's Satan:

> I knew, and know my hour is come, but not
> To render up my soul to such as thee:
> Away! I'll die as I have lived—alone.
>
>   . . .
>
> Thou hast no power upon me, *that* I feel;
> Thou never shalt possess me, *that* I know:
> What I have done is done; I bear within
> A torture which could nothing gain from thine:
> The mind which is immortal makes itself
> Requital for its good or evil thoughts,—
> Is its own origin of ill and end
> And its own place and time. (3.4.125–132)

Again Manfred has heightened his predicament by showing how powerful he is compared to other forces, yet, ironically, how powerless he is to overcome the consequences of his sinful act. When he finally dies the pathos is almost unbearable. He asks for the abbot's hand, and as the abbot touches Manfred, he remarks almost casually, "Old man! 'tis not so difficult to die" (3.4.151).

Such was Manfred's leavetaking, and when Byron's editor cut this line Byron was incensed. He demanded its restoration, saying that "the whole moral and effect" of the poem had been destroyed.[6] It had been. Manfred's sin is beyond exculpation, beyond penitence, beyond even understanding. It is a "sin" that even a man more powerful than all others cannot forget, nor be forgiven for. The text makes it clear: incest is a sin that transcends all life, making death its only expiation.

It may seem paradoxical that one of the most socially revolutionary, and certainly one of the most supposedly sexually "liberated" characters in the whole nineteenth century should be so fixed in his view of the inviolability of the incest taboo, but such is the case. Here in art, at least, Byron is not posing; he is speaking (possibly) from experience and he wants us to know it. We are to pity him as well as learn from him. While we usually think of Byron and the Byronic hero as the open-shirted libertine ready to try any new challenge to conservative mores, here in *Manfred* he is the archsupporter of familial sex roles.

Because this is not the usual view of Byron as sexual renegade, it may be instructive to see how sibling incest is treated in other works of Byron. Joanna Rapf makes a provocative point in "The Byronic Heroine: Incest and the Creative Process." She contends that there are three kinds of women in the Byronic canon: the "perfecta," like Donna Inez in *Don Juan*; the demonic, like Gulbayez in *D. J.*; and the ideal, like Haidée in *D. J.*, Leila in *The Giaour*, Zuleika in *The Bride of Abydos*, and Gulnare and Medora in *The Corsair*.[7] The ideal woman is dark, tempestuous, noble, spiritual, and defiant. She is also inspiration—the muse. She is as well the Byronic hero's double, his anima, his female half. So in worshipping her he celebrates poetic revelation, but she is as well his repressed sensitive self—his sister. So to follow his genius he must violate and finally destroy part of his self. In each case when the Byronic hero meets his ideal love his love proves fatal for her. In making incestuous passion the prerequisite for his creative fulfillment, Byron ironically proves far more censorious than his contemporaries. The implication is clear. The only path to creation is the destruction of what you love most. The artist is forever caught in a Hobson's choice—to create is to murder, not to create is to die. Is this complexity a reflection of Byron's guilt, his homosexuality, his fatalism, his ironic stance, or a repression of some deeper ambiguous desire?

Since the Freudians, most notably Otto Rank, would contend that sibling incest is in itself a displacement of oedipal desire, we might go back one step to look at the only mother-son pattern in the Byron oeuvre. We may recall that mother-son incest is extremely rare outside of literature. When it does appear in instances other than those in Greek tragedy, it usually follows the pattern of the Don Carlos dramas, which retell the story of Crown Prince Don Carlos and his stepmother, the second wife of King Philip II of Spain. Although Thomas Otway had earlier introduced an English version, Schiller popularized the story for the romantics. Essentially, the Don Carlos saga is a psychologically buffered version of parental incest because the mother-son relationship occurs with no possibility of consanguinity.

This configuration, full now of post-Freudian continuities, is being revived by the psychologists as the "Phaedra complex." It seems clear that Byron, fully aware of the Don Carlos tradition in German and English letters, was himself attempting to trace the dynamics of sibling incest back to its primary form. In 1815, just as his relationship with his wife was becoming unmanageable, thanks in large part to his deepening affection (sexual or not) for Augusta, he set to work on *Parisina*. Although this work was based rather closely on a fifteenth-century tragedy of incest, it was to prove to an eager public that rumors of Byron's scandalous behavior were based firmly in reality. What it proved to Byron, however, is a more interesting question.

Parisina retells a story reported by Edward Gibbon in *Antiquities of the House of Brunswick* in which the Marquis of Este discovers the incestuous love between his wife, Parisina, and his bastard son, Hugo. In Gibbon's truncated rendition the focus is on the Marquis, who is portrayed as a figure of some sympathy, having a disreputable son and an unfaithful wife. But in Byron's verse drama attention shifts predictably to the lovers' plight. With a goodly admixture of Romeo and Juliet superimposed on the story, we find that Hugo, the valiant and princely son, was engaged to Parisina long before his father pushed him aside. To make matters worse, this is not the first time father has played villain to son: he earlier reneged on nuptial promises to Hugo's biological mother. By not marrying her and "making her honest" he wrecked her life and made her son a bastard. The fact that Parisina and Hugo are star-crossed young lovers and the father is a tyrant certainly mitigates the horrors of incest, but such transgressions still demand punishment. If ever there was a context in which incest could be exploited as arbitrary, this is it. But Hugo is beheaded, Parisina enters self-exile, and the father/husband lives out his years in solitude and melancholy.

If one were looking for the expected—Byron revelling in broken taboos—one would once again be disappointed. Like *Manfred, Parisina* is socially and sexually conservative. Oddly enough, the older male protagonists—one a violator of his family, the other cuckolded by his family—share strangely similar fates. Superhuman Manfred suffers superhuman guilt; the tyrannical Marquis suffers tyrannical isolation. At the end, the paterfamilias is like a massive oak, we are told, struck to the trunk's center as if fused by lightning, blasted to the heart's core, while Manfred lives out his life as "a blighted trunk upon a cursed root." Anyone, it seems, who commits or even comes close to the forbidden act is forever cauterized to the core.

When you examine the archromantic rebel's treatment of incest you find an archconservative standpoint. True, Byron is certainly daring to introduce the subject, but its repressive resolution is Procrustean. Incest, whether parent-child or sibling, is simply insupportable. Essentially what gave Byron his reputation as advocate is twofold: he may or may not have committed the act, and, more importantly, he was willing to write about the subject in the polite forms of verse. As is often the case, the mere mention of a tabooed subject, whether it be illicit drugs, illicit beliefs or illicit sex, gives one the reputation of advocacy—especially if one is an aristocrat. As sensationalist magazines daily attest, the content of what is reported is very often less important than that it *is* reported and *who* it is reported about.

Although Byron is very sympathetic with the victim of incest (in fact, Byron was almost professionally sympathetic with victims of any tyranny, be it state sanctioned as with the Greeks at the hands of the Turks, or socially imposed as with the social constraints surrounding his Childe Harold or Don Juan), in only one instance does he seem in any way neutral to forbidden relations. In *Cain*, almost as if determined to find the possible exception, Byron makes the case for the necessity of consanguinity. However, while Byron portrays Cain's love for his sister, Adah, as necessary for the survival of the species, he also emphasizes that this kind of love must be denied to their progeny. Here is the grief-stricken Adah as she realizes

that the love she has shared with her brother must be forever
renounced by all who follow:

> Oh my God!
> Shall they not love and bring forth things that love
> Out of their love? Have they not drawn milk
> Out of this bosom? Was not he, their father,
> Born of the same sole womb in the same hour
> With me? Did we not love each other? And
> In multiplying our being multiply
> Things which will love each other as we love
> Them, and as I love thee, my Cain? (1.367–375)

As in Jacobean "blood and thunder" tragedies, such as Ford's
'Tis Pity She's a Whore, or in Restoration melodramas such as
Dryden's *Don Sebastian*, Byron plays out the forbidden scenario not to advocate or condemn, but rather to create the
inevitability of pathos—to generate the victim par excellence
in the unresolvable dilemma. In this sense we see that Byron
is far closer to the tradition of the romantic, and especially the
early gothic, novel than he is to any profound unfolding of
the *Geschwister-Komplex*.[8]

In romantic poetry it was not Byron but Shelley who was
the sexual revolutionary, the philosopher of gender, the articulate examiner of selfhood and self-love. If the traditional novel
(not the gothic, which tells another story) was the middle-class
medium of social conservatism which absorbed the verse dramas of Byron into popular culture, then it was visionary poetry, especially the lyrical excesses of Shelley, that played out
the sexual curiosities with a minimum of censorship. As if relieved of social repercussions, the ethereal realms of the heavens became the context in which to unwind themes otherwise
forbidden. Only here, literally above the horizon, could the
poet violate private mores in semipublic. The romantic desire,
not only to introduce but to sustain relationships once thought
so horrible that they could only result in tragedy, was at last
provided a habitation—the same locale where such relationships flourished in classical mythology.

In this century we have tended to separate Shelley's extreme views of sexuality from those of his colleagues, if only because they are often so radical and so shocking. In large part because of the Humanists and then the New Critics, Shelley has too often been seen as characterized by Arnold—"a beautiful but *ineffectual* angel." But in the last twenty years Shelley has been viewed as anything but "ineffectual." To the most recent generation of romantic scholars, Shelley has emerged, together with Blake, as a commentator on quintessentially modern problems.[9] Shelley was not unique in his assessment of family roles, especially in his interest in both the prescribed patterns derived from role-playing and its extension into intrafamilial tabooed sexual relations. Both subjects had precedents in art poetry, as we have seen, and even in the traditional novel incest phobia is exploited for titillation from *Moll Flanders* to *Joseph Andrews*. Usually the situation develops thus: we follow young lovers who discover that yes they were, no they were not, yes they were, no they were not siblings. What separates Shelley is his radical departure from this literary model. He was willing to tell the story in the forbidden way, the affirmative way—yes, they were siblings.

It should be mentioned that in some authors prior to Shelley, the poeticization of this configuration was also moving dangerously close to the point where the lovers realize, and accept, that they really are related. Although these works were composed by poets seemingly unconscious of the danger, we might pause to consider them for they seem to be crossing the same terrain. Certainly the two poets who inadvertently traveled on this "wrong path" were Wordsworth and Coleridge. I say "inadvertently" because at that stage of composition not only did they not know the direction English letters would take, but there is every reason to believe they did not even know what they themselves were unfolding as subjects of concern.

That the sister would provide first the ideal companion and then the ultimate completion of self, was a hypothesis being tested first in the gothic novel and then, at the turn of the century, in the art poem. Some of this interest in valorizing siblings resulted from the cross-pollination of genres; some was extraliterary, founded in biography. The romantic poets' sisters were very important influences in their brothers' lives. The "family cult of friendship" was a central part of the early nineteenth-century *Weltanschauung* for the middle class as well as for the aristocracy. The family was such a solid social and financial unit that it was quite normal for a girl to think of refusing to marry a man she loved because her brother might not like it. This was the stuff of novels because it was first the stuff of life, as the Brontës, the Lambs, and Elizabeth Barrett and her eldest brother could all testify. As Augusta Leigh was for Byron, and Elizabeth was for Shelley, so Dorothy was for William Wordsworth.

Of all these sisters, Dorothy played the most crucial role in her brother's creative life, and arguably the most important role in all his life. Twenty years ago when F. W. Bateson suggested in the second edition of *Wordsworth: A Re-interpretation* (1956) that this role had pseudosexual overtones, some members of the scholarly community were incensed. Biographical interpretations have always been an acceptable approach, but this was going too far. Bateson, however, was so convincing that his interpretation still finds a responsive audience, as the recent spate of letters to the *Times Literary Supplement* attests.[10] It is not my concern to psychoanalyze the poets, or to explore the connections of biography to art. I am interested in what impulse in romanticism should have been strong enough to partially efface the power of the taboo—not the taboo on the act, but the taboo on mentioning, implying, or even thinking of, the act.

In Wordsworth's so-called "Lucy poems" (*She Dwelt Among the Untrodden Ways, I Travelled Among Unknown Men, Strange Fits of Passion Have I Known, Three Years She Grew in Sun and Shower, A Slumber Did My Spirit Seal*), we may see played out the paradoxical compulsion to mourn the passing of what the poet considers the lost innocence of youth mixed in with what appears to be sexual longing. The poet's melancholy loss is heightened by establishing the figure of Lucy as the missing piece of some obscure puzzle of incomplete personality. In other words, she seems almost his soul sister, once an intimate part of his consciousness, now hopelessly lost even to memory. In *Tintern Abbey* this "other" is clearly depicted in Wordsworth's characterization of his sister Dorothy. As he concludes his rapture to Nature he tells how his own consciousness has expanded to comprehend the "sense sublime." As Wordsworth finishes this rather grand, and to some critics self-serving, pronouncement of his own sensitivity he turns to Dorothy and claims that,

> thou my dearest Friend
> My dear dear Friend; . . . in thy voice I catch
> The language of my former heart, and read
> My former pleasures in the shooting lights
> Of thy wild eyes. Oh! yet a little while
> May I behold in thee what I was once,
> My dear, dear Sister! (115–121)

Again, it certainly could be, and has been, argued that this emotional burst is couched in perfectly appropriate language for a generation that was much less concerned with sibling distance and roles. However, considering what we know about the depth of their affection, and that this depth was of concern to their contemporaries, it is possible to speculate on sexual undertones. For instance, as already noted, Molly Lefebure, author of *Samuel Taylor Coleridge: A Bondage of Opium*, has contended that Coleridge was distressed in April 1799 with the "melancholy & hipp'd" relationship of the Wordsworths in Germany. Brother and sister had spent part of the year together while Coleridge was wandering through the libraries of Germany. Lefebure does not contend that Coleridge suspected actual incest, but posits the possibilities, as has Donald Reiman of the Pforzheimer Library, of "incestuous longings."[11]

Considering *Tintern Abbey* in conjunction with the Lucy poems, it may appear that Wordsworth wants the relationship both ways. He wants his mature individual vision that finally encompasses "Thoughts that do often lie too deep for tears" (*Intimations Ode*). He also wants what has been lost along the way; he wants the other self, his imaginative, natural self, his anima, his feminine self personified, if you will, his Dorothy. Although he may protest that his verbal self, his religious self, his thoughtful self, his male self has been adequate compensation for the loss of this "other," we may suspect otherwise. Like the fictional René, the real-life Wordsworth seems to sense that nothing can really bring back "the hour/Of splendour in the grass," because that splendor quite possibly has overtones of forbidden emotions and relationships.

With this in mind as a possibility, it may be instructive to set aside the Dorothy of *Tintern Abbey*, and the Dorothy of the *Journals*, and the Dorothy of *The Prelude*, and look at the possibly displaced Dorothy of the Lucy poems.[12] The Lucy poems are all genre works, all elegies in which the poet, with almost deceptive candor, expresses six instances of intense feelings of loss. In English literature there had never before been such elegies; in fact, pre-Wordsworthian elegies are exactly the opposite. From classical times onward, the genre usually demanded a prescribed pattern resolving present loss by promising consolation in future life. Usually the grieving poet is vouchsafed a reassuring conclusion in which the spirit/soul of the departed is at last free of this dreary world and made happily one with the world beyond. One can see why the elegiac genre and the Christian religion were so compatible. Not so for Wordsworth; for him there is no easy deliverance into future worlds, instead only the sad "memory of what has been,/And never more will be."

Because the Dorothy-as-Lucy reading has already been detailed in Bateson's *Wordsworth: A Re-interpretation* and has been so much discussed that its thesis has become almost a postulate in the criticism of the Lucy poems, I will detail only one of the six poems. What I say is in no way original and I include it more to display the temper of romantic longing than because it specifically influenced the same theme as it unfolded in the works of others. Each poet projects his personal, and to a lesser extent his age's, sensibility and, although each poem owes its vitality to a set of unique "facts," both are still part of a wider cultural flow. I don't mean to belabor the obvious, but the unfashionable concept of *Zeitgeist* is clearly the basis of periodization in both the arts and history and is the implied assumption upon which criticism, as opposed to explication, is based.

In *Strange Fits of Passion* we have right from the title the announcement of a possible irregularity of feeling. The first stanza only reinforces the eccentricity of what may be forbidden feelings:

> Strange fits of passion have I known:
> And I will dare to tell,
> But in the Lover's ear alone,
> What once to me befell.

The rest of the poem details in a markedly emotionless manner the journey of the poet across a field and up a hill to Lucy's cottage. Beneath the ostensible stillness of his solitary trek, however, is another journey, a journey across the thresholds of consciousness through a world of powerful feeling. This inner journey is presented as it often is in art, especially in romantic art, through a cluster of natural symbols. On this allegorical level the image of the moon is central. We are told that, as the poet climbs the hill and nears Lucy's cottage, the moon, which earlier seemed to hover above the house, now rapidly drops from sight, leaving the poet in eerie darkness. Then, suddenly, the emotion of the second journey floods into the first and the poet is startled:

> What fond and wayward thoughts will slide
> Into a Lover's head!
> "O mercy!" to myself I cried,
> "If Lucy should be dead!"

Here the "strange fit of passion" abruptly ends.[13] In marked distinction to earlier elegies, there is absolutely no attempt to continue on toward any resolution. At the moment of greatest tension we are stopped in our tracks, stranded, stunned.

Why? Is it because the poet has lost interest? Because he is after only the emotion? Because he knows that explanations of death are invariably anticlimactic? Or is it because in the attempt to explain powerful feeling intelligible only to a special "Lover" (cf. first and last stanzas), Wordsworth is led here, as he was in *Tintern Abbey*, back to the one person who was once part of his self, part of his inner mirror, but who is now outside and unacceptable as the object of certain feelings? Hence the poem celebrates her demise, her death, so to speak, because longer life would prove intolerable. Could Wordsworth's repression of incestuous feeling explain the elegiac tone and genre used to commemorate the passing of a loved one, not from physical life, but from the emotional one, while also expressing the concomitant sorrow in giving up the "heart's desire" for separateness?

However the Lucy poems are interpreted (and there is an often vehement reaction to this kind of interpretation, most persuasively put forward by one of Wordsworth's more knowledgeable biographers, Mary Moorman) the possibility at least remains.[14] What is especially provocative is that the romantics may have been discovering that, although their language and culture had only one word to describe the taboo on intrafamilial relations, namely "incest," sibling relationships are fundamentally different from those of parent and child. What we may have uncovered in Wordsworth's description of irreconcilable loss was as well the echo of the Sturm und Drang of Continental culture, most especially as articulated by Goethe and Schiller, which was spreading throughout the West. What Wordsworth found in the sibling relationship as a source of inexplicable loss would continue to intrigue such disparate artists in the Anglo-American tradition as Leigh Hunt, Emily Brontë, Poe, Dickens, and Hawthorne, and would continue to do so well into our own century.

Such is definitely not the case with parental incest. While both the English gothic novelists and the English art poets are willing, or even eager, to play out the fictional possibilities of the once repressed brother/sister fantasies, when the attention turns to parent/child incest there is first real hesitancy, and then later palpable horror. When this configuration is played out only disaster and tragedy result. A cursory review of the most obvious texts reveals the ramifications of violating this aspect of the taboo to be both violent and fierce. Here, in these texts, we can see that parental incest which happens most regularly in "real life" is most vehemently condemned in fiction. In fact, the only medium where we find the story of parental incest told without catastrophe is in the pornographic novel. Even there, however, it is implicitly censored by being self-consciously treated with distance and disdain.

That William Blake's mythology should include incestuous mating is as predictable as that incest should appear in Byron's *Cain*. When any Ur-myth returns us to the beginnings of creation we will perforce end up, as we do in Christianity, in an Edenic setting tacitly accepting the inevitable: the only means of reproduction is incestuous. So if the mythic emanations of the descendants of Albion replicate through lines too close for social comfort, it is not because Blake was carrying revolution home to the family, but rather because he was making the only expeditious resolution of a population problem. A case could even be made that Blake's ostensibly nonsexual emanation process, which characterizes generation in the Prophetic Books, shows his unwillingness to approach the literal taboo. It seems just as likely that in the creation of his mythic families Blake just wasn't very interested in the actual sex act at all.

Not so, however, when Blake turns his attention to the world of sensation around him. In describing *this* world, the palpable world that we consider "real" and that Blake considered ultimately worthless, parent-child incest becomes the metaphoric engine that drives human life on to hopeless eternity.

In *The Mental Traveller* Blake details how our world, the world that Empiricists promoted as the only sensible and hence actual one, really worked. Because Blake wishes to deny this world any purpose, the Mental Traveller describes its very hopelessness in terms of never-ending family violation. This "fallen" world functions as a perpetual motion machine in which the sexes invade each other's privacy, reverse each other's growth, and then repeat the act in opposite roles. Here

is how the two-stroke engine of the Urizenic world operates.
First, the male cycle is described. At birth a male child is en-
trusted to an old female crone who nails him to a rock Pro-
metheuslike, binds his head with thorns Christlike, and then
proceeds to devour his energy until she becomes younger and
he ages. He grows up as she grows younger. When they are
of approximately the same age, sex occurs. Here in Blake's
words is the process:

> And if the Babe is born a Boy
> He's given to a Woman Old,
> Who nails him down upon a rock,
> Catches his shrieks in cups of gold.
>
> She binds iron thorns around his head,
> She pierces both his hands & feet
> She cuts his heart out at his side
> To make it feel both cold & heat.
>
> Her fingers number every Nerve,
> Just as a Miser counts his gold;
> She lives upon his shrieks & cries,
> And she grows young as he grows old.
>
> Till he becomes a bleeding youth,
> And she becomes a Virgin bright;
> Then he rends up his Manacles
> And binds her down for his delight.
>
> He plants himself in all her Nerves,
> Just as a Husbandman his mould;
> And she becomes his dwelling place
> And Garden fruitful seventy fold. (9–28)

After this literal and figurative combustion, he grows still
older until he is an "aged Shadow," while she continues to be
rejuvenated until she returns to innocent girlhood. Then in
stanzas marked by their Blakean gnomic concision, the second
sexually combustive act occurs between these two, except that
now it is the aged man who violates the woman who seems

to be his daughter. This girl appears to him as a babe in the fire from which he plucks her, and then he fondles her in his arms. The whole world seems to vibrate in dread of some act to come. While the specific incestuous act is hazy, the results are not:

> And to allay his freezing Age
> The Poor Man takes her in his arms;
> The Cottage fades before his sight.
> The Garden & its lovely Charms.
>
> The Guests are scatter'd thro' the land,
> For the Eye altering alters all;
> The Senses roll themselves in fear,
> And the flat Earth becomes a Ball. (56–64)

Somehow the surrounding universe reverberates from this event as presumably it had earlier when the aged crone and the young male mated. Although the relationship is now not mother-son but father-daughter, the momentum of expansion and contraction is maintained. He grows younger, she older, and the poem ends promising us more of the same, a return to exactly how it all began, the selfsame sexual dynamics that were first seen by the Mental Traveller at the outset. The male baby, born of the old man and young girl, is abandoned:

> And none can touch that frowning form,
> Except it be a Woman Old;
> She nails him down upon the Rock,
> And all is done as I have told. (101–104)

It is generally thought (this is about the most one can ever claim for consensus in Blake scholarship) that *The Mental Traveller* is Blake's searing condemnation of the hopelessness of a world understood only through the senses. Here we are presented with an eternal cycle of horrible hopelessness. This will be our world, promises Blake, should we refuse to use the visionary imagination that leads us into "an immense world of delight, clos'd by your senses five." That Blake should in-

terpret the cycle of family violence as an allegory describing
mankind at its most pathetic, is tribute both to Blake's knowledge of domestic life gone amok and to his understanding of
the nature of horror. Additionally, that Blake should have found
in incest the most expressive analogy for meaningless and
mindless life is a tribute to the then powerful, and still powerful, mandate forbidding parent-child relations. Incest is as
well the apt mythologem describing the capricious and cruel
exploitation of youth, and Blake's treatment is remarkably
modern in its clinical description of child abuse as an almost
communicable disease.

The frisson of incest, so rarely mentioned in neoclassical
times, became almost a leitmotif invoked when a particular
effect was desired. As we see in Blake, the effect was not just
the gothic delight in abrupt discontinuities; the shock was as
well in the service of exploring the ligatures that hold society,
especially the family, together. And very often this in turn led
to an exploration of how the various parts of the self were
united. In other more modern words, the unraveling of incest
motifs often unfolds what Lacanians refer to as the mirror-
imaging of the self, a reflection of knowledge about the self as
well as an image of the magnified self, society itself.

Blake seems consciously to exploit this micro/macro inter-
relationship as Shelley will later do in *The Cenci*, so we might
look at a work between these two that seems inadvertently to
recapitulate the same configuration. In *Christabel*, Coleridge's
only family-oriented fantasy, we see similar relationships played
out in a submerged manner. This is not, however, to suggest
that *Christabel* is a more conservative retelling of family romance; it may be one of the most radical. What sets *Christabel*
apart from earlier instances, such as those in Jacobean or Restoration drama, or even in many of the gothic novels, is that
while in the earlier works incest functioned as a means to titillate the audience with an unexpected sexual configuration
only to quickly reset the norm, in *Christabel* Coleridge seems
willing to play them out without resolution. What "protected"
the earlier drama and the then contemporary gothics was the
realization that the censor/publisher/audience would never al-

low such a situation to actually develop, and what "protects" *Christabel* is that we are reading a poem that is unfinished. In contradistinction to "finished" works, we are willing to accept bizarre rearrangements of family because we know that what we suspect can never come to pass. *Christabel* is forever incomplete.

Such a withholding of judgment, such a suspension of conditioned censorship is, of course, the allure of fantasy. We are granted safe passage to the world of make-believe, secure in the belief that it is only made up, only a figment of our imagination, only a dream. This poetic displacement is rather like the cinema in which images unreel before us in the dark, forming, in a sense, a cinema vérité of the psyche. It is not happenstance that critics have mentioned the similarities of the movie and of the dream to *Christabel*.[15]

In *Christabel* we see into a midnight world of dreams. The central activity occurs in the misty darkness between mysterious characters of strange physical allure, but of almost no palpability. The two central characters, both women, the virginal Christabel and the matronly Geraldine, are almost disembodied, waiflike, spirits who play out a relationship so bizarre that we may be unable, as well as unwilling, to reconstruct their actions accurately in the light of day.

So here, focusing on the specific roles of these women, is the story as it disassembles family relations. On a dark and eerie night a young lady, who is soon to be married, ventures forth from the safety of her father's castle into the dark woods. There, we are told, she will pray for the wellbeing of her "betrothed knight" who is away, presumably at battle. This is Christabel and, although her name would have us believe she is a figure of innocence, her initial acts encourage us to suspect otherwise. We might question not only what such a nice young lady is doing in a place like this in the middle of the night, but also why she has chosen such a forbidding place to pray. She chooses to kneel in prayer at the base of a huge oak tree. This is hardly a Christian place of worship; it has long been suggested by numerous critics that something druidic is in the air. Regardless of the inappropriateness of place and action, out from behind this tree glides Geraldine, a figure, like her name, of powerful contradictions. Like Christabel she is regal, and like Christabel we wonder what she is doing alone in this dark forest. Her explanation makes about as much sense as Christabel's. She explains that she has been kidnapped and then abandoned, but both Christabel and the reader may well have second thoughts. It is clear that Geraldine would much rather make contact—literally, she wants to touch Christabel—than to explain her whereabouts. Christabel does touch Geraldine and a bond begins to form, a bond that, as we shall see, has rather precise mother-child overtones.

To understand these overtones we must follow Christabel and Geraldine back to the castle. Along the way we are provided a catalog of images that should alert us, as well as Christabel, to impending disaster. Geraldine sinks at the threshold and must be carried into the castle by Christabel; Geraldine cannot pray to the Virgin Mary in thanksgiving; the family dog moans dolorously as she passes by; the dying embers of the fire shine bright as she passes; and as Christabel trims the taper of her bedroom candle, Geraldine sees a carving of a Christian angel and again visibly droops. It should be clear to Christabel what is clear to us: Geraldine is some sort of demon in human form, some sort of witch. But what sort, and what business does she have with Christabel?

At this point the already surrealistic poem breaks into an almost dreamlike digression. We learn that Christabel's mother died the very day that she was born, and that on her deathbed she declared that she would hear the castle clock strike twelve on her daughter's wedding night. We have already heard the clock strike twelve. Are we supposed to believe that Geraldine is somehow the wedding partner? We know this cannot be true because we have been assured from line 30 on that Christabel's betrothed is far away. These are two women, not a male and a female. How can they be "wed?" Just as Christabel is reiterating her mother's last words, and wishing she were there to help her, the mother's spirit suddenly appears—at least to Geraldine.

> But soon with altered voice, said she [Geraldine]—
> "Off, wandering mother! Peak and pine!
> I have power to bid thee flee."
> Alas! what ails poor Geraldine?
> Why she the bodiless dead espy?
> And why with hollow voice cries she,
> "Off, woman, off! this hour is mine—
> Though thou her guardian spirit be,
> Off, woman, off! 'tis given to me." (203–213)

Could it be that somehow there is a connection between the bridegroom, whom we have been assured Geraldine cannot be, and the mother, whom as well Geraldine cannot be?

Such connections between the bridegroom, the "real" mother, and Geraldine may well exist. Indeed, there is still more to come that encourages such a reading. The women, one innocent and mysteriously affianced, and the other a maternal *Doppelgänger* and strangely androgynous (even the names), now prepare for bed—a nuptial scene that simply cannot be a nuptial scene. Christabel, whose father's castle surely has a guest room, has insisted that Geraldine spend the night with her, and Geraldine, having eagerly accepted, now undresses. Christabel, in bed, watches:

> So half-way on her elbow did recline
> To look at the lady Geraldine.
> Beneath the lamp the lady bowed,
> And slowly rolled her eyes around;
> Then drawing in her breath aloud,
> Like one that shuddered, she unbound
> The cincture from beneath her breast:
> Her silken robe, and inner vest,
> Dropt to her feet, and full in view,
> Behold! her bosom and half her side—
> A sight to dream of, not to tell!
> O shield her shield sweet Christabel! (243–254)

Exactly what Christabel sees has been the subject of almost two centuries of conjecture. This much is certain. One of Ger-

aldine's breasts, her literal and figurative organ of mother-
hood, is deformed. It is Christabel's "touch" to that bosom
which simultaneously captivates Christabel and returns Geraldine to such robust health that the next morning her breast
seems to be restored to normal—the next morning while
dressing, we are told, Geraldine's "girded vests/Grew tight
beneath her heaving breasts" (380–381).

What exactly is their relationship? And what exactly have
they done during the night? Although we are earlier led to
conjecture that Geraldine represents Christabel's wildly displaced "husband"—after all, the references to impending
nuptials cannot be missed—their relationship seems also to be
that of mother and child. In fact, we are even told that they
passed the night together "as a mother with her child" (301).

Part II of *Christabel* only reinforces this parental relationship.
As Geraldine becomes first friend and then future lover to
Christabel's father, she becomes still more a surrogate mother
to Christabel. Of course, we know this can't be true—hasn't
Christabel's real mother earlier come to Christabel's aid? But,
as with dream intrusions of opposites, this rebuslike organization seems more to deflect what we must not admit than to
deny it. In the poem, as in the dream, the dreamer/poet gets
it both ways. Although Christabel attempts to protect her buf-
foonish father by alerting him to the danger presented by
Geraldine, she is strangely restrained by Geraldine's spell, a
possession somehow connected with the touch of the bosom.
As Christabel attempts to speak, she sees Geraldine's bosom
again:

> Which when she viewed, a vision fell
> Upon the soul of Christabel,
> The vision of fear, the touch and pain!
> She shrunk and shuddered, and saw again—
> (Ah, woe is me! Was it for thee,
> Thou gentle maid! such sights to see?)
> Again she saw that bosom old,
> Again she felt that bosom cold
> And drew in her breath with a hissing sound:
> Whereat the Knight turned wildly round,

> And nothing saw, but his own sweet maid
> With eyes upraised, as one that prayed. (451–542)

Finally in desperation Christabel falls at her father's feet beseeching him: "By my mother's soul do I entreat/That thou send this woman away!" (616–617). Once again as if to deny what seems hopelessly undeniable the "real" mother is invoked to discharge the "false" mother.

But too late. Whatever deed has been done, has been done. Like the parent who is willing to overlook child abuse by the spouse in order to preserve the status quo, Leoline discharges Christabel in an intemperate fury. The conclusion to Part II attempts a feeble epilogue by explaining paternal wrath as excess love, but it isn't convincing. There really can be no termination to this family relationship as it has unfolded. Christabel and Geraldine are on the one hand "lovers," and on the other hand, parent and child—an untenable situation.

Although Coleridge claimed in *Table Talk* (July 6, 1833) that he "always had the plan entire from beginning to end in my mind," we may suspect differently. Rather like his declarations elsewhere (as in *Kubla Khan*, for instance) that he could write his way to conclusion if only the "damsel with a dulcimer" would play to him longer, it may be that certain subjects have no desinence, no final chord. Like life, art, even with its symmetries and drive toward resolution, cannot resolve the enigma of parent-child sex regardless of circumstances.

Whatever parent-child incest may have represented to romantic artists—oppression, degradation, possibly even reunion—the very irreconcilability of the act made it a touchstone of individual, familial and, by extension, social concerns. Coleridge had played out the forbidden scenario as a dream, a fantasy, where the two major participants are almost like coins in a Chinese box. They are of interchangeable sex but not of interchangeable roles. So while Christabel can be thought of as feminine or masculine, as can Geraldine, they are always contemporary in age. Yet their relationship is one of parent and child. Whether their action is oedipal, Electral, or lesbian, the violation is of youth, of innocence (albeit not of complete innocence) by a knowing adult. This act of parent violating child is in no way like sibling incest, and hence reformation of familial roles, to say nothing of any resolution, is out of the question. These acts do not end; they disintegrate.

It was Percy Shelley, more than any other romantic poet, who carried the two unfolding incest outlines, one sibling, the other parental, to their extremes. In *The Cenci* he extended Coleridge's fantastic parent-child paradigm until it ended in the disintegration of individual, family, and society. In *The Revolt of Islam* he re-wove the solipsistic union of selves, already attempted consciously by Byron and unconsciously by Wordsworth, until he pictured the final synthesis of the sexes.

In spite of all Shelley's attitudinizing and pronouncements (notably in the pamphlet *On Love*) about the nature of human affection, it must be acknowledged that in his poetry he anatomized the dynamics of the modern family and described a great deal that had been implied but never stated in later romanticism. Although the Victorians viewed this Shelley as the agent provocateur, the sexual rebel, the predecessor of Swinburne and the later Decadents, Shelley is more appropriately seen as the last of the romantics and the first of the moderns. In his studies of family life, he shows what had earlier only been implied: the horror of child abuse; the possible salvation of sibling affection.

Shelley's verse drama *The Cenci* has remained a curiosity of romantic art. On one hand it is one of the few plays written in the first part of the nineteenth century that *could* have been performed on stage (in other words, it was not written as was *Manfred* as a "closet drama" only to be read), yet it was never acted until staged by the Shelley Society in 1886.[16] Rivaling its strange nonhistory of performance is its equally strange history of composition. *The Cenci* was written while Shelley was between Act III and IV of *Prometheus Unbound*. This is a startling juxtaposition because *Prometheus* is one of the most wonderfully rhapsodic pieces of romantic optimism ever envisioned in English, while *The Cenci* is possibly the most morbid and melancholy piece ever conceived in the nineteenth century. Additionally, what makes *The Cenci* such an enduring paradox is that Shelley was purposefully attempting not to befuddle by complexity, but to lay bare the hidden dynamics of family life. In fact, he writes in the Preface that he consciously sought to "obscure nothing by metaphysics," yet as we shall see, *The Cenci* is one of the most "metaphysical" dissections of the family ever attempted.

To open the family up to view, Shelley turned to a story already well known: the sixteenth-century tale of paternalistic oppression inflicted on innocent members by a tyrannical nobleman, Count Cenci. Shelley was neither the first nor the last to be drawn to the Cenci family, but he did add a level to the original that has endured.[17] Shelley added the one ingredient that made the play unactable and, to many critics, unattractive. He added overt incest between father and daughter. Incest had always been implied, however, for the Cenci story is essentially the Lear saga run amok. A father, driven by his own inadequacies, dedicates himself to the systematic testing of his wife, his sons, and finally his daughter. When they resist him, he turns vindictive. He kills most of the sons, and rapes the daughter. As this story was repeated in both art and popular cultures, the daughter, Beatrice, finally conspires with her mother and a surviving brother to slay the tyrant. They succeed in having him murdered, but are themselves discovered and one by one punished by the pope. The pope, the ultimate father, is more concerned with protecting his power (he has grown rich selling pardons to men like Cenci) than in dispensing justice. His patriarchal system prevails: the Cenci women are destroyed but not defeated, ironically undone by their misdirected desire to right the scales of justice.

I pass by the genuine artistic and moral complexities of *The Cenci*, notably the philosophical attempt to explore the nature of Beatrice's casuistry, to concentrate on the family extirpation by sexual violation. For it is in the nonmetaphoric and brutally actualized incest that we see that even a poet who is attempting to stage a tragedy of family struggle cannot transform this act of sexual violation into something explicable. Paternal incest, by its very nature, seems so sadistic an act that it mandates not catharsis but melodrama. More broadly speaking, parental incest is such a heinous act that unless it is cocooned in layers of confusion as in *Christabel*, or played out as a case of mistaken identity as in the gothic, it cannot be properly framed in our fiction. As we shall see, even the pornographic novel, which depends on aggressive subversion of sexual standards, doesn't know how to frame the act.

Paternal incest, which happens in "real life" with frequency, is portrayed in romantic art culture not as unfeeling, or ignorant, or even self-aggrandizing, but rather as categorically evil. It is not the result of tragic flaw or accident, but of pure malice. Cenci is no Faust or, better yet, no Manfred; he cannot be understood as the misguided solipsist, a deranged Heathcliff. For a father to knowingly violate his unwilling daughter he must be a fiend, and that is exactly how Shelley portrays him. More specifically, Cenci is a rather particular kind of fiend; a character out of the gothic. He is a vampire— a Count Dracula before his time, bleeding innocence dry. Shelley pays the artistic price for such necessary exaggeration, for once the perpetrator has been so removed from our sympathies, his acts become more mythic than believable, and his victim perforce is transformed from human to angel. When the victimizer becomes a Schedoni or a Montoni, his prey turns equally unrealistic; she is transformed into a paragon of virtue, a character too pure to exist even in the pages of a Harlequin romance.

In *The Cenci* the violation of such purity is played almost entirely on stage, leaving little to speculation. After the murderous count has had to purchase still more pardons from the pope at the rate of a third of his dukedom, he rants to his personal cardinal of his own transcendent malice.

> All men delight in sensual luxury,
> All men enjoy revenge; and most exult
> Over tortures they can never feel—
> Flattering their secret peace with others' pain.
> But I delight in nothing else. I love
> The sight of agony, and the sense of joy,
> When this shall be another's, and that mine.
>   . . .
> When I was young I thought of nothing else
> But pleasure; and I fed on honey sweets:

> Men, by St. Thomas! cannot live like bees,
> And I grew tired:—yet, til I killed a foe,
> And heard his groans, and heard his children's groans,
> Knew I not what delight was else on earth,
> Which now delights me little. I the rather
> Look on such pangs as terror ill conceals,
> The dry fixed eyeball; the pale quivering lip,
> Which tell me that the spirit weeps within
> Tears better than the bloody sweat of Christ.
> I rarely kill the body, which preserves,
> Like a strong prison, the soul within my power,
> Wherein I feed it with the breath of fear
> For hourly pain. (1.1.77–83,103–117)

For one who so needs to seek pleasure from the pain of others, Cenci has run out of victims. He has murdered his sons, demoralized his wife, spread contagion to all around him; his only remaining hope is to violate his daughter, Beatrice. As the evening wears on he prepares himself for the violation of his daughter's virginity by preparing this perverse Eucharist:

> (*Filling a bowl of wine, and lifting it up*) Oh, thou bright
>   wine whose purple splendour leaps
> And bubbles gaily in this golden bowl
> Under the lamplight, as my spirits do,
> o hear the death of my accursed sons!
> Could I believe thou wert their mingled blood,
> Then would I taste thee like a sacrament,
> And pledge with thee the mighty Devil in Hell,
> Who, if a father's curses, as men say,
> Climb with swift wings after their children's souls,
> And drag them from the very throne of Heaven,
> Now triumphs in my triumph! (1.3.77–87)

Cenci is a man who has carried malevolence to an art form. Yet, he has one last act of savagery left in him. He commands Beatrice to "meet [him] at midnight and alone," and there and then, offstage, he ravages her. The next morning Beatrice is unable to tell her mother what Cenci had done. "He has trampled me/Under his feet" (2.1.64–65) is all that she can admit, but her mother knows better. But, like any intimidated spouse of a child victimizer, she cannot accept such information, let alone confront her husband with it. Instead, both women pretend the husband/father is not what they know he is: a sexual tyrant. As Cenci has violated Beatrice's body, his seminal evil proceeds to transform her very perception. Again, like the victim of parental abuse, Beatrice takes her sense of reality from her father. She no longer is sure of what she sees, of what she feels, even of what has happened. As Act 3 opens Beatrice reports:

> My God!
> The beautiful blue heaven is flecked with blood!
> The sunshine on the floor is black! The Air
> Is changed to vapours such as the dead breathe
> In charnel pits! Pah! I am choked! There creeps
> A clinging, black, contaminating mist
> About me . . . 'tis substantial, heavy, thick,
> I cannot pluck it from me. (3.1.12–18)

The image of blood and semen, so unavoidably linked in the vampire myth that the victim is reborn as a double of the victimizer, now unfolds as an elaborate analogy not for Dracula and his virgin, but for father and daughter. Beatrice laments:

> O blood, which art my father's blood,
> Circling through these contaminated veins,
> If thou, poured forth on the polluted earth,
> Could wash away the crime, and punishment
> By which I suffer . . . no that cannot be! (3.1.95–99)

But she realizes there can be no purgative for what has happened, no spermaticide for his evil; that nothing, not penance, nor escape, nor suicide can undo what has been done.

While Beatrice suffers, Cenci celebrates his conquest. He glories in his perversity to his God:

> (Kneeling)   God!
> Hear me! If this most specious mass of flesh,
> Which Thou hast made my daughter; this my blood,
> This particle of my divided being;
> Whose sight infects and poisons me; this devil
> Which sprung from me as from a hell, was meant
> To aught good use; if her bright loveliness
> Was kindled to illumine this dark world;
> [then] I pray Thee for my sake
> As Thou the common God and Father art
> Of her, and me, and all; reverse that doom! (4.1.114–126)

Cenci promises all if He, the father triumphant, will allow him, the father temporal, dominion over their creation. Meanwhile, to his wife, Cenci goes still farther, expressing the hope that Beatrice will be fecund and gestate his atrocity:

> And my deep imprecation! May it be
> A hideous likeness of herself, that as
> From a distorting mirror, she may see
> Her image mixed with what she most abhors,
> Smiling upon her from her nursing breast. (4.1.145–149)

Clearly, Cenci is departing from anything ever imagined, let alone seen, in real life and entering the hyperbolic world of gothic excess. His villainy is just too much to comprehend, and we lose all "touch" with him.

Yet, as Cenci has become progressively satanic, Beatrice has become progressively less the heroine of melodrama. She comes to realize that this demon is too evil to live, that she and her mother and brother must take it upon themselves to rid the world of this pestilence. The family hires some thugs to murder Cenci in his sleep. The thugs succeed, and while we in the audience may applaud their rebalancing the scales of justice, Shelley does not. In fact, just the opposite. As an ardent pacifist he deplores Beatrice's use of force under *any* circumstances, even if the object of this force is unmitigated brutality. In the Preface he even refers to the act of vengeance as

Beatrice's "pernicious mistake." What would he have her do instead? To find the answer we may have to look beyond *The Cenci* to what Shelley was writing elsewhere.

At the very time Shelley was describing the plight of Beatrice he was also confronting the enormous dilemma of Prometheus. In *Prometheus Unbound* Shelley proffers what to him is finally the only productive response to evil: forgiveness and compassion. It is Prometheus's forgiveness of Jupiter that causes the apocalypse of Act 4. Presumably, had Beatrice returned to her father adamant but forgiving, he would have been crushed under the weight of his own self-hatred. Evil exists only when pitted against opposition; remove that opposition, substitute passive resistance and, Shelley would have us believe, evil will crumble like Ozymandias's midsection. It just takes a little more time.

Whether or not such a rapprochement would have followed if Beatrice had been docile is for others to speculate about. What is clear is that to reach such a moral impasse of evil versus good Shelley has used an act so barbaric that patricide seems an appropriate response. Beatrice is condemned to die for killing the father in a trial presided over by another father (the judge), in turn supported by yet another father (the pope), thus reinforcing the theme of paternalistic oppression from on high. This oppression has its immediate focus on the act of violation, and its ironic denouement in the conviction of the victim who is only seeking redress. Cenci was correct in saying that he would succeed in corrupting Beatrice for, indeed, she must stoop to vengeance, however justified it may seem. In so developing the effects of incest Shelley reminds us that incest is an apt mythologem for family life out of control, the inevitable extreme of patriarchy.

If daughter rape extends one possibility of family romance, then sibling love extends the other. Although the term "incest" may be used to categorize them both, for Shelley the acts are diametrically opposed. If we can evaluate his views by his art (a critical act Shelley would have insisted on) then parent-child sex is despicable to the nth degree but sibling love, even a love implying sexual relations, is the ultimate self-completion. Such an act finally restores what single sexuality has rent asunder: it returns us to a primal unity where male and female are no longer oppositions but continuities. This romantic view of incest, promulgated explicitly by Chateaubriand and implicitly by Wordsworth, reaches its fullest advocacy with Shelley. Certainly one could assert that until recently no other artist has so embraced its supposedly palliative powers with quite his enthusiasm. Yet, as we may see, Shelley ultimately celebrates sibling reunification in a world far removed from the dull reality of what we now know, a world exempt from the anxieties of social consequences.

As with its relatively sudden appearance elsewhere in romanticism, sibling incest repeatedly surfaces in Shelley's work as the result of often contradictory forces. There have been a number of explanations for its recurrence, of which the most obvious is biographical. Shelley was from childhood the idolized brother of his four younger sisters, the overlooked issue of his confused mother, and the almost lifelong antagonist of his father. From Thomas Jefferson Hogg's garbled rendition of Shelley's letters, which implied that Shelley desired a physical affair with his sister Elizabeth, to Shelley's artistic collaboration with Elizabeth, which resulted in his first poetical publication, *Original Poetry* by "Victor and Cazire," to Benjamin Hayden's speculations that Shelley "would lie with his sister," to the "league of incest" stories circulated about the Byron-Shelley entourage by Southey, there does seem to be a basis for more than sensationalistic speculation that Shelley really desired what should be repressed.[18] The early interactions of the Shelley family do seem almost a case study of the centripetal forces of a family out of sexual balance. Instead of growing outward into independence, the children, most notably the only son, Percy, were forced inward toward each other. Percy was the only one who exploded into rebellion. It should be noted that, as with Wordsworth and Coleridge, this pattern was also repeated in many nineteenth-century families and was not always the result of a domineering father (witness the other fatherless romantics) so much as it was the consequence of a confined area of social movement.

In addition, as Harold Bloom has argued in *The Anxiety of Influence*, the sensitive artists of the early nineteenth century, who earlier had to displace this familial confusion elsewhere, were now relatively free to play out the pressures of poetic anxiety. They were actually inspired by recreating it. Thanks to political and social restructuring, the canon of what could and should constitute art had opened, and new possibilities of subject matter and treatment were available. Equally influential as regards the subject of family sex was the gothic novel— a then recent mutation in the none-too-stable medium of prose fiction. The gothic allowed, even encouraged, sublimated familial scenarios to be played out protected by both audience (the young female who didn't know what she was reading) and the genre (the gothic was *mandated* to shock). Here there were no masters to rewrite, only a form without content. In a sense, the romantic poet co-opted the now mentionable subject of family sex and used it in the service of the struggle for self-knowledge, which led either to destruction (paternal incest) or to redemption (sibling incest). The salvation that Christianity had effected through the father was now to be found through the sister who, as well, took on attributes of a pagan earth-mother. The romantic orphan, looking for a parent, found his sister.

No artist articulates this new consciousness more often and with more fervor than did Shelley. The passions that animate his questers for perfect unity, from the poet in *Alastor* to the poet in *Epipsychidion*, connect the literary tradition of courtly love with the new freedom of the gothic to express hitherto unmentionable relationships. Sibling incest is not so much social as it is psychological, not so much literal as literary, not so much actual as metaphorical. Yet, for all the poeticizing, one gets the distinct sense that Shelley ultimately viewed the taboo on sibling relations as a mixed blessing. It inhibited as much as it resolved. Along the way, however, it provided a context in which to express the postrevolutionary anxiety about the isolation of the individual.

Shelley's early ambivalence about the taboo is clearly played out in *Alastor*. Here he portrays an ephebic poet questing, as did Keats' Endymion, for absolute truth and beauty. Along the way, and a very circuitous way it is, he dreams of a "veiled maid" who not only seems his mirror image, but as well speaks with a "voice . . . like the voice of [my] own soul" (153). Throughout the remainder of the poem the poet manqué struggles to find his anima, his antitype, his female self, but in vain. He finally washes up on far-away shores as alone and lonely as when he started his quest for selfhood. It seems clear that Shelley realizes the paradox of struggling to enter the mirror, as it were, of sexuality since Alastor is subtitled "Or the Spirit of Solitude." Ironically, the search for completion via incest here seems only to aggravate the self's singularity.

Although Shelley's interest in untangling and/or extending family relations seems at times almost obsessive (he will re-work the theme in Epipsychidion and Rosalind and Helen), it is most fully explained in a work written just after Alastor, Laon and Cythna, later retitled The Revolt of Islam. It is almost as if, unable to explore the ramifications fully in one text, Shelley would amplify aspects of the subject out of sequence in the next. Each subsequent poem seems a "trying out" of the same subject, but with a different emphasis, almost as if he were convinced he could "get it right" if he could only arrange the siblings properly. Whatever the reason, Laon and Cythna (1817), the template of The Revolt of Islam (1818), is well worth examining. If The Cenci takes father-daughter incest to extremes of horror, then The Revolt of Islam takes sibling incest to the extremes of human perfectibility.

Although there is plot aplenty, Laon and Cythna essentially traces the fortunes of two star-crossed lovers who rise up from the debacle of the French revolution to continue the struggle for Apocalypse. The poem is a moral allegory with good and evil personified in the forms of young exuberant idealists and repressive older tyrants. As the cantos progress we hear the sad tale first of Cythna, who has risen to power but is unfulfilled in her dreams of ideal love, then of melancholy Laon, who has been disappointed by friends, by family, by faith, and by state. All that endures for either is the memory of an earlier balmy childhood love unbesmirched by tyranny, unstained by parental repression. They seem to have been like shadows of each other in childhood, antitypes of the same organism, androgynies. They spent their days in each other's company and their nights in each other's arms. Then, abruptly, their pubescent life together was interrupted by the brutal State. Cyntha was made a slave of tyrants, Laon escaped into a melancholy exile. Seven years later Laon is able to return to his homeland, thanks in large part to the liberation movement led by a mysterious young woman. Once back with his own people Laon preaches nonviolence and is so successful that a new human brotherhood arises and struggles toward Utopia. But, alas, the established regime is not so easily rent asunder. The king, once saved from lynching by Laon, now routs the peace-loving, weaponless, vegetarian dreamers. All are massacred except Laon, who is again saved by a mysterious female appropriately astride "a black Tartarian horse of giant frame." His savior is, of course, Cythna who earlier had been the liberator of the oppressed populace. Laon is naturally overjoyed at being saved, to say nothing about being saved by his sister.

But what is not "natural" and what scandalized first Shelley's publisher, as well as early reviewers who happened on both versions, was that this is clearly an amorous relationship between siblings. In addition, the relationship is physically consummated. A meteor lights the way above so we may be sure to see what is happening below:

> A wandering Meteor by some wild wind sent,
>   Hung high in the green dome, to which it lent
> A faint and pallid lustre; while the song
>   Of blasts, in which its blue hair quivering bent,
>   Strewed strangest sounds the moving leaves among;
> A wondrous light, the sound as of a spirit's tongue.
>
> The Meteor showed the leaves on which we sate
>   And Cythna's glowing arms, and the thick ties
> Of her soft hair, which bent with gathered weight
>   My neck near hers, her dark and deepening eyes,
>   Which, as twin phantoms of one star that lies

O'er a dim well, move, though the star reposes,
  Swam in our mute and liquid ecstasies,
Her marble brow, and eager lips, like roses,
With their own fragrance pale, which Spring but half uncloses.

The Meteor to its far morass returned:
  The beating of our veins one interval
Made still; and then I felt the blood that burned
  Within her frame, mingle with mine, and fall
  Around my heart like fire; and over all
A mist was spread, the sickness of a deep
  And speechless swoon of joy, as might befall
Two disunited spirits when they leap
In union from this earth's obscure and fading sleep. (2617–2640)

Not only does such a tabooed sexual relationship occur, but it also seems to bear fruit. I say "seems" because later a child of dubious parentage will appear and cause scholars no end of lineage disputes.[19]

Shelley clearly knew that even without progeny this union, entered into by knowing siblings, would not go unchallenged by his current readers, or, for that matter, his future readers. Although Shelley might argue in the Preface the relativistic nature of *all* values, it is difficult to let this one pass by. Shelley must have realized this even as he was composing the text, for two stanzas before the incestuous act he emphatically reiterates the Pauline coda: "To the pure all things are pure" (2596). Perhaps the incestuous act was an attempt to carry such an argument to extremes. Whatever the explanation, a fundamental taboo had been violated, and if Shelley didn't appreciate the consequences, his publisher did. Charles Ollier refused to release the printed text of *Laon and Cythna*. A few copies slipped past, copies he was unable to recall, and it is from that version that we recognize the basis of *The Revolt of Islam*.

Shelley did not make the changes happily. Thomas Love Peacock reported that he "contested the proposed alterations step by step" and emendations on the manuscript itself seem to bear out this reluctance.[20] Whether or not Shelley earlier had qualms about the absolute literalness of "to the pure all things are pure," when he was faced with the prospect of the aborted publication, he assented, insisting, however, that the poem was ruined.[21]

The story of Laon and Cythna still has many cantos to go, and the action continues into a veritable phantasmagoria so typical of Shelley when he is not sure of what he wants to say. Through a series of flashbacks and hallucinations we learn that Cythna probably has mothered a child, yet, this child, a daughter, seems almost a supernumerary on the stage. She passes us by with no thematic, let alone biological development. Instead of following the widening family circle, Shelley moves in the other direction: the family is collapsed. A new tyrant comes to power, and Laon, fearful of losing what little family he has, pleads that they be allowed to emigrate to America. In the next canto, however, despite the pleading of the daughter, the family is burnt at the stake, one by one. In a *puella ex machina* ending, the child leads the winged intertwined spirits of her parents above the corrupted earth into the empyrean for eternal life and love together.

Are they transported out of this world because they have committed acts so noble, so pure that they cannot exist in the putrid, sordid world of humankind? Or are they transported because they have violated one of the most fundamental reproductive codes of this species, and Shelley unconsciously realizes they can no longer coexist with others? Certainly in contemporary criticism most critics have taken Shelley at his word when, in the original Preface, he explained his motives thus:

> In the personal conduct of my Hero and Heroine, there is one circumstance which was intended to startle the reader from the trance of ordinary life. It was my object to break through the crust of those outworn opinions on which established institutions depend. I have appealed therefore to the most universal of all feelings, and have endeavoured to strengthen the moral sense, by forbidding its energies in seeking to avoid actions which are only crimes of convention. It is because there

is so great a multitude of artificial vices that there are so few real virtues. Those feelings alone which are benevolent or malevolent, are essentially good or bad.

In spite of Shelley's protestations that he is really attempting to "break through the crust of those outworn opinions," one can see that the break is really not as tidy as he supposes. He would like to see incest as a violation of society's law—he calls it a "crime of convention"—but not as a violation of the laws of nature. After all, it is nature's law which will rise triumphant after the law of custom and convention is suppressed. But Shelley seems unsure how deep the prohibition goes. He says elsewhere, with reference to a work by Calderón:

> Incest is like many other *incorrect* things a very poetical circumstance. It may be the excess of love or of hate. It may be that defiance of every thing for the sake of another which clothes itself in the glory of the highest heroism, or it may be the cynical rage which confounding the good & bad in existing opinions breaks through them for the purpose of rioting in selfishness & antipathy.[22]

In *Laon and Cythna* Shelley seems to have found out, almost in spite of himself, that incest is not like atheism or anarchism; it is not simply a "crust" of custom. If it were, the poem could well have ended happily without removing the protagonists from this world to deposit them beyond the reach of consequences. They could have found resolution on earth. This is, after all, how *Endymion*, the companion poem by Keats (supposedly written as a result of a bargain between the two poets to create extended fantasies), finally concludes. Endymion must leave Poena, his sister, in order to finally be reunited with a sister surrogate in the guise of the Indian Maid. In the hurry-up confusion of Keats' ending, Endymion, who has twice "broken the mortal bars" to find "perfection" with yet another sister figure, Cynthia, the goddess of love beyond the clouds, is finally returned to earth aware at last that such perfection is unattainable for mortals. Narcissism has limits. But not so for Laon. Laon conducts his relationships, not with projected *Doppelgänger* in the skies, but with his real sister here on earth. Almost in spite of himself, Shelley finds, as did Byron with Manfred, that such protagonists must suffer exile first, then escape past the flesh if they really wish to continue their love. The fire must burn out the dust. Incest may be, as Shelley proposed in the Preface, the result of "all sympathies harmoniously blended," but one should add that such are the harmonies of the heavenly spheres, not those of humankind. It was not happenstance that for the ancient poets only the gods escaped the consequences of consanguinity. Intuitively, at least, the romantic poets also came to understand the importance of limits. As we shall now see, the common reader did not have to depend on intuition.

CHAPTER 4

"I SHALL BE WITH YOU ON YOUR WEDDING NIGHT": INCEST IN NINETEENTH-CENTURY POPULAR CULTURE

> To know whether his idea of *adultery* or *incest* be right will a man seek it anywhere among things existing? Or is it true because anyone has been witness to such an action? No; but it suffices here that men have put together such a collection into one complex *idea* that makes the *archetype* and specific *idea*, whether ever any such action were committed *in rerum natura* or no.
> —John Locke, *Names of Mixed Modes and Relations*

IT IS ONE THING for John Locke to say that we share certain ideas that have no basis in natural reality; it is quite another to explain the how and why of that sharing. If the taboo on incest is ideological, as Locke implies, how is that consciousness created, let alone shared? As we have seen, the high culture artists were of little help. Still more particularly, how could someone like John Locke claim that incest is an idea when all around him he is being told it is an act abhorred by nature and abominated by God? To find the answer we need turn from art literature, which has always expressed its ambiguous messages to a privileged audience in a hard-to-decipher code, to popular culture which has communicated its understandings in just the opposite manner. Mass culture depends on audience unawareness that judgments are being made, shared, and enforced.

Had you been living in nineteenth-century England, and had you been leafing through your *Book of Common Prayer*, your eye might well have caught what was often printed on the last page. Chances are you would pass it by, but if you were young and curious you might have read it carefully, for it details thirty specific people you are forbidden to marry. Or to put the matter in the proper adolescent perspective: here are thirty people not to have sex with, not to think "those thoughts" about.

Most of the list makes no *biologic* sense whatsoever. Almost fifty percent of those named bear no genetic linkage to the individual; even more intriguing, there is absolutely no mention made of first and second cousins. It may be that these cousins are not only tolerated but accepted as mates because they provide the necessary knots that prevent family wealth from slipping away.[1] Yet, as an attempt at prior sexual restraint, the list of unacceptable degrees of relationship is both a warning for the young not to be foolish with family members as well as a rather precise definition of exactly who is considered "family." That a young man today would think there is nothing wrong with marrying a nephew's wife, or even a wife's sister, tells much about how the family has shrunk. Two hundred years ago the network of kinship and affinity extended one entire human orbit farther than it does today, and two hundred years before that it encompassed yet another circle. In fact, there have been times in Western culture when the circle extended out to enclose sixth cousins.[2]

Still, what is the chart doing in the *Book of Common Prayer*, the vade mecum of Anglicans? Although it purports to relate what has been "forbidden in scriptures," such is not the case. Biblical injunctions and prohibitions are nothing if not irregular and inconsistent. While it is true that we are often ordered not to "lie with" or "uncover the nakedness" of specific family members, we are also provided a catalog of exceptions. The incestuous necessity of Adam and Eve may certainly be understood and forgiven, as may the situation of Lot and his

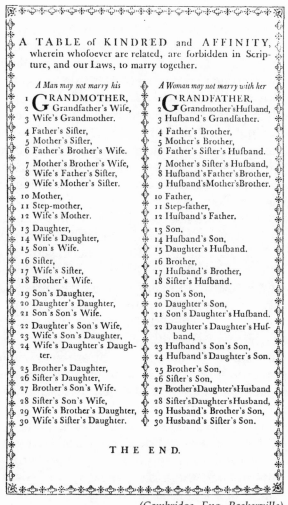

A TABLE of KINDRED and AFFINITY, wherein whofoever are related, are forbidden in Scripture, and our Laws, to marry together.

A Man may not marry his	A Woman may not marry with her
1 GRANDMOTHER,	1 GRANDFATHER,
2 Grandfather's Wife,	2 Grandmother's Hufband,
3 Wife's Grandmother.	3 Hufband's Grandfather.
4 Father's Sifter,	4 Father's Brother,
5 Mother's Sifter,	5 Mother's Brother,
6 Father's Brother's Wife.	6 Father's Sifter's Hufband.
7 Mother's Brother's Wife,	7 Mother's Sifter's Hufband,
8 Wife's Father's Sifter,	8 Hufband's Father's Brother,
9 Wife's Mother's Sifter.	9 Hufband's Mother's Brother.
10 Mother,	10 Father,
11 Step-mother,	11 Step-father,
12 Wife's Mother.	12 Hufband's Father.
13 Daughter,	13 Son,
14 Wife's Daughter,	14 Hufband's Son,
15 Son's Wife.	15 Daughter's Hufband.
16 Sifter,	16 Brother,
17 Wife's Sifter,	17 Hufband's Brother,
18 Brother's Wife.	18 Sifter's Hufband.
19 Son's Daughter,	19 Son's Son,
20 Daughter's Daughter,	20 Daughter's Son,
21 Son's Son's Wife.	21 Son's Daughter's Hufband.
22 Daughter's Son's Wife,	22 Daughter's Daughter's Hufband,
23 Wife's Son's Daughter,	23 Hufband's Son's Son,
24 Wife's Daughter's Daughter.	24 Hufband's Daughter's Son.
25 Brother's Daughter,	25 Brother's Son,
26 Sifter's Daughter,	26 Sifter's Son,
27 Brother's Son's Wife.	27 Brother's Daughter's Husband
28 Sifter's Son's Wife,	28 Sifter's Daughter's Husband,
29 Wife's Brother's Daughter,	29 Husband's Brother's Son,
30 Wife's Sifter's Daughter.	30 Husband's Sifter's Son.

THE END.

(Cambridge, Eng. Baskerville)

The Book of Common Prayer, 1761

daughters (Gen. 19:30–38). After all, anything is acceptable that preserves the race from extinction. But what of the half-siblings Abraham and Sarah (Gen. 20:12), or uncle-niece pairs like Nahor and Milcha (Gen. 11:27,29), aunt-nephew pairs like Amram and Jochebed (Exod. 6:20), or even the brother-sister rape of Amnon and Tamar (II Sam. 13:2, 14, 28–29)?[3]

More to the point is the conclusion of the heading which
states that the Table is also a listing of what "our law" has
forbidden. The antecedent of "our" is ambiguous—is it the
church's law or the law of the land? For, while "incest is one
of the earliest crimes known to the law along with murder by
magic and a few sacral offenses," as the legal scholar A. S.
Diamond had noted, it was one of the last to be codified in
English criminal law.[4] In fact, only after 1908 does incest become a crime recognized and punished by the civil authori-
ties. Until modern times incest, like bestiality, witchcraft, and
adultery, was a crime against God and therefore handled within
the ecclesiastical domain.

The jurisdictional history of incest is almost as uneven as
the biblical treatment. Until the sixteenth century the church
was the undisputed arbiter of such internecine crimes, but when
Henry VIII wished a divorce from Anne Boleyn he had no
specific church doctrine to support his case. After he had broken with the Catholic church, the "laws of custom" were repudiated and nothing substituted in their place. So Henry had
to rely on what was already established through generations
of prohibitions, and the risk was worth it. Since Henry needed
a more powerful pretext than adultery, he trumped up the
charge of incest as well. He contended that Anne was the willing, even eager, recipient of her brother's sexual advances.
Surely, Henry must have felt uneasy in this accusation, knowing that he himself was the descendant of a consanguineous
line mixed since the offspring of Charles the Bald. Worse yet,
he had contemplated the incestuous union of his illegitimate
son, the Duke of Richmond, with his half-sister Mary. And
this is to say nothing of the fact that he himself had earlier
married his brother's widow, Catherine. But Henry was desperate and, although tarred with the brush, he could hope
that his accusation was more potent than public memory.

Anne was charged with three crimes: treason, adultery, and
incest. It was alleged that George Boleyn, Viscount Rochford,
had on at least one occasion spent several hours in her bed-
chamber and that "the queen . . . procured and incited her
own natural brother . . . to violate her, alluring him with her

tongue in the said George's mouth, and the said George's tongue in hers."[5] For this, and for mentioning in public court that Anne had told him that Henry was impotent, George was beheaded. Such also was the fate of his sister. In the whorl of gossip and rumor that followed, it was even suggested that Anne herself was the illegitimate daughter of Henry, for it was known that he had dallied for some time with Anne's mother, Elizabeth of Norfolk.

Little wonder then that in the 1560s Archbishop Parker should promulgate the *Table of Kindred and Affinity* within the endboards of the *Book of Common Prayer*. Based on what had transpired, it was good politics for all to know exactly where family sexual distinctions were to be made. The acts regarding succession (25 Henry VIII c. 22) surely pertained to families in general, and so where better to make such matters known than in the *Prayer Book*. The fact, however, that by the early seventeenth century the list was sometimes not included attests to the limbo into which these prohibitions had passed. Queen Elizabeth, Anne Boleyn's daughter, mindful of her mother's fate, repealed the death penalty for incest and introduced fines instead. But a generation later, during the Commonwealth (1640–1660), the death penalty was reinstated "in order to destroy this monstrous sin." That too was swept away by the repeal of much of the moral legislation of Cromwell during the Restoration. By 1835, after the crime had been shifted like a bad penny from institution to institution, an act was passed (5 and 6 William IV c. 54) which restored the church as the governing and punishing body of such offenses. To make doubly sure, the Matrimonial Causes Act of 1857 reasserted the church's dominion in all related areas.

So by the nineteenth century the *Table of Kindred and Affinity*, now given the imprimatur of the Queen's bench, stood again for the regulation of unacceptable degrees of consanguinity. How much real effect this had can be seen in the implications of Blackstone's memorable phrase on the subject: family strife, when carried to court, is most usually resolved by the "feeble coercion of the spiritual courts, according to the rules of canon law."[6] Intrafamilial traumas remained in this miasma until just after the turn of the twentieth century. As a result of often aggressive lobbying for the rights of victims of child abuse, the state finally accepted responsibility for both categorizing and enforcing family boundaries. First in 1903, and then in 1908, legislation was introduced, and ultimately passed, that made the "rather . . . unpleasant subject" something that was going to have to be considered in the public courts. At last, by our century, it was clear that the definition of incest was no longer tied to the sacraments or to church history. It was instead a function first of individual rights to bodily privacy and then of public moral standards.

It is tempting to ascribe the zigzagging of jurisdictional authority to the studied neglect of specific human problems by uncaring institutions. It is almost as easy to go one step farther and view child abuse in Marxist terms of exploitative economic systems. For the poor incest is denounced since it disrupts the cohesion of inexpensive labor; for the ruling class in which incest is unacknowledged, but accepted, it becomes a means of preserving and augmenting family capital. Eighteenth- and nineteenth-century social stability was to a considerable degree the result of manipulation of proletarian family life by the lord of the castle, town father, priest, and family patriarch. It is a perverse testament to this class oppression that social stability should result. Of course, by the late 1840s the social fabric was unraveling all across Europe, but it had held tight for generations. Or one might offer the feminist correlary to this argument that as long as male-dominated institutions were in control of women and children, the women and children would be treated like chattel and systematically exploited. How can you punish someone for abusing his own property?

These explanations have all been put forward recently and all make good sense, but there is another, more subtle explanation for the seeming failure of social and religious institutions to concern themselves about domestic matters which has to do with philosophical assumptions of the nature of morality itself.[7] In the eighteenth century the specific moral question of suitable sex partners was subsumed into the broader proposition of the nature of moral sense. Did we, or did we not, have an inner faculty that, like a gyroscope, would keep our actions on an even keel along a precharted course? Incest was an appropriate exemplum for categorical discussion because few other human acts are so susceptible to the nature versus nurture dichotomy. In the eighteenth century the terms were changed to providence versus custom, and understanding their place in explanations of human behavior may resolve much of the confusion about how, and where, and by what rights, should physical invasions and intimidations of family members be understood and finally adjudicated.

On the side of ascribing custom as the basis of sexual habits were those such as Bernard Mandeville who, in *A Search into the Nature of Society* (1723), asserted that the incest prohibition resulted primarily from the force of habit. There is no mandate in nature forbidding consanguineous intercourse other than that which has been made customary. We are, after all, like bees who have been instructed by repetition in how to make our hives stable. The beekeeper does not tell the bees how to arrange their society; they learn from each other, and from the past. Morality is what is customary: my morals are not the morals of the ancient Egyptians, but they are equally serviceable in my hive.[8]

This remarkably modern culturological argument was soon countered by those who, like the framers of the *Table of Kindred and Affinity*, believed the prohibition to be part of an earthly sense, which was also a sense engendered by the Creator and mandated in the Bible. The prohibition is not simply *natural*; it is mandated from Above. The consequences of familial instability as well as the lessons of, say, Leviticus, essentially point out the divine way. Here is Francis Hutcheson in *An Inquiry Concerning Beauty and Virtue* (1725) discussing the importance of what today would be called "natural consequences":

Had we no *moral Sense natural* to us, we should only look upon *Incest* as hurtful to our selves and shun it, and never hate other *incestuous Persons*, more than we do a *broken Merchant*; so that still this Abhorrence supposes a *Sense* of *moral good*. And further, it is true, that many who abhor *Incest* do not know, or reflect upon the natural tendency of some sorts of *Incest* to the *publick Detriment*; but wherever it is hated, it is apprehended as offensive to the DEITY, and that it exposes the Person concern'd to his just Vengeance. Now it is universally acknowledged to be the grossest Ingratitude and Baseness, in any Creature, to counteract the Will of the DEITY, to whom it is under such Obligations. This then is plainly *a moral evil Quality* apprehended in *Incest*, and reducible to the general Foundation of *Malice*, or rather Want of Benevolence. Nay further, where this Opinion, "that *Incest* is offensive to the DEITY," prevails, *Incest* must have another direct Contrariety to *Benevolence*; since we must *apprehend* the *Incestuous*, as exposing an Associate, who should be dear to him by the Ties of *Nature*, to the lowest State of *Misery*, and *Baseness*, *Infamy* and *Punishment*. (pp. 212–214)

It should be noted that both Mandeville and Hutcheson start with the premise that the aversion is somehow "natural." They differ in the attribution and in the amount of "reminding" man needs of this sanction. Sometimes the reminding occurs naturally; sometimes it has to be consciously or unconsciously reinforced.

Almost twenty years later Hutcheson was no longer so sure that the aversion was not God-given. In *A Short Introduction to Moral Philosophy* (1742) he seems to recognize the social utility of the taboo as it provides stability for the family, or, rather, that the lack of the taboo causes friction. Hutcheson is forced to this reconsideration, in part, by having to explain why the taboo operates in non-Christian cultures. In his waffling, Hutcheson finally has to agree, as did Dryden in *Religio laici*, that there was an original divine law that, while it has been diffused into different systems, is still operable. In fact, the incest prohibition, instead of asserting the force of custom, or even attesting to the validity of consequence, can be seen, thanks to its supposed universality, as the basis of a singular divinity.

This argument continued to be made throughout the century, never centering on the sexual act of violation or breach of trust, as much as on what the act presupposes about a divine law. From time to time it was suggested that divine law ought to need no institutional affirmation, a suggestion made by no less a gentleman philosopher than Lord Bolingbroke, who asserted that the "shame" engendered by the act clearly meant the prohibition was social. Just as man covers his genitals and copulates in private, so he shuns consanguinity: ". . . this abhorrence is artificial, and . . . has been inspired by human laws, by prejudice and habit." Still, one can see there is little or no concern for the plight of the victim; the moral concern remains, in the worst sense, academic. Bolingbroke was simply not interested in incest per se, but rather in mapping the boundaries that constitute human behavior. He was, incidentally, just as interested in the deleterious effects of marriage too far from the family center. Such marriages, he claimed, also weakened the fabric of the family. Here Bolingbroke tips his aristocratic hand. Distant marriage, he argued, will not "preserve possessions and wealth in the families to which they belong, . . . [but will] suffer them to be carried by any female caprice into others."[9]

With the rise of animal husbandry, newer and biologically more cogent explanations were offered to explain the enigmatic taboo. In a mid-century treatise, *The Horse*, the French naturalist George Buffon unfolded an analogy hitherto sidestepped. Could we argue from observing animal behavior that man's incest aversion was endemic in organisms above a certain degree? Clearly, both those who maintained the taboo was divinely ordered, and those who thought it a result of the force of habit had skirted this argument. And well they should, for it was equally detrimental to both sides. The religious would maintain that the central point of their religion was that man *does not* behave like the animals. He is on earth to subdue the lower beasts, not to act like them. Meanwhile the exponents of the custom argument were hardly supported by the premise that custom was omnipresent in nature, else how could they distinguish a "moral sense" in humanity? The scientist Buffon didn't care; he was interested in observing horses and from his observations he concluded:

Policy, unless when derived from physical considerations, never extends in a manner so general and so absolute. But, if men once discovered by experience that their race degenerated, when intercourse was permitted among children of the same family, they would soon regard the alliances of different families as a law established by Nature. In a word, we may presume from analogy, that, in most climates, men, like other animals, would degenerate after a certain number of generations.[10]

For all its appeal to logic, however, this argument is wrong-headed. The bloodlines of carefully linebred horses will improve in most observable qualities like stamina or speed. No matter; the willingness to extrapolate from nonhuman to human, from animal to man, was the unavoidable result of the empirical method. The scientific approach, informed by biology, proved so powerful that it even seeped into the nascent political science of revolution. Here, for instance, is Thomas Paine, making a biopolitical argument about class structure:

Aristocracy has a tendency to degenerate the human species. By the universal economy of nature it is known, and by the instance of the Jews it is proved, that the human species has a tendency to degenerate, in any small number of persons, when separated from the general stock of society, and intermarrying constantly with each other.[11]

What Hutcheson had called *Horror naturalis* seemed about to carry the day; the argument was over. Maybe God initiated the prohibition; nature maintains it. In either case, the courts of man have no right interfering with the law of God as it operates through nature. The biological explanation had everything both parties could want—except truth. How could we explain such cultures as those of the Incas, Phoenicians, Egyptians, Persians, and, more embarrassing still for neoclassicists, the Athenians, who accepted, even encouraged, a diluted form of incestuous mating. Unfortunately, however, the promise was soon shattered. As animal studies, especially studies of what was rapidly becoming the obsession of German, Middle European, and English aristocracy, namely the breeding of race horses, were becoming more comprehensive, the argument of Buffon that consanguinity leads to degeneracy was undermined. The implications for the aristocracy were profound. As a result of experiments with horses in Hungary, even the German theologian J. D. Michaelis was forced to conclude that when a stallion "covers a mare of his own getting, that is, the father his daughter, no degeneracy or diminution of size, has been observed to follow, nor yet any other detrimental consequence whatever."[12]

By the time of the romantic poets all the categorical arguments had crumbled, worn away by their own contradictions, undermined by too many historical exceptions, and threatened by their own economies of simplification. To the best of my knowledge, never once does any theologian or naturalist attempt to determine the incidence of human incest. Never once in the entire century, for instance, does *Lancet* or the *Journal of the Statistical Society of London* report evidence of the darker side of family life. This most logical step would have to wait until the 1880s when the National Society for the Prevention of Cruelty to Children attempted to produce a statistical tally on its efforts to reform working and living conditions. This lack of concern about gathering a data base first and *then* arguing a case was because both sides really did not care about the act other than how it functioned as an exemplum of other forces operating on human behavior.

Through the efforts of social historians such as Lawrence Stone and a new generation of computer-assisted family historians, we are now getting a sense of what early nineteenth-century domestic life must have been like.[13] Our most trustworthy extrapolations are being made from the study of late nineteenth-century bureaucratic documents. The rise of the modern state carried with it the need to classify and categorize and file away data. Predictably enough, what bulk information we have comes from the attempts of a modern central bureaucracy to confine, and/or control, the most potentially concussive development of industrial life: the sprawling urban slum.

In order to construct and implement legislation to deal with

such modern phenomena as urban orphans, child exploitation, housing codes, and life lived literally on the street rather
than near the green, organizations such as the City Corpora-
tion, the Privy Council, the House of Lords, and numerous
Royal Commissions were forced to study families which had
no permanent homes. For the first time "things done in secret," "unmentionable acts," were made known to what was
usually a committee of men, themselves part of an aristocracy
that had made many of these selfsame acts a method of class
protection, a way to ensure purity of blood and passage of
possessions. Child abuse in the upper classes was every bit as
brutal and quite possibly every bit as frequent as that in the
lower classes, but harder to identify as it was often done in
the name of sport, education, or eccentricity. In 1903 when
the first of the laws prohibiting and punishing incest was promulgated, most people still believed that such unnatural acts
were characteristic only of the deprived urban family.

Incest was too gross an act to accept as part of the human
condition, and so it was explained away as the result of the
slum itself; too many people in too small a space. Incest was
thought to be a function of proximity. Beatrice Webb, who
would sit on the Royal Commission on the Poor Law and with
her husband Sidney write the influential Minority Report, re-
called how she, in writing her reports, had to omit all references to

> the prevalence of incest in one-roomed tenements. The fact that
> some of my workmates—young girls, who were in no way
> mentally defective, who were, on the contrary, just as keen-
> witted and generous-hearted as my own circle of friends—could
> chaff each other about having babies by their fathers and broth-
> ers, was a gruesome example of the effect of debased social
> environment on personal character and family life. . . . The
> violation of little children was another not infrequent result . . .
> to put it bluntly, sexual promiscuity, and even sexual perver-
> sion, are almost unavoidable among men and women of aver-
> age character and intelligence crowded into the one-roomed
> tenements of slum areas.[14]

For the first time in European culture humans had been herded together for extended periods of cohabitation and, in *post hoc ergo propter hoc* reasoning, the crowding was thought to cause these new sexual aberrations. Mrs. Webb was not alone in jumping to the conclusion that proximity alone produced perversion. Here is Lord Shaftesbury addressing the Church of England's Young Men's Society and making the same link: "Talk of morality amongst people who herd—men, women, and children—together, with no regard of age or sex, in one narrow, confined apartment! You might as well talk of cleanliness in a sty, or of limpid purity in the contents of a cesspool."[15]

The speculation that sexual behavior was more observable, or even more magnified, in urban settings, was too complicated an argument to make. It was just as probable, knowing what we do about the "kibbutz factor," that there were unique pressures at least *against* sibling incest. But no such sophistication was needed; Ockham's razor would clearly have any sensible observer conclude that incest occurrence was primarily a function of population density.[16]

What cinched the causality argument, however, was exactly what should have made legislators curious about the extent of sexual oppression: the objective investigations of bureaucratic functionaries. For developing along with the slums were sanitary inspectors, poor-law guardians, philanthropists, truancy officers, street clergy, and a host of those in the salvation armies of the compassionate, drawn out of middle class parlors. Most of them were willing to, or directed to, "file a report" on what they saw. They were willing to tell what they saw not only because they were earnest in what they did, but also because they were quite sure that slum-family behavior could never be confused with their own.

So here is Shaftesbury again, now reporting in 1861 to the House of Lords:

It is impossible, my Lords, to exaggerate the physical and moral evils that result from this state of things [in London slums]

. . . I would not for all the world mention all the details of
what I have heard, or . . . seen, in these scenes of wretched-
ness. But there are to be found adults of both sexes, living and
sleeping in the same room, every social and every domestic
necessity being performed there; grown-up sons sleeping with
their mothers, brothers, and sisters, sleeping very often, not in
the same apartment only, but in the same bed. My Lords, I am
stating that which I know to be the truth, and which is not to
be gainsaid, when I state that incestuous crime is frightfully
common in various parts of this Metropolis—common to the
greatest extent in the range of these courts [London].[17]

The same plaint can be heard in documents published by the
Association of Medical Officers of Health in 1868 (overcrowding has meant that "sex and consanguinity count for nothing"); the 1882 testimony before the Select Committee on the
Protection of Young Girls by John Horsley, Chaplain of the
Clerkenwell prison (incest was "common," but not "very
common," whatever that means); numerous witnesses before
the Royal Commission on the Housing of the Working Classes
(most importantly Rev. Andrew Mearns whose report "The
Bitter Cry of Outcast London" had asserted that "incest is
common and no form of vice or sexuality causes surprise or
attracts attention"); and as well a series of *Lancet* letters and
articles which sounded an alarm at least to curious men of
science.

But what could be done? As long as incest was considered
in the spiritual domain the temporal courts had no jurisdic-
tion. Worse still, the church treated incest as an act of sacra-
mental transgression, not of physical violation. The sin was to
marry your kin, not to rape her. Again, here is the careless
distinction being made between incest and exogamy. So the
punishment was, as far as the ecclesiastical courts were concerned, annulment and only then possible penance. Furthermore, as Anthony Wohl has found, in the few cases that were
ever brought to court, penance was usually waived after full
court costs had been paid.[18]

The fact of the matter was that neither church nor state really cared to be involved in what so clearly was a messy situation. Call attention to the high incidence of child molestation and you essentially call attention to the fact that your conceptions about divinely inspired moral law or industrial progress were ill-conceived. Both institutions had a vested interest in maintaining the myth of family inviolability and family integrity, and so the helpless child victim was kept at arm's length. Worse yet, to rescue that child not only meant that the family shield would be cracked, but also that these institutions would have to arrange care and protection for the victim. This was no simple matter, as the church had known for generations and as the state was just finding out.

What began at the end of the eighteenth century as a profound resettling of family roles in which the child was seen not as a deformed adult, but as an innocent struggling to be formed, continued as the romantics repeatedly referred to youngsters as lambs, divine philosophers, fathers of men, and concluded as the Victorian novelists portrayed children as credulous angels exploited by older villains but triumphant in the end. This change in attitude had its concomitant effects in popular culture. Concern was transformed into legislation. As part of the general outcry over child exploitation, the National Society for the Prevention of Cruelty to Children flooded Parliament with "moral statistics" as well as with impassioned testimony. In 1908, the Incest Act (8 Edward 7 ch xlv) at last defined both act (focusing on the usually female victim but exempting stepchildren) and punishment (imprisonment of no more than seven years and no less than three). The social crusade against sweatshops, prostitution, drunkenness, gambling, and other "sins of the flesh" had drawn its dragnet around child molestation as well and forced an unwilling and, as it would turn out, largely powerless state bureaucracy to resolve this unmentionable problem of the working classes.

What had transpired between the late eighteenth-century debate on moral versus biological determinism, in which incest was more a case in point than a subject, and late nineteenth-century legislative action, in which incest was a social concern limited to urban crowding, was the gradual assimilation of family sex partners into the concerns of popular culture. As we have seen, art culture, the private aristocratic culture, had shown some interest, mainly in sensationalizing the act as a new subject of rebellious independence at the turn of the century. This interest had proved short-lived. On the one hand, after Shelley had spoken what could a poet say that was startling? On the other hand, once the problem was seen to be real and serious what could a poet *want* to say?

One can almost see the rapid transformation of the incest motif from a subject of art culture to a topic of a burgeoning social science by looking at Tennyson's "Locksley Hall" poems. In the first of the two poems (1842), a young man bemoans his lost opportunities, most specifically his lost love. He laments the forbidden love he has had for his cousin Amy, who has been forced by her family to marry another.[19] The poem only hints of what these unspecified, but powerful, reasons really were. The plaintive lover moans:

> Better thou and I were lying, hidden from the heart's disgrace,
> Rolled in one another's arms, and silent in a last embrace.
>
> Cursed by the social wants that sin against the strength of youth!
> Cursed be the social lies that warp us from the living truth!
>
> Cursed be the sickly forms that err from honest Nature's rule!
> Cursed by the gold that gilds the straitened forehead of the fool!
>
> Well—'tis well that I should bluster!—Hadst thou less unworthy proved—
> Would to God—for I had loved thee more than wife was loved.
>
> Am I mad, that I should cherish, that which bears but bitter fruit?
> I will pluck it from my bosom, though my heart be at the root.
> (57–66)

Since the situation is hopeless, he accepts the restriction with an adolescent pout and prepares to find happiness in some far-away land. In *Locksley Hall: Sixty Years After* he has gone away and returned sadder but wiser, and, of course, richer. He has mellowed into a grandfatherly curmudgeon. We overhear him telling his grandson, who has also been jilted, that the young man's shock is nothing compared to his own. The love the old man had for cousin Amy will never be duplicated in this world and most definitely not by this new parvenu generation. He then launches into a diatribe on the corruption of modern life, condemning newfangled politics, philosophy, religion, fashion, and all the subversions of authority that older people have always blamed on the young. Then he returns again to his prohibited love for Amy. After a momentary pause, he addresses his grandson in what by the 1880s had become a standard indictment of urban life:

> Is it well that while we range with Science, glorying in the Time,
> City children soak and blacken soul and sense in city slime?
>
> There among the glooming alleys Progress halts on palsied feet,
> Crime and hunger cast our maidens by the thousand on the street.
>
> There the Master scrimps his haggard sempstress of her daily bread,
> There a single sordid attic holds the living and the dead.
>
> There the smouldering fire of fever creeps across the rotted floor,
> And the crowded couch of incest in the warrens of the poor.
> (217–224)

Finally, more out of exhaustion of topics than anything else, the old man turns over the key to the youngster telling him, "Follow Light, and do the Right" (277), and presumably shuffles off to sleep and death.

In terms of the sensationalism of incest, it is clear that the old man, unconsciously at least, connects his love of Amy with the perverse modern "love" of city life, but Tennyson, now poet laureate, has no interest either in exploiting the forbid-den, or in explaining the current state of affairs. It is almost as if Tennyson, having initiated a subject that he recognizes as having once been poetically, and now politically, potent, isn't willing to pursue either approach further.[20] The once po-etic subject of incest had become co-opted by the vulgar press and the commonest reader, first in gothic and then in porno-graphic novels. The gothic, written by now forgotten hands, and the pornographic, written by hands never known, had returned the "unpleasant subject" to whispers, innuendo, and the euphemisms so prized by Mrs. Grundy. Tennyson clearly knew what these two burgeoning genres had done. His two "Locksley Hall" poems show his hesitancy to deal with a sub-ject of past artistic interest, but now of popular anxiety. The poeticization of incest had become prosaic and had reentered low culture in such a tarnished state that it could no longer be treated metaphorically. For the next generation treatments of incest would be only carried in vernacular media, in slang forms of transmission.

"Popular culture" is such a loaded term that it might be best to, if not tighten it up, then at least acknowledge its loose-ness. To the defenders and protectors of sacerdotal texts, namely college professors, popular culture usually has been translated into its derogatory diminutive "pop culture," im-plying that, like "pop art," it is a fluke, interesting only as a passing whim. It should not be studied seriously because it is, by its very nature, superficial. Popular culture is culture that is obvious and what is obvious is what needs no gloss, no footnote, no critical exegesis. Since the stuff was never in-tended to be taken seriously, how can it be studied? But just as the term "kiddie lit" does disservice to the legitimate study of the readings of childhood, so "pop culture" mistakes what often have been the really important messages we pass around. These messages are all the more important because we are often unconscious of their meaning, as well as of the depth of their power. They cannot be forgotten because without them we would have no memory of how to behave.

Popular culture, mass culture, majority culture, is that stuff, be it verbal, visual, tactile, or auditory, which is produced in bulk to be consumed in bulk. It is culinary entertainment which is meant to satisfy the appetites, if not the hungers, of the multitude. It is to be devoured, not tasted. Since I am interested in the function of the incest taboo as it is conducted in verbal texts, I will concentrate on the gothic novel, which forms a telling counterpart to romantic poetry.

Since mass production is crucial to the success of any medium of popular culture, the novel was greatly influenced by technological developments in print and paper production, to say nothing of distribution. The railway book store was as influential then as the coaxial cable is now. Stereotyping, paperbacks, cheap paper, permanent inks, movie rights—all caused profound shifts in form and content. Additionally, with popular culture the marketplace itself determines what will be produced in the future as well as in the present. "Will it sell?" is what the publisher asks, not "Is it important?" Popular culture topics thus are commodities, behaving more like soybean futures than "short time's endless monuments." Tastes are predicted and exploited by what entrepreneurs surmise about the market.

What makes this all so important to the student of human behavior is that the process is vaguely reminiscent of the patterns of dream life. As dreamers repeat certain sequences and images until some garbled message has been decoded by the unconscious, so too does popular culture repeat and repeat until the audience "understands" and changes channels. Authorship and craft are beside the point: who knows and who cares? Content is all, and we can judge the power of that content only by checking effect and frequency. Is this a show that we will keep watching even in rerun after rerun? Is this a dream we have dreamed before? Is this a novel just like the novel we just put down? If it is, it probably is passing information around that we want and need in order to be socialized in some manner. Popular culture is not the best that can be thought, but the best that we can remember.

Another analogy: as fairy tales prepare the juvenile audience for adolescence, so do horror myths prepare us for adulthood. We see most of these myths now played out as in dreams in the darkness of the movie theater, but in the nineteenth century they were carried on screens of paper unreeling in lines of print. From its beginnings with Samuel Richardson, the novel was an arcade for popular culture, exploiting as it did first the curiosities of adolescent females and then of the general populace. In fact, the Harlequin romance is much more a "novel" than the art novels we teach as the "traditional" novel. The popular audience for the novel has migrated elsewhere, attracted to the more exciting manipulation of images in electronic media. However, the one audience that has not really been effaced by television, or the movies, is the audience that has remained nurtured by a rather particular form of the novel: the gothic. That is because the gothic was to the nineteenth century what the soap opera is to us—a fantastic exemplum of the bourgeois family under pressure.

Even if one is unwilling to admit that the gothic has social utility, one must concede that the gothic has remained a powerful socializing force through many generations of popular culture. It is in such robust health that the *New York Times* bestseller list had to be broken down to accommodate the glut of such mass market fiction. Stephen King and his confreres have made their mark not only in publishing, where they outsell all others, but in Hollywood. The adaptation of the gothic to celluloid has made it overall the most lucrative genre. A generation ago, perhaps as a result of the world wars, which produced real horror, the gothic was slightly different, bordering on what is called "weird fiction." This pulp was pushed aside with the rise of movie studios such as Universal and AIP and Hammer, which filled their coffers by adapting gothic novels like *Frankenstein, Dracula,* and *Dr. Jekyll and Mr. Hyde* to film and then by producing sequel after sequel. It should be noted that in the 1890s there was a similar surge, a surge which first produced the classic texts of *Dracula* and *Dr. Jekyll,* from which the adaptations proliferated. I am not interested in these relatively recent pulses of gothic enthusiasm, but rather in the first gush which flowed through the mid-eighteenth century and crested in the first twenty years of the nineteenth. It is here that we see the incest prohibition assimilated with other forms of domestic family life and carried to a curious and demanding audience via the popular novel.

After a notably quiet start in the 1760s, gothic fiction burst forth with such vigor that it dominated the early nineteenth-century novel, forcing more conservative forms to take refuge in such safe harbors as the novel of manners (Jane Austen) or the historical novel (Walter Scott). The gothic, and its cousins, the sentimental novel and the romance, were so popular that before the turn of the century poetic and novelistic satires were almost as current as the real stuff. That Jane Austen's *Northanger Abbey* could turn the conventions inside out while at the same time behaving like a "real gothic" tells much about the assimilation of the gothic into popular culture. By 1800 the clichés had an independent life of their own.

I have no interest in cataloging most of those formula novels—such long-suffering critics as Birkhead, Ralio, Summers, and Varma have already done that—nor do I want to trace the precursors of the gothic in the English and German novel. But I do want to give a quick sense of the general atmosphere within the gothic before showing how the incest phobia functions in general, and then how it operates within a specific work, Mary Shelley's *Frankenstein*.

The world of the gothic is a world almost overwhelmed with dread. The sense of apprehension, of vague impending disaster, makes this genre strangely alluring because, as opposed to other genres, this one pictures our own fallen world, the real world, the corrupt world. Within the seemingly safe fantasy of what we can always convince ourselves is just gothic claptrap, we can play out the anxieties of our own nighttime fears and follow our own forbidden curiosities. However much we may intellectualize about the gothic's ick and boo, however much we think of it as an indulgence in kitsch and coincidence, there have been times in our lives, especially in adolescence, when we have recognized that the stories it tells are not so far away and that some of its described distress is our own.

This distress is almost always generated within a home, or

more specifically, within a family. The outer world reinforces this sense of foreboding: castles, ruins, cliffs, passageways, earth opening up beneath our feet, secret towers, and most of all, darkness, interminable darkness. Twilight and blackness are the colors of the gothic because things we dread happen in houses at night. The old haunted house is a cliché today because yesterday we understood that that was the place, the locus of horror. Occurring within darkness is violation, not necessarily actual, but imagined. In the gothic the ultimate violation, death, is always obsessively present, but sexual violation lurks in the shadows and plays a much more important part.

Sexual violation of whom? Here we are led to one of the two eidolons in the gothic cast of characters: the isolated female protagonist and the isolating older male. The ingenue is often orphaned or of mysterious parentage, always virginal, adolescent, and sensitive. In confinement, she is confronted with this older man, perhaps a wanderer, priest, landlord, robber, noble, or even a creature from another world. If he is from her own world, and if his relationship is explained, he will be a paternal or avuncular figure. He is driven by desire, sexual desire which he may or may not be able to control. In either case, he does not *want* to control this desire. He is rarely ashamed of himself or of his actions. He is almost totally unselfconscious. Often he is more than capricious. He is demonic and evil precisely because he enjoys these illicit desires, these unmentioned urges, precisely because he has refused to sublimate. What becomes progressively obvious, as you consume more and more of these novels, is that this central relationship is essentially that of father-daughter from *both* their points of view.

Now clearly, this is not always the case, but as Ann B. Tracy has demonstrated in *The Gothic Novel 1790–1830*, the father-daughter paradigm is the most frequent. After all, older man chasing young girl has been the occasion of shrieks since days in the cave, and given the novel's adolescent female audience, it was inevitable that a whole genre would be constructed to conduct both the thrill and the horror of this concussion.

There is also a less important interaction that is of interest here, and that is the relationship between the female heroine and her socially acceptable suitor, the young courtier. Ostensibly he is interested in courtship, marriage, and family, not sex. In the sentimental novel and in the romance this interaction can be played out to a happy ending, but in the gothic it often involves a series of false recognition scenes between now-they-are, now-they-are-not siblings. What makes this subplot so revealing of family sexual repression is that in the "primary" gothic, in the high gothic from *The Castle of Otranto* to *Dracula*, the paternal character personified by a Manfred, Dracula, Wolfstein, or Schedoni pursues the innocent female to *his* demise, and maybe her own as well. The foul patriarch is destroyed literally or figuratively by being sent to a monastery for perpetual penance. However, in the siblings-who-don't-know-they-are-siblings story, ultimate resolution is possible even if the incest taboo is violated.

Clearly, society seems far more forgiving of ignorance in the service of youth than consummation in the service of power. If the youngsters never consummate the act, they will usually both be saved. If they mistakenly consummate the act, the male usually will be exiled. If the male knowingly consummates the act, he will meet with disaster. (The female will never, that I know of, knowingly violate the taboo.) In other words, paternal incest is absolutely scorned both in act and imagination and threat, but sibling incest is, if not tolerated, at least not always stigmatized. To witness the basis of these generalizations, let us look at the texts.

For reasons obvious to those who have read in the gothic tradition, no scholar has ever systematically evaluated the function of incest in the English *Schauerroman*, other than to assert that it most assuredly exists. At the risk of writing gothic commentary on gothic novels (ceaseless citation of ceaseless dangers), I should like very briefly to outline the familial patterns as they unfolded in the first burst of gothic enthusiasm between 1780 and 1820. Then I will treat in depth the only first generation gothic novel to have jumped the literary tracks and entered popular culture with an independent life of its

own: Mary Shelley's *Frankenstein*. We will see that incest was
so much a part of the gothic ethos that by the time Mary Shelley entered the famous bargain to compose a "shocker," incest was already a stock assumption. In 1816, if you were
eighteen years old and had read your youthful fill of this kind
of entertainment, violation of the incest taboo was an expected method of shock delivery.

As noted earlier in reference to general cultural patterns,
paternal incest was treated in nineteenth-century culture as if
it were different in both kind and degree from sibling incest.
More than any other genre, the gothic seems to prove this
supposition, for even when the sexual risk is minimal, daughters and daughter surrogates must steer clear of fathers. This
concern for the sexual safety of the ingenue is expressed almost from the first pen stroke and remains to this day one of
the central lessons repeated time and again in texts which ostensibly have no moralizing to do.

In Horace Walpole's *Castle of Otranto* (1765), considered by
many the prototext of the genre, the usurping patriarch,
Manfred, attempts to separate from his wife in order to court
the sexual favors of his future daughter-in-law, Isabella.
Manfred has been "almost a father" to the young girl all her
life and Isabella is so unnerved that she seeks sanctuary in the
local church. There is no doubt that Manfred's subsequent
hallucinations and bizarre behavior are related to his forbidden desires, as is his later barefaced attempt to trade his own
daughter to Isabella's father in return for Isabella's hand, or
more exactly, her body. And so when Manfred finally stabs
his own daughter, mistaking her for Isabella, the sexual relationship is clear to more readers than just the Freudians. Ultimately, Manfred is shown to be wicked in the extreme, and
the "usurper," in all manifold meanings, of Otranto. Once exposed, he must follow the only course of action open to those
who act on these desires, at least in the gothic. He must enter
a "religious house" to spend the rest of his days doing penance—an exile from his family.

By the turn of the eighteenth century this intrafamilial configuration was being unraveled, as it had been in the romance

tradition, from the young female's point of view. It is the tale of Clarissa when her Lovelace is none other than her father. Feminists may decry the seeming absence of their own *Bildungsromans*, but in so doing they overlook the gothic. In this genre girls *must* grow up.[21] So in 1798 Elizabeth Sophia Tomlins traces the route of her heroine, Rosalind de Tracy, through three volumes of maturation in which all important action centers on finding an appropriate spouse. Because Rosalind was orphaned, her guardian, Sir Raymond Cecil, has chosen just the mate—an over-eager neighbor who is priapically insistent on matrimony. This superannuated courtesan, Signor Mondovini, has already sneaked into Rosalind's boudoir and grabbed her in the dark; now he wishes to do the same in daylight. Rosalind will have none of him and, after many pages have turned, she learns that Mondovini is really her father. Rosalind is stunned. Her father is forced to marry a lunatic, and a monument is erected to the memory of the departed mother/wife.

An interesting twist in the family romance occurs in *St. Botolph's Priory* (1806), by T. J. Horsley Curties, which tells of another innocent, Roselma, who is urged by her stepfather to marry M. DeRochemond, much to Roselma and her mother's distress. DeRochemond is in such unseemly haste that he says the wedding simply cannot be postponed even by a minute. But halfway through the hurry-up ceremony, a huge figure in black appears announcing that Roselma must not wed this man. Forget this rubbish, says DeRochemond, let the vows be said. If any problem develops, we'll just not consummate the act. Roselma does not object and the ceremony continues. Roselma's mother, however, becomes hysterical and dies, and two volumes later we realize why: DeRochemond is Roselma's uncle who supposedly has killed Roselma's father in order to marry her mother. Now he is after Roselma. Little wonder the mother was such an embarrassment at the wedding! But who was the huge man in black who did not stop the ill-fated wedding? He was none other than Roselma's father who, it seems, had escaped his brother's attack but did not have the courage to protect his own daughter. No need to feel sorry for poor Ro-

selma—after DeRochemond dies, she marries the well-behaved
Marquis of Valmont and lives happily ever after. After all, she
was totally innocent in thought and deed.

By the nineteenth century two motifs seem associated with
father-daughter incest as it is recapitulated in the gothic: the
frisson associated with the act is so damaging to the family
that it falls apart if the father is allowed to persist too long;
and often the father figure is so upsetting to contemplate that
the role is displaced to uncle. This switch may also be because
in nonmobile families, uncles really did provide a threat to the
sexual well-being of young females. In either case, from the
point of view of the storyteller, the shock of father-daughter,
or father surrogate-daughter surrogate incest, is so powerful
that the only way to get the story out is to continually dilute
the relationship.

As an example of how powerful even a veiled reference to
paternalistic oppression can be, witness *The Mysterious Monk*
written by C. A. Bolen in 1826. Here we follow poor Ella as
she is pursued by King John, no less, whom she supposes to
be her father. For symmetry's sake, she is also pursued by the
pope, who has the same designs. Ella is able to withstand the
onslaughts of both her temporal and spiritual fathers. A year
before in *The Castle Chapel*, a secondary character, Rose, was
spirited off by her long-lost but now found and homicidal father, who presses his suit. Finally, he relents and offers to
marry her off to a young man whom he earlier had perse-
cuted, but Rose is so confused and mortified by what her father has done that she dies of a broken heart. Ella and Rose,
like their sisters in the sentimental novel, are sought after by
men; what replaces the romance conventions in the gothic is
that the men in the gothic are none other than the ones who
are supposed to be their protectors. The guardian has become
what needs to be guarded against, and in such a topsy-turvy
world the only sane response is neurosis.

If the gothic tells us anything it is what "too close for comfort" really means. So Mrs. Carver's *The Horrors of Oakdale Abbey* (1797) tells the story of poor Laura who is pursued by Lord
Oakdale, who becomes by turns employer, suitor, and uncle.

Laura finds this last relationship repulsive and only his death frees her to do her heart's desire: to marry her cousin. In Francis Lathom's *The Mysterious Freebooter* (1806) young Rosalind must fend off an attack from a rogue who turns out to be her father-in-law. In George Walker's *Don Raphael* (1803) Cornelia and her look-alike sister Christina come to tragic ends. One is a suicide and the other almost becomes a nun because they unknowingly allow their father, the crazed Don Raphael, to pay them court. As well, in Regina Maria Roche's *Nocturnal Visit* (1800) Jacintha is sent by her long-lost mother-in-law, who is not really her mother-in-law but thinks she is, to a distant castle in the Pyrenees to keep her away from Lord Gwytherin, who is yet another of these agressive fathers.

To be sure, the gothic novel by its commitment to shock may have been forced to describe the breaking of family bonds, but it was not forced to mandate the requisite trip to the nunnery for the girl, or to the asylum or worse for the male. As we have seen, the father, or displaced father, invades the privacy of the ingenue and by virtue of his authority and her weakness (a weakness exaggerated by her usually being abandoned, or at least motherless) is able to intimidate and profoundly unsettle her sense of well-being. Although to the best of my knowledge the sexual act very rarely occurs, it is always clear that this is what he contemplates. He is invariably the instigator, the eager actor. Never is she the seductive Lolita, and never is he a clumsy Humbert.

The taboo is also enforced with rigor when the father/father-in-law/surrogate father is projected one degree further to become an uncle. If Walpole's *Otranto* is the most famous of the paternal configurations, then Ann Radcliffe's *The Italian* (1797) is the avuncular counterpart. Although the relationship between Schedoni and Ellena is played out initially as father-daughter, especially after Schedoni sees what he takes to be a miniature of himself worn around Ellena's neck, the relationship is so powerful that even Schedoni seems to recoil until the roles are reestablished. In reality, as we learn from Ellena's mother, Schedoni is only an uncle, a relationship that Schedoni clearly prefers. Even so the shock so disturbs Ellena that it is only her abiding love for Vivaldi that protects her by allowing quick exit from one oppressive relationship and immediate entry into a protective one.

The Italian was not the only story in which Mrs. Radcliffe had played out this familial scenario. Six years earlier, in one of the very first of the full-scale gothic romances, *The Romance of the Forest*, Adeline is supposed to be the "natural child" of her suitor, the Marquis de Montalt. Again, the relationship is removed a notch by showing them to be uncle and niece, but the effect achieved is a father-daughter concussion. What is especially shocking about this relationship is that once the Marquis knows that Adeline is close kin, his response is no longer amorous but violently destructive. Rather like Schedoni, the older rogue male links sex and violence quite literally. He explodes in libidinous fury. To paraphrase Bard Bracy in *Christabel*: child abuse is the other side of excessive and inappropriate child love. His illicit passion is literally self-destructive; he poisons himself.

No doubt we carry the father-daughter incest taboo in the unconscious codes of everyday linguistic interchange. Think of the buried meaning of the cliché, "he's old enough to be her father." Essentially, the gothic extends the idiom until the buried story is partially uncovered, then quickly hidden again. The relative paucity of unabashed father-daughter plots, compared, say, to uncle-niece ones, may attest to how much effacement, or how much displacement, our society seems to need. In this context, it is interesting to speculate about the point at which the gothic mode intersects the romance tradition, for we might well find that as the older man's paternalistic relationship fades, the gothic recedes and the sentimental begins. Think, for instance, of Charlotte Brontë's *Jane Eyre*, where, although the father-daughter paradigm is always in place, the story obviously details how much literal and figurative weakening Rochester must endure before he is a suitable partner for Jane.

To give some idea of how popular the uncle-niece configuration was at the turn of the century, here is a brief descriptive chronology. In Eliza Parsons' *Castle of Wolfenbach* (1793),

Mathilda is pursued by her uncle through two volumes until he is forced to confess his illicit love, grow penitent, and vow a monastic future; in Joseph Fox's *Santa-Maria, or, The Mysterious Pregnancy* (1797), it is Maria who is molested by her uncle, Contarini, who, for this and other nefarious acts, is beheaded; in Mrs. R. M. P. Yorke's *The Romance of Smyra* (1801), Alizra is drugged and raped by uncle Don Joseph, an act that results in the demise of both (he by the state and she by his poison); and in T. J. Horsley Curties' *Ancient Records* (1801), Rosaline must steer clear of wicked uncle Randolf if she is to escape the prison of her decaying family.

Admittedly, I am not doing justice to these often incredibly turgid plots, but I do think one general message to young women can be culled from these novels with regard to relationships with an older male relative: always stay away from him regardless of what he says. He has power. He has control. The caveat to the older man seems only slightly less strict, but easier to comply with. Be careful not to be caught and exposed. In the gothic, young women live in constant risk of defilement not by a breathless Don Juan, as in the romance tradition, but by a father or an uncle. Are there dim shadows of the primal horde being cast here? Like the folk ballad it so often resembles, the gothic deals with sin, guilt, and immediate retribution. The most particular sin is family sex, the most guilt-producing arrangement is of the father-daughter variety, and the retribution is unambiguous and almost without exception. Do "it" just once, the gothic seems to say in its own particular vernacular, and you will do nothing else, ever again. Come *close* to doing "it," and there may be hope. The male may be forever stigmatized, the female may be lucky enough (depending on degree of collusion) to find, or start, another family in which her role can be stabilized.

Another lesson seems to be that the greater the age difference, the more vehement the social stipulations. December and April relationships are not on the calendar of stable families, no matter how eager December may be. But what happens when the ages are equalized while the family bonds are still tightly tied? What happens when sibling incest occurs, or is implied, or just contemplated? This relationship also abruptly jars the sense of family role playing. Sibling incest, however, does not call forth such horror or such penalty. In fact, this relationship can sometimes pass through the communal sieve of morality and, if not end "happily ever after," at least be acknowledged to be a forgivable mistake.

Although this kind of statistic is probably misleading as well as unimportant, in the early gothics there are approximately three times as many instances of sibling incest as there are of father/uncle-daughter/niece variety.[22] This may simply mean that the plot possibilities were more exciting, more easily manipulated between coevals than where the ages were disparate. It may just as easily indicate an audience predisposition for certain renditions in preference to others. Such a preference would be important to establish because the early gothic audience seems to have been predominantly female. If so, could the higher incidence of sibling encounters indicate a willingness at least to countenance what was clearly objectionable when the participants were of the father figure-daughter surrogate type? And could this in turn mean that the interfamilial tension is markedly less when brother-sister roles become confused with the roles of lovers? After all, our language, the cryptograph of social memory, broadly classifies them with the same term, "sibling," while there is no single term to describe parent and child.

The validity of such speculation, however, may soon be called into question when we realize that, although incidents of sibling incest in the gothic novel may far outnumber all others, there is little uniformity in the treatment. I have been able to catalog four distinct types: 1) consummated brother-sister incest that inspires horror; 2) nonconsummated brother-sister affairs that end in pathos; 3) sibling relationships that are imagined as, then shown not to be, incestuous, and result in romance; and 4) consummated brother-sister incest that occurs with no attendant horror, apparently in the service of plot development elsewhere. I should like to describe an example of each of these moving from 1) horror (*The Monk*), through 2) mutual recognition of consanguinity (*The Farmer of Inglewood*

Forest), to 3) false recognition (*The Mystery, or, Forty Years Ago*), to 4) mutual recognition and short-lived acceptance (*Ernestus Berchtold, or, The Modern Oedipus*).

If *Otranto* is the most famous of the general father-daughter variety, and if *The Italian* is the most famous of the avuncular type, then Matthew Lewis's *The Monk* (1796) is the most important of the sibling incest category. It is also a rare example, along with Ian Crookenden's *Horrible Revenge* (1808), of sibling incest which is contrived to produce outright horror. In *The Monk*, the most unmonkish miscreant, Ambrosio, is in a sense blameless as his desires are sanctioned and protected by a minion of Satan, Matilda. Still, his desire for his long-lost sister, Antonia, is initially his own, and the consummated incest must be charged to the lust and sexual recklessness that underlie his otherwise insufferable piety. In addition, that he should also kill his mother in the process of sibling rape indicates that we need hardly see his actions as anything other than hyperbole. Yet in that exaggeration is a core of such violent antisocial behavior so repulsive that even Lucifer finds it disgusting. Monk's development of fallen family life prefigures the Sadean transformation of nineteenth-century pornography—barbarism in the service of titillation.[23]

Typical of a gothic entanglement about twenty degrees less intense than *The Monk* is Elizabeth Helme's *The Farmer of Inglewood Forest* (1796). Like Frances Jamieson's *The House of Ravenspur* (1822), Anna Mackenzie's *The Irish Guardian* (1809), Mary Meeke's *Midnight Weddings* (1802), Mary Robinson's *Vancenza* (1792), and Francis Lathom's wonderfully titled *Astonishment!!!* (1802), the frisson here is generated by allowing brother and sister, or surrogate siblings, not to consummate the incestuous act but to contemplate it. If *The Monk* ends awash in dreck, in excess of fright, these novels end, at best, in tragic hokum. The male may not be heroic, but he is decent. It is his willingness to contemplate such an act of familial discord that forces a finale reminiscent of the heroic demise of the unwanted suitor in the romance tradition. He commits suicide.

In *The Farmer of Inglewood Forest*, Edwin and his sister, Emma, leave the pastoral quiet of rural life and venture into the mecca of dissolute pleasures, London. En route, they turn their backs on their neighborhood sweethearts in order to seek the thrills of the flesh. Rather like Wordsworth's Luke in *Michael*, they rise, shine, evaporate, and fall even more quickly than Dr. Johnson could have predicted. In a matter of months Edwin has become a notorious profligate, Emma an abused prostitute. As they separately live out their lives of fallen promise, corrupting country values with city filth, their paths inevitably cross. Unknown to them, they become patroness and client. They almost commit incest. But they are saved at the last minute by authorial fiat: Edwin is too drunk and Emma has had a warning dream and begs off. From such sexual proximity, however (as well as from the usual raunchy behavior that city life calls forth), a price is to be extracted. Emma returns home to die a penitent while Edwin does the manly counterpart and shoots himself. Incest in this type of gothic novel is not titillating as in *The Monk*, but is, rather, an exemplum of the depths of human depravity, a situation more indicative of the perversion of social values than of lust.

With the third and by far the most popular type of gothic, incest phobia is exploited by parents and guardians as a wedge to keep young lovers apart. Novels of this kind really belong to the romance tradition, and it is only the intrusion of the incest motif that moves them off to the margin of propriety and makes them shockers. Added to all the other inhibitions in the romance that have kept the young from copulation, or, more politely, from marriage, such as parental refusal, overwhelming distance, incarceration, military service, lapses of memory, religion, marriage to others, and disinheritance threats, consanguinity was added in the late eighteenth century as yet another fear. What makes incest inhibitions historically so interesting is that they entered prose fiction at the same time that the cultural idealization of sibling love was also finding its way into art poetry. We have seen this in the romantic verse of Byron and Shelley and we see it a little later in the novel. These two strains often mix, as we observe in the child lovers of Scott, Dickens, Thackeray, and Hardy.

It was in the gothic, however, that the experiments were first performed. In Thomas Gaspey's *The Mystery, or, Forty Years Ago* (1820), Charles Harley falls in love with his neighbor, Amelia Henderson, and when he asks her father, Sir George, if they may proceed, he is given a surprising and abrupt "No!" To make a long story (three volumes worth) rather short, Charles goes to the African jungle to collect his thoughts; there he meets Smithers, an English missionary. Smithers gives him some papers from which, when Charles returns home and gives the papers to Sir George, he learns something rather unexpected. Sir George had said "No!" because he thought Charles to be his bastard son. But now, thanks to what is contained in these papers, all recognize the mistaken identity. The relieved lovers marry at once.

In living out this plot Charles and Amelia join Alphonso and Maria of Stephen Cullen's *The Haunted Priory* (1794), in which a birthmark replaces Smithers' papers; Margiana and Ethelred of Mrs. S. Sykes' *Margiana* (1808), in which special papers appear just in time to prove "sister" is not really sister; Enrico and Laurette of Eleanor Sleath's *The Orphan of the Rhine* (1798), in which the mysterious LaRoque must explain the secret of their separate lineage; and a manor house full of such young lovers who must wait patiently, or not so patiently, for Smithers' papers to arrive. Whether it be a miniature painting, a nurse remembering swapped babies, or monks with prodigious powers of recall, or the favorite of all—the birthmark—the missing element is always introduced at the point of reader exhaustion to show that if the course of true love does not run smooth, it almost always runs out into the same romantic sea. As long, that is, as it is not diverted by the hasty physical actions of the lovers. These gothic novels all seem to say the same thing to youth: wait it out, be careful, stay apart.

The only novel I know of in which incest is committed without immediate disaster is John William Polidori's *Ernestus Berchtold, or, The Modern Prometheus* (1819). This work is a curiosity for extraliterary reasons. Polidori was Byron's personal physician who traveled with the poet during the early days of the Byronic hegira to the continent in 1816. Polidori was also present in the Villa Diodati during that wet June evening when

Byron, Percy Shelley, Mary Godwin, and her half-sister Claire
Claremont struck the bargain that each would write a tale calculated to horrify in the manner of the then popular German
chillers. Byron's contribution was the fragment of a vampire
tale which Polidori re-formed and published two years later
under Byron's name in the April issue of *Colburn's New Monthly
Magazine*.[24] Shelley and Claire Claremont both wrote pieces now
thankfully forgotten (thankfully, that is, if they were like Shelley's earlier attempts in the genre and what we might expect
from the flighty Claire). Mary Godwin, not quite yet Mary
Shelley, wrote the tale that would break away from the gothic
novel tradition and enter popular culture with a vengeance—
Frankenstein. It seems that it was here in this company, in what
was bandied about as a "league of incest" by outsiders, that
the irascible young Polidori first conceived of *Ernestus Berchtold*.[25]

With the exception of some recent interest, Polidori's contribution has been almost completely forgotten, which is not
unusual considering the content. It is, however, just that content that proves so interesting in examining the romantic ambivalence about the consequences of incest. Ernestus and Julia,
orphaned twins, have been raised by the priest Berchtold with
only the highest of moral standards. As we know from *The
Monk*, as well as from reams of gothic sagas, the higher the
moral expectations, the lower the results. Ernestus is soon led
astray by the alluring Louisa, led, in fact, into the army, and
from there into the regiment of Louisa's brother, Oliveri, who,
in turn, is led back to Ernestus's sister, Julia. Seductions abound
and the consequences are dire: Julia's traumatic pregnancy and
death in childbirth.

Ernestus and Louisa are luckier; they marry and hope to start
a new life together. As part of their domesticity, they decide
to decorate their apartment with the portraits of their parents:
one of Ernestus's mother and one of Louisa's father. They do
indeed live happily for a while as man and wife, but then there
occurs the inevitable visit from a relative. This time it is from
Louisa's father who recognizes the portrait of Ernestus's mother
as the woman by whom he had fathered twins many years ago.

The happy marriage is shattered and what had been a bitter-sweet memory of the affair between Julia and Oliveri is rendered repulsive. The twins, with the highest of moral educations, have committed not just the lowest of acts, incest, but double incest. Strangely, at least in this genre, nothing very terrible now happens. The father, who had been a quack scientist, renounces all antisocial behavior; Louisa dies not of a broken heart or of an excess of guilt, but from having lived "too much"; and Ernestus is left hoping for a melancholy reunion with her in the afterlife. What should, and usually does, call down the fiercest of penalties—suicide, madness, monastic life—is accepted with relative equanimity.

Ernestus Berchtold is clearly the exception that proves the rule. Far more often sibling physical attraction is dealt with quickly and forcibly, even ruthlessly. In fact, one of the most romantic of gothic novels, really the most romantic of all nineteenth-century novels, may depend on the incest phobia to churn the central action. The question in *Wuthering Heights* is why do Catherine Earnshaw and Heathcliff not respond physically to each other? Arguably, there is no more powerful love ever described in English literature. The fact that these two strong-willed and independent characters never do much more than look at each other with intense and furious love is perplexing even to the most forgiving of the Brontëans. About thirty years ago Eric Solomon in "The Incest Theme in *Wuthering Heights*" suggested an answer which has been updated by William Goetz in "Genealogy and Incest in *Wuthering Heights*." Incest avoidance is what drives these two lovers apart just as their passion drives them together. This explanation may resolve some, but by no means all, of the novel's thorny cruxes. It explains, for instance, why Mr. Earnshaw brought Heathcliff back to Wuthering Heights from the slums of Liverpool when such generosity was hardly in his character; why Nelly Dean comments about Earnshaw that "he took to the child *strangely*," this "poor fatherless child, as *he* called him;" and what may subconsciously be the meaning of Catherine's extraordinary, "Nelly, I am Heathcliff!" exclamation. Is this the plaint of a lover or the unconscious confession of a sibling? We will never know, but this much we do know: here is a novel literally riddled with overlapping alliances, merging appellation systems (the endless mix-up of names), complex exchange systems, and bizarre kinships all of which center on a core of incestuous ferment. Here is a novel in which Heathcliff marries his love's sister-in-law; his wife's son marries her brother's daughter; the second generation Catherine marries her brother's son; and certainly these events pass through the conscious censors of both author and reader with little concern. It is not so idle to speculate about how deeply the incestuous motif penetrates this most enigmatic of gothic novels.[26]

By the time Emily Brontë's *Wuthering Heights* appeared at mid-century, the incest configuration had become well established in the art novel.[27] From Defoe's *Moll Flanders* (marriage to brother-in-law) and Fielding's *Joseph Andrews* (Fanny and Joseph) and *Tom Jones* (the supposed relation of Tom to Mrs. Waters) in the eighteenth century, it spread as far as Burney's *Evelina* (Evelina and Mr. Marcartney are supposed siblings), Mackenzie's *The Man of the World* (uncle-niece incest), Scott's *St. Ronan's Well* (siblings Mowbray and Clara), and then into the mid-Victorian novels like Thackeray's *Henry Esmond*. The essence of this rambling and overlooked novel, as Walter Pater first noted, is the shifting of a mother-son relationship into that of husband-wife when Henry finally marries Lady Castlewood.[28]

Russell M. Goldfarb has argued in "Charles Dickens: Orphans, Incest, and Repression" that incest—more often implied than stated—is present in most of the child relationships of the famous Dickens novels. But the most extraordinary of the High Victorian instances is surely in George Eliot's *The Mill on the Floss*. Although Henry James may have been frustrated and annoyed by the ending, who can forget Maggie and Tom Tulliver clutching each other in passionate embrace as they are swept into the whirlpool of the flooded river Floss? What have they done to be so consumed by nature? Is this a rewriting of *Wuthering Heights*? There is much in the novel, as David Smith has argued, to have us conclude that "the organizing principle of *The Mill on the Floss* is the unconscious incestuous passion."[29] Think only of Maggie's childhood passion for Tom, her guilt over these feelings, the deflection of feeling toward Philip, the guilt, self-punishment and renunciation, and, most of all, the suggestive flood death scene. As the observers on shore beseech Maggie and Tom to "Get out of the current," they are literally swept into each other's arms, into sexual excitement, and into death. "'It is coming, Maggie!' Tom said, in a deep hoarse voice, loosing the oars and clasping her." The omniscient narrator opines that "brother and sister had gone down in an embrace never to be parted." The townspeople make sure the point is not missed. They have the tombstone inscribed: "In their death they were not divided."

Incest also clearly figures in the popular culture tradition not only in the gothic, as we have seen, but also in the send-up of the gothic which by the early nineteenth century was almost as vibrant as the "real stuff." The parody was as apt to come from the pen of a practitioner, as with Lewis' *Giles Jollup, the Grave*, as from that of a detractor, as with Jane Austen's *Northanger Abbey*. Here, for instance, are the concluding lines of Mary Alcock's *Receipt for Writing a Novel* (1799):

> Now at your fable's close devise
> Some grand event to give surprise—
> Suppose your hero knows no mother—
> Suppose he proves the heroine's brother—
> This at one stroke dissolves each tie,
> At length when every woe's expended,
> And your last volume's nearly ended,
> Clear the mistake, and introduce
> Some tatt'ling nurse to cut the noose,
> The spell is broke—again they meet
> Expiring at each other's feet;
> Their friends lie breathless on the floor—
> You drop your pen; you can no more—
> And ere your reader can recover,
> They're married—and your history's over.(73–88)[30]

Shared by both art and popular cultures is a work that has transcended them both: *Frankenstein*. Like the vampire saga, this story quickly shed the printed text to appear on the stage, then on celluloid, and is now omnipresent. It has proved so powerful that it can catch on to any mode of transmission: comics, bubblegum cards, even a breakfast cereal—"Frankenberries." The Frankenstein story has become one of the central myths of our time, changing as our fears change. Here is the gothic novel made allegorical. It is now read as a warning about science, about the dangers of organ transplants, gene splicing, and DNA research. But this too will doubtless change as our fears change. Inside this ever-changing text is one of the repositories of adolescent information about life and its attendant confusions. Not only is the text of the myth about confusion, sexual confusion (after all, how can just one person create life?), but the supertextual world is also characterized by confusion; it is, after all, a myth consumed by a pre-adolescent audience. For instance, ask any twelve-year-old who "Frankenstein" is and you will be told it is the monster—it is not, of course; it is the protagonist. Then, if you ask about this protagonist, you will probably be told that he is an older man, a doctor, a mad scientist. He is not: he is a very callow youth. And if you ask how the audience feels about the "monster," you will probably learn a very important fact. You will learn that this character (like the other horror monster, the vampire) is a figure of some sympathy. Although it might seem logical to return to the text to resolve these ambiguities, the printed text is not sufficient. We need to examine the entire saga to see where the excitement comes from, how it gets embedded into the various renditions, and how it continues to exist there regardless of the medium of transmission. What we will see is that, as with Dracula, the other central myth of adolescents, the excitement of Frankenstein is generated around a core of forbidden sexuality.

The generating text of the Frankenstein myth is, as George Levine has written, "one of the great freaks of English literature."[31] Mary Shelley's *Frankenstein, or, The Modern Prometheus* is awkwardly written, inconsistently plotted, peopled with a host of seemingly superfluous characters, and full of the kind of inappropriate longueurs that characterize artistic immaturity. It is a gothic novel, to be sure, but instead of a monstrous antagonist it has a *real* monster. The story is delivered to us, however, as if it were a typical chiller. A young man, Robert Walton, writes his sister a verbatim account of what a young scientist, Victor Frankenstein, has accomplished in creating a "monster," who in turn has given young Frankenstein a verbatim account of what has happened to him during four years of the eighteenth century in Europe. This Chinese box narrative safely cocoons "meaning" inside a double layer of stories. Yet, in spite of (and because of) all the obscuring effects of these buried narratives and the ironic juxtapositions of narrators, there is not enough authorial control to save the multiple tales from some incredible silliness while presenting some profound truths. Students of absurdities have a field day wondering how Victor could create a being eight feet tall from the body parts of ordinary men (to say nothing of the fact that Victor might well have started creating life first on a less sophisticated level); how this creature could become fluent in English and French in less than a year (we are told he just happens to find the books—Milton, Plutarch, Goethe); why Victor did not create a female partner sans reproductive apparatus to quiet the monster; how the monster finds Victor's journal or a regular-sized cloak that happens to fit someone of his prodigious size; and all of this is to completely overlook the implausibilities (nay, impossibilities) of some of the time sequences and the wild coincidences of serendipitous meetings.

In this story, coincidence—so much a staple of the gothic anyway—is raised, I think deliberately, beyond the limits of credulity. In fact, it is taken to the level of dream life, where, after all, Mary Shelley says the story was first enacted. However, hidden between the ludicrous coincidences is a subtext of compelling interest that has nothing coincidental about it at all; in fact, it is ruthlessly predetermined. A young man creates a being and then spurns this creation, making it monstrous. Much is made of the fact that this love deprivation has transformed prelapsarian Adam into Satan: "Remember that I am thy creature," says the monster. "I ought to be thy Adam, but I am rather the fallen angel, whom thou drivest from joy for no misdeed" (p. 95).[32] In his role as satanic scourge, the monster throttles Victor's brother William and frames Justine, a family friend; harasses Victor for more than a year; strangles Elizabeth, Victor's new bride, on their wedding night, and leads Victor off on a continental chase that ends in the Arctic wastes, where Victor expires and the monster finally immolates himself.

Now what is so interesting about this story, or more particularly, why should it have held our impassioned interest for so many generations? Why and how did this gothic novel gain the velocity necessary to escape the printed text? To find the answer we need to return to the most exciting part of the story, the creation of the monster, and then watch carefully what this creature really does. For we may find that instead of being Victor's antagonist, he is in fact his best friend, protecting the callow youth from what we have seen in other gothics is the fate of those who desire, or even contemplate, the taking of forbidden partners. What separates *Frankenstein* from its type is that this forbidden action is always implied, never stated.

Here is the entire creation scene as it is condensed into just a few sentences at the beginning of chapter five:

> I had worked hard for nearly two years, for the sole purpose of infusing life into an inanimate body. For this I had deprived myself of rest and health. I had desired it with an ardor that far exceeded moderation; but now that I had finished, the beauty of the dream vanished, and breathless horror and disgust filled my heart. Unable to endure the aspect of the being I had created, I rushed out of the room. (p. 56)

The young scientist, Victor, abandons his creation ostensibly because it is unaesthetic, because it has "watery eyes that seemed almost of the same colour as the dun-white sockets in which they were set, [a] shriveled complexion and straight black lips." Never once does Victor think that what he has done is presumptuous or Faustian, or sacrilegious—only modern critics think that. In fact, Victor really doesn't know why he made this creature in the first place, other than it was the result of "my obsession." Initially, he doesn't even think the creature monstrous and so repeatedly calls him a "daemon," a word which originally meant a neutral spirit, before becoming appropriated by the Christian fathers to mean evil spirit, as in "demon."[33]

Once "born" the creature must be "educated," and his schooling occurs in the rather awkward episodes where the eight-foot daemon is literally slid in behind the De Lacey household to participate passively in a surrogate family. This is more than a convenient narrative device to resolve such problems as language and socialization; this is a way to mature him to Victor's level so that by the time he leaves, or rather is ejected from, the bosom of the family, he is Victor's coeval, ready to fulfill Victor's secret curiosities. The metamorphosis from noble savage to awkward adolescent (separated from the family) takes only a few months in his sped-up life, but he is now fully ready to do what every teenager wants to do—he can at last "get even" with those who have restrained him; he can find out on his own exactly where the boundaries inside the family really are.

But who is "getting even" with whom—is it the daemon with Victor, or Victor (via his creature) with his family? What the monster does is in no way capricious; rather, from Victor's point of view, it is the fulfillment of desire as well as of curiosity. The monster's first victim is Victor's baby brother, William. Admittedly, the monster is in a foul mood when he happens on William (who has been wounded while helping a little girl), but William does not make him feel any better by telling the creature to leave him alone; he is, after all, the son of M. Frankenstein, municipal magistrate. That's enough for the monster; it's all over for William and he is strangled straightaway. In the monster's words: "I grasped his [William's] throat to silence him, and in a moment he lay dead at my feet. I gazed on my victim and my heart swelled with exultation and hellish triumph. . . ." By wild happenstance, around the child's neck is a locket with a picture of Mrs. Frankenstein (Victor and William's mother), and the monster grasps it and gazes in rapt attention:

I took it; it was a portrait of a most lovely woman. In spite of
my malignity, it softened and attracted me. For a few moments
I gazed with delight on her dark eyes, fringed by deep lashes,
and her lovely lips; but presently my rage returned; I remembered that I was forever deprived of the delights that such
beautiful creatures could bestow and that she whose resemblance I contemplated would, in regarding me, have changed
that air of divine benignity to one expressive of disgust and
affright. (p. 136)

The mere sight of Victor's mother is sufficient to melt the
monster's rage. Now, just happening to pass by, is Justine,
Victor's surrogate sister, who has been cared for by the Frankenstein family.[34] She stops for a short early morning nap—it
takes all of a minute—in a nearby shed, and the daemon "places
the portrait securely in one of the folds of her dress." It is a
propitious act, which eventually leads to Justine's being tried
and convicted of William's murder. Strangely enough, however, it will be Victor who admits responsibility. For later he
learns that, sick with a fever (repressed guilt?), he has called
himself "the murderer of William, of Justine" (p. 169). Precisely what he means we do not learn at that point, but we
already have a hint that the monster is dutifully acting out the
curiosities, if not the desires, of his creator.

We are now given a short reprieve during which Victor re-
ceives a most peculiar letter from home. His father writes:

I confess, my son, that I have always looked forward to your
marriage with ["your cousin" in the 1818 text] our dear Elizabeth as the tie of our domestic comfort and the stay of my
declining years. You were attached to each other from your
earliest infancy; you studied together, and appeared, in dispositions and tastes, entirely suited to one another. But so blind
is the experience of man that what I conceived to be the best
assistants to my plan may have entirely destroyed it. You, perhaps, regard her as your sister, without any wish that she might
become your wife. Nay, you may have met with another whom
you may love; and considering yourself as bound in honour to
Elizabeth, this struggle may occasion that poignant misery which
you appear to feel. (p. 144)

To be sure, in the 1831 edition Mary Shelley has struck the word "cousin," but the damage, so to speak, has been done: a truth has leaked through. As we know, cousins were not forbidden to marry, and frequently did. Elizabeth is somehow another member of the family, but what member? To find out we need to recall Victor's previous relations with Elizabeth. Here, for instance, is her induction into the "family circle":

> On the evening previous to her being brought to my home, my mother had said playfully, "I have a pretty present for my Victor—tomorrow he shall have it." And when, on the morrow, she presented Elizabeth to me as her promised gift, I, with childish seriousness, interpreted her words literally and looked upon Elizabeth as mine—mine to protect, love, and cherish. All praises bestowed on her I received as made to a possession of my own. We called each other familiarly by the name of cousin. No word, no expression could body forth the kind of relation in which she stood to me—my more than sister, since till death she was to be mine only. (p. 35)

So it is with good reason that Victor responds to his father's suggestion "with horror and dismay," for Elizabeth seems more than a cousin, more like a sister, and, perhaps, even like a mother.

Victor has a pressing problem before he can consider a wife, however. The daemon has first demanded a mate of his own. Consistent with his earlier problem-solving behavior, Victor first swoons at the news and then embarks on a leisurely trip that takes him across the continent to England and then up to the Orkney Islands. Here in splendid isolation he engages in the "filthy process" of creation (p. 156), this time to make a companion for the monster—the female who will become in a much later cinematic operation (thanks to popular confusion of the proper name) the eponymic "Bride of Frankenstein."

Victor typically has second thoughts and recants on his promise. His love-sick daemon is distraught and first implores, then threatens, but to no avail; Victor will not be swayed. Finally, as the creature turns on his heel to go, he makes one last promise to his creator: "I will go; but remem-

ber, I shall be with you on your wedding night" (p. 161). This
is a powerfully ambiguous threat; surely the monster is promising vengeance, but on whom—Victor or the bride? Victor—
ever the egotist—thinks the intended victim will be himself,
but he acts as if it were to be his wife. We know better; if the
monster wanted Victor's life, he could have it any time he
wished. The monster wants the bride, and Victor subconsciously knows it.

After this threat Victor falls into the requisite "deep sleep,"
and the plot is driven through some rather conventional gothic
territory. The monster kills Victor's best friend, Henry Clerval,
and frames Victor (who is freed, thanks to the good offices of
his father); Victor makes some desultory attempts at suicide;
but most important he is gently nudged by Elizabeth to think
again about the unthinkable. She writes:

> You well know, Victor, that our union had been the favourite
> plan of your parents ever since our infancy. We were told this
> when young, and taught to look forward to it as an event that
> would certainly take place. We were affectionate playfellows
> during childhood, and, I believe, dear and valued friends to
> one another as we grew older. But as brother and sister often
> entertain a lively affection towards each other without desiring
> a more intimate union, may not such also be our case? Tell me,
> dearest Victor. Answer me, I conjure you, by our mutual hap-
> piness, with simple truth—Do you not love another? (p. 178)

Although Victor knows that the monster has always been true
to his Delphic threats, he writes back to Elizabeth of his willingness, but warns her:

> I have one secret, Elizabeth, a dreadful one; when revealed to
> you, it will chill your frame with horror, and then, far from
> being surprised at my misery, you will not only wonder that I
> survive what I have endured. I will confide this tale of misery
> and terror to you the day after our marriage shall take place,
> for, my sweet cousin, there must be perfect confidence be-
> tween us. (p. 180)

Just whom is he trying to protect—himself or her?

The wedding day arrives and with it, of course, Victor's an-hedonic dread. Surely such dread is the dread of incest—the brother/sister references have been an unmistakable motif, even though we have often had to look beneath the pentimento of the 1831 revisions. Simply put, by ravaging the family the monster has cleared the way for Victor to experience a level of sexuality that has been tabooed, while at the same time promising to appear on the wedding night to make sure the "marriage" is not consummated. The frisson is generated not only by the idea of sibling incest but also by hints of the oe-dipal relationship as well. We know this cannot be. We have been assured that Victor's real mother has died from a disease carried into the family by Elizabeth, her "present" for her son, and that her dying wish was that her son marry this very girl. A mother would never allow anything horrible to happen; wasn't even Christabel's mother there to protect her from Ger-aldine?

To find out how Victor really perceives Elizabeth, rather than how his mother wants him to, we need to recall the dream he had during his post-monster-creation swoon. Here is the dream complete with the daemon's cameo appearance:

> I was disturbed by the wildest dreams. I thought I saw Eliza-beth, in the bloom of health, walking in the streets of Ingol-stadt. Delighted and surprised, I embraced her, but as I im-printed the first kiss on her lips, they became livid with the hue of death; her features appeared to change, and I thought that I held the corpse of my dead mother in my arms; a shroud enveloped her form, and I saw the grave-worms crawling in the folds of the flannel. I started from my sleep with horror; a cold dew covered my forehead, my teeth chattered, and every limb became convulsed; when, by the dim and yellow light of the moon, as it forced its way through the window shutters, I beheld the wretch—the miserable monster whom I had cre-ated. He held up the curtain of the bed; and his eyes, if eyes they may be called, were fixed on me. His jaws opened, and he muttered some inarticulate sounds, while a grin wrinkled

his cheeks. He might have spoken, but I did not hear; one hand
was stretched out, seemingly to detain me, but I escaped and
rushed downstairs. (p. 57)

When this element is considered, Victor's familial relationships appear at last to fall into place; for if Elizabeth is the
displaced sister, let alone mother, then Victor will not be able
to consummate the marriage without utter psychological disintegration. No gothic has ever allowed a known situation of
incest to develop to consummation. Only the pornographic
novel can sustain that eventuality and, even there, as we shall
see, it is accomplished in the service of wholesale social subversion. But Victor is still curious and he wants, as does the
dreamer, to get as close as possible to the forbidden event.
Ironically, it is the monster who will protect him, just as he
had earlier befriended him in Victor's dream. All along the
daemon has acted out Victor's wishes. He has destroyed family and friends, all in preparation for this central encounter of
Victor's fantasy. And now, here on Victor's wedding night,
Victor is so close to the sexually forbidden that he is under-
standably hebephrenic. Elizabeth inquires, "What is it that ag-
itates you, my dear Victor?" and her husband can only reply:
". . . this night is dreadful, very dreadful" (p. 185). He now
leaves her, ostensibly to look for the monster; the monster
conveniently takes his cue and dispatches Elizabeth; Victor returns, swoons at the sight of his dear departed, then covers
her face with a handkerchief and for the first time in their
entire relationship he "embraced her with ardour" (p. 186).
Now, however, there is guilt as well as horror to deal with.

The scene trembles with, as Coleridge said of his own incest
dreams, "desire with loathing strangely mix't." Victor knows
what the monster has promised, yet goes ahead with the marriage. Victor knows the monster will be there on his wedding
night, yet he does not stay in the room to protect his bride.
Like the little boy who has been told not to stand too close to
the fire, Victor's first response is to inch closer. Little wonder
he gets burned. He has had more sexual excitement than he

can withstand, and like his cohorts in the genre, he dissembles.

If we had any doubts about the *Doppelgänger* connection between Victor and the monster, the last quarter of the novel resolves them.[35] For from now on Victor pursues the monster to set things right, just as earlier the monster had dogged Victor for what he felt was just. First the shadow chases the man, then the man chases the shadow. Victor's repressed desires have broken the surface and he must now try to bury them again. It is almost as if Victor's ego, having liberated his monstrous id, now feels compelled to return to some psychological stasis. But his superego, so to speak, will have none of it now and so unity is denied. Victor monomaniacally pursues his "devil" (the "daemon" has become "demon") to the ends of the civilized world, "more as a task enjoined by heaven, as a mechanical impulse of some power of which I was unconscious, than as the ardent desire of my soul" (pp. 194–195).

Here, appropriately, Victor's narrative ends, and we are returned to Robert Walton's epistolary frame. Victor is rescued from the ice floe of insanity just long enough to warn Walton, another curious seeker after forbidden partners, to turn back. The relationship between Robert Walton and his sister Mrs. Saville (is there a pun here?) mimics the role of Victor Frankenstein and his "sister" Elizabeth, as many critics have noted. Once again the *Doppelgänger* transformation and implied incestuous relationships indicate not so much the author's weakness in delineating character as it does her almost obsessive compulsion to rework the familial relationships until she "gets it right."[36] Victor expires, but the monster lingers on to let us know that even now he is not satisfied. He tells the ephebic Walton:

You, who call Frankenstein your friend, seem to have a knowledge of my crimes and his misfortunes. But in the detail which he gave you of them he could not sum up the hours and months of misery which I endured wasting in impotent passions. For while I destroyed his hopes, I did not satisfy my own desires.

> They were forever ardent and craving; still I desired love and
> fellowship, and I was still spurned. Was there no injustice in
> this? Am I to be thought the only criminal, when all human-
> kind sinned against me? (p. 210)

But separated from his other half, his shadow, the monster
wanders off, presumably to immolate himself.

When the pieces of this gothic puzzle are put together, they
reveal a buried design in keeping with other less sophisticated
attempts with the same material. This design may explain such
peculiarities as why the monster reacts to the locket picture of
Frankenstein's mother; why Elizabeth is textually displaced from
"mother" to "sister" to "cousin" to "foundling"; why the
monster reappears on the *wedding* night; and why the final
symbiosis of monster and man is so fantastic, even dreamlike.
All this also explains, I think, why the story in all its manifold
print and cinematic versions should appeal to the ignorant,
but curious, adolescent audience. For it is clear that just such
an audience is especially concerned about the choice between
following their curiosities (Victor), which will lead to knowledge and horror, or being restrained (Robert Walton), which
will lead away from certain sexual knowledge but promise social safety. Once Victor's fictive journey is over, once his rite
of initiation is finished, it should be clear to us which path we
ought to follow. Although the text exists in the limbo of adolescence, lingering between the two choices without passing
obvious judgment, we know that if we are going to be "mature" we must learn from Victor to follow Robert.

Had the monster not literally interposed his self between
Victor and Elizabeth and had Victor been able to consummate
marriage, there is no telling how *Frankenstein* would have
ended. There is "no telling" because this is a tale never told—
at least not in "polite" literature. Not once in English or
American prose fiction in the nineteenth century does consummated incest ever extend beyond the act into a continuous
story. The act is simply so powerful that it stops all protagonists, if not literally, then figuratively, in their tracks. Certainly, Melville made a heroic attempt to extend sequences in

Pierre but ended up either with mish-mash (if you don't like Melville) or a misguided parody of romanticism (if you do). The problem essentially is that the shock of consummated incest is so powerful that once the current has passed, only numb anticlimax can result. There is a genre, however, that depends on both climax and anticlimax, and it is there that the incest configuration found continuation not along a storyline, but in mindless repetition.

The gothic and the pornographic are not at all dissimilar. Essentially they both attempt audience excitement, the former by irreconcilable shock, the latter by voyeuristic titillation. They both attempt their frisson by concentrating on what the traditional novel had revealed as the allure of fictional experience—imagined events quickly leading to a pitch of action. Predictably, the short story, which struggles for what Poe called "that certain unique effect," was a most efficient carrier of these two charges. In fact, gothic and pornographic novels are essentially linked short stories held together by a saw-toothed pattern of crescendos, be they of unexpected collisions of antagonists as in the gothic, or of off-limit sexual partners as in the pornographic. Very often, of course, the gothic shock *is* the pornographic seduction—well censored, but clearly in place, and the place, more often than not, is square in the middle of the family.

In order to maximize these bursts, the encounters must be carefully arranged to violate norms and expectations. The gothic draws from a catalog of imagery based mainly on childhood fears—darkness, knives, stairs, shadows, narrow passageways, tombs—while the pornographic has its own devices, which usually detail human anatomy in a state of arousal: swelling breasts, tumescent members, moistness, and the like. Both modes depend on evoking and then ritualizing these images as they pair their protagonists with properly shocking partners. Hence incestuous partners figure prominently. Whereas the gothic usually presents this situation from the girl's point of view, the pornographic most often takes the boy's. Therefore the lowering uncle or father, or the curious brother of the gothic is replaced by the pubescent sister and the cornucopian mother in the pornographic. The genres share something still more profound. In their mandate to subvert social norms as well as to generate a specific physiological effect, they are led to essentially the same story line—family romance run amok.

To be more specific, the center of pressure in both forms is the bourgeois family. From this family come both the newly literate and prosperous readers eager, or at least curious, to see what anarchy can do to the measured forms they have been carefully instructed to cherish. In the only detailed study of the incest theme in nineteenth century English literature, *Forbidden Fruit*, Henry Miles conjectures that incest was the third most prevalent fantasy around which Victorian pornography was spun. Less popular than heterosexual and homosexual encounters, and more popular than flagellation, sadism, sadomasochism, and fetishism, incest holds a place of particular import to Victorians. For, as Miles contends,

> There is little doubt that the fictional treatment of incest in the 19th century served as a form of protest literature, whether conscious or not, opposing the cosy artificial world of the Victorian family presented by the penny novels and general fiction of the circulating libraries. The golden haired child becomes the little monster; the insipid prim, wholly domesticated maternal figure becomes a new Messalina; the stern or indulgent father not only seduces but is seduced by his sexually satanic offspring. The picture is reversed; the glove puppets are turned inside out. (p. 9–10)[37]

Like the gothic before it, the pornographic, especially as activated by the crossing of incest barriers, gathers significance not because the forbidden act is contemplated with enthusiasm, but because the idea of the act, the concept of breaching norms and inverting roles, becomes part of a more comprehensive attempt to rend asunder the conventions not just of family life, but of society itself.

When one looks at English pornographic novels, novels quite unlike a genuine sexual autobiography such as *My Secret Life*, which mentions everything *but* incest, one sees that tradition and family are only convened in order to be subverted. The requisite "Long, long ago in the land beyond the trees . . ." introduction of the gothic is replaced by the "For as long as I can remember I have always adored my sister . . . ." From here the script proceeds with the enthusiasm of a magnet for the iron of seduction until all parties are attracted and exhausted. It's all done in such good fun. Here is a typically jovial episode from *Sheaves from an Old Escritoire* (c. 1887) in which siblings Norah and her brother Willy meet in Tunbridge Wells, of all places.

> "Norah," said he, "there's such a nice chap next door. He is the only son of an old fool who lives by himself. Bob Green is his name. He's down from Oxford on his holidays and we play tennis together. He wants me to introduce him to you. Perhaps he will fall in love with you and what fun it would be if you were to let him have a poke! You can see his bedroom window opposite."
>
> "Well, Willy, I will let you introduce him to me if you will put your monstrous thing into my pussie," Norah replied.
>
> Thereupon Willy pushed her down and lifting her night-dress, at the same time pushing her legs wide open, he inserted his cock which was now firm and still again into her expectant cunt. (p. 10–11)

Even in such a throwaway episode, we can see that the codes of social order are introduced only to be disordered. Oxford, tennis, "nice chap," holidays, even the gratuitous use of "again" in the last line, connote the upper levels of established order, levels aspired to by the rising middle class. As with the descriptive apparatus of "the old dark manse with the dank cellar" which the gothic jerry-rigs in order to portray a family in shambles, the pornographic builds on an equally contrived bungalow and fills it with a cheery group of close kin eager to violate sexual prohibition *not* by force but by fantasy. In fact, in a relatively late entry, *The Power of Mesmerism* (1880), which has the telling imprint "Printed for the Nihilists, Moscow," hypnotism is invoked as the means by which young Frank is able to cajole first his sister, then mother, uncles, aunts, cous-

ins, into enthusiastic, albeit robotic, orgies. This is all done
with a fire on the hearth, chintz on the sofa, and sod quietly
growing on the roof.

The Victorian pornography of incest is so uniformly jovial,
so much of the waxed smile and perpetual leer, that it is almost impossible to separate participants, let alone incidents.
It is also, as Miles repeatedly points out, so mechanical that
one soon realizes that the incest is essentially beside the point;
it is included primarily as the necessary limit to be surpassed.
"I bet you think I can't seduce my mother/sister/niece," the
interior speaker, usually a testosterone-driven young male,
seems to be wagering with the reader, and the reader, of course,
is always going to underestimate. Incest is the means to the
end, not the end in itself. It is the social limit to be sabotaged,
the bridge to be burned, so that there can be no turning back
to normalcy.

Here in one of the watershed works, *Philosophy in the Bedroom* (1795), the Marquis de Sade sets the direction for the
flood to come. An old roué, Dolmance explains life's nui-
sances to the ingenue, Eugenie:

> Can one so regard Nature's gentlest unions, the very ones
> she consistently prescribes to us and advises most warmly? Just
> think, Eugenie, how, after the vast afflictions our planet at some
> time knew, did the human race perpetuate itself, if not through
> incest? Do we not find the examples and the very proofs in the
> books which Christianity respects most highly? How else could
> the families of Adam and Noah have been preserved? Look
> closely at universal customs: everywhere you will find incest
> authorized, even considered a wise law, proper to cement fam-
> ily ties. If, in a word, love is born of resemblance, where can it
> be more perfectly found than between brother and sister, fa-
> ther and daughter? Incest is banned from our midst by an ill-
> founded policy based on the fear that families might become
> too powerful. Let us not so deceive ourselves as to mistake for
> natural law that which is dictated only by selfish interest or
> ambition; let us delve into our hearts—it is always there that I
> bid pedantic moralists go. Let us but question this sacred organ
> and we shall discover that there is nothing more exquisite than
> carnal connection within the family. It will not do for us to be

blind to a brother's feeling for his sister, or a father's love for his daughter: in vain shall they disguise their feelings behind a mask of legitimate tenderness—the unique sentiment in them is the most violent of loves, the only one that Nature has planted in their hearts. Let us therefore double, nay, triple these delectable incests and fearlessly multiply them: let us give ourselves and the object of our desires, the greater pleasure there shall be in enjoying it. (pp. 28–29)

This is the vintage hyperbole of pornography, the ultimate transvaluation of family sex—the very health of the family *demands* incest. One hears the same Sadean argument not just throughout nineteenth-century pornography, but in twentieth-century sexology as well. This is, after all, the argument of the "pro-incest" lobby carried to the nth degree. The nuclear family needs the cement of sexual contact.[38] Iconoclasm in the service of liberation is a narcotic to contemporary Western imagination.

Here is the same appeal to a perverted family authority in *Forbidden Fruit* (c. 1905), in which the mother herself delivers the message to her son, young Master Percy, this time shifting the blame to the institution of the church:

". . . but Percy never a word to anyone if you love me; this is so naughty, so wicked to do."

"Naughty? Wicked? How can it be so to play with my Mama?"

"Fathers or mothers must not have their children like this, nor even brothers their sisters; it is thought awful, called 'incest,' in fact. The clergyman would say we were cursed—but that is all nonsense. We know better; it's their business to call everybody sinners." (p. 87)

This stance is assumed again in *Letters from Three Maids*, as young Master Randolph turns the tables on his mother. In a letter, he writes,

My Good Mother,
It seemed to me that you were in a melancholy mood, speaking of yourself as a poor mother, and such things. I cannot fancy whence these thoughts come, for it seems to me that my

sister and I benefited from the closeness we shared with you.
We are both healthy and not likely to fall prey to unscrupulous
people as are other children who are sometimes too sheltered
from what are natural urges and instincts. I cannot see why it
is that a young man should forego every form of fucking until
he has come upon manhood, at which [time] he is to marry
and to know the whole works at once without ever having done
it. It is nonsense it seems to me. Parents instruct their children
in good manners, in conversation and dancing, girls learn to
cook and sew from their mothers, and boys are brought into
the business by their fathers, but fucking is neglected, as though
it mattered not, when in truth I suspect it gives more good or
bad to a marriage than any other art or practice. And we cannot credit you with that sort of negligence for which I am grateful and would be even if I did not admire you as a mistress.

It intrigues me that you should think of pairing my sister and
I. I have known all along of your dallying with her, but I think
you have not told her about us, am I right? We shall have to
talk about this further when you are returned, but I can say it
is pleasant to think about, for she is a pretty girl, inheriting
many good qualities from you and some others from her father, who is a handsome man too. I can confess that I have
taken note of her little figure and greatly admire the lines of it.
. . . (p. 131)

Once the excitement of removing the wedge of role prohibitions has been accomplished, the sex machines labor onward to inevitable exhaustion. In *The Romance of Lust* (1873–
1876) we have four volumes, some 611 pages worth, of almost
obsessive dedication to all the forms of incest *except* that of
actual mother-son. In other words, the freedom-loving narrator will tell of other oedipal escapades, but strangely enough
has experienced none of this kind himself. Typical of the for-
mulaic scenes, composed in what seem to be almost kennings,
is the following:

I was conducted to my room and left alone to recruit my forces
with a good night's rest. I may here incidentally mention that
it was a rule of Uncle and Aunt, very rarely departed from, to
send their favourites to their lonely couches as a means of re-

storing their powers, and reinvigorating them for daylight encounters—both the dear creatures loving to have the fullest
daylight on all the charms of their participants in pleasure, at
the same time yielding an equally undisguised inspection of
their own. . . .

I slept on this occasion with a deep and continuous slumber
until I was awakened by my uncle who came to summon me
to the arms of his wife who, in the splendour of her full-blown
charms awaited me in her own bed, naked as the day she was
born. Her arms outstretched, she invited me to the full enjoy-
ment of her glorious person. My uncle drew my night shirt
over my head, and in a moment I was locked in the embrace
of that superb creature. We were both too hot to wait further
preliminaries, but were at it in furious haste, and rapidly paid
our first tributes to the god of love. My uncle had acted as
postillion to both of us . . . this double operation made the
dear lascivious creature spend again in a very few movements,
and giving her hardly time to discharge, I fucked on with double force, and with a prick as hard as wood, as fast as I could
work. This furious onset, which was the most exciting thing
she knew of, rapidly caused a third discharge. To prevent my
own prick from spending too quickly, I held somewhat back;
then again we went at it fast and furious, and the dear lustful
creature, with cries of joy, spent again with me, and fainted
from excess of pleasure. . . . (pp. 64–65)

Charles steam-engines his way through the entire family,
missing only his mother and ending finally by marrying his
daughter:

Now in my old age, she is the comfort of my life and the
mother of my beautiful son whom we have named Charlie
Nixon, in memory both of my adored first wife and my guardian, through whom he will inherit great wealth. The dear little
fellow is now eighteen years of age, handsome, well grown,
and very well furnished, although not so monstrous in that
way as his father. His dear mother has initiated him in every
delight, and he has all the fire of lust that his old father had
before him . . . . We are thus a happy family, bound by the
strong ties of double incestuous lust. (p. 70)

The *Romance of Lust* is to pornography what *The Monk* is to the gothic; it is a rip-roaring buzz-saw cutting through convention with a mindless enthusiasm. It was so extraordinarily furious that it was paid the ultimate compliment a parody can achieve: a parody of it was written. In *Letters from Three Maids* (c. 1890) young Charles is replaced by young Randolph, but the rest of the cast of regulars remains the same: sisters, mother, aunts, uncles, nieces—all ride a merry-go-round of interchangeable partners. Whether Randolph is writing Mommy, Aunt Gwendolyn, or Sister Louisa, *et al.*, the text and tone are the same. Here is a sample.

> *My Dearest Sister Louisa*, How delighted I was to receive your letter, since it told me not only that you and Mother had reached Paris safely on your holiday, but moreover, offered those sweet words to my ears; for I confess, it was a joy to me to know how unhappy you are on this accursed journey which has separated us, if only for a few weeks. But it is such a crucial time, having so recently discovered the true depth of love which we feel for each other, which goes far beyond that pale affection common to brothers and sisters and which I late thought was all that existed between us. Oh, how I remember that night— was it only this summer—when I came unannounced into your chamber and found you not, as I had expected, fully garbed, but rather standing in that magnificent unclothedness with which I have since been haunted. My beloved, you know that I have been wicked in the past, for I confess to you all my goings, as you confess all to me. But I say in all honesty, I feel that all those other maids were but a prelude to you, a preparation that would thus enable me to fully appreciate all that you had to offer, and that would entrain me to better provide you with the pleasure you so richly deserve.
>
> My beloved, I can understand that you have been and will continue to be quite deluged with temptations, for while you are away from me who could satisfy those lusty urges which seem common to our blood; and you are with our mother who, we both know, is a woman of nearly unchecked licentiousness, despite the air which she affects, for we know that she lives but for fucking, and will fuck with anyone, given a minute to hide herself away, or even assurance that no one will look, and

I do not think we could enumerate the men that she has had right here in her husband's (and our father's) home. So you will no doubt have to contend with that as well, and it is hard to sleep with sounds of fucking from the next chamber disturbing one, and when one is without any similar recourse; and too, you are in a land where men have no courtesy toward a lady of refinement, but think only of bedding her, so that a creature of your loveliness will be set upon at every minute. . . . —Your impatient brother, *Randolph*. (pp.123–124)

The similarity of all the scenes betrays that it is not incest that is desired, it is taboos, any taboos, that can be broken and forbidden excitement extracted.

Whether it be father-daughter incest, as in *Sweet Seventeen* (1910), or uncle-niece, as in *The Autobiography of a Flea* (c. 1887), or siblings, as in *Her Brothers Two* (1970), the act of incest in pornography is as far removed from the real event as the gothic is from actual danger. That incest is one of the chosen paths to titillation testifies primarily not to its sexual, but social, force and power. The prohibition is overthrown not by pent-up desire, but by manipulation. The shriek of the gothic is every bit as contrived as the sigh of the pornographic. To get that exclamation at its most frenetic, the schlockmeisters in both traditions depended, as they still do, on the violation of the incest restraint.[39]

CHAPTER 5

"THE DISEASE OF THE LAST OF THE USHERS": INCEST IN NINETEENTH-CENTURY AMERICAN CULTURE

Thus the basic question becomes: *Why, by and large, don't human beings like it* [incest] *much*? Why, in the vast majority of societies, do they take *some* trouble, however vague, to discourage incestuous unions, even though most human beings are probably not going to indulge in such unions? . . . *Unease* and *avoidance* seem to be the common denominators—not fierce desire held in check by even fiercer sanctions or lust reined in by the power of taboo. The universal root phenomenon appears to be the *ease with which it rouses our unease.* —Robin Fox, *The Red Lamp of Incest*

IF THE UNEASE we feel in contemplating incest is partially cultural, and if culture carries these feelings from generation to generation through the creation of a shared grammar, will different verbal texts from different cultures betray different methods of avoidance? If the taboo is ideological, will different political and economic systems generate different expressions? Will there even be observable variances within similar cultures as to how unease is communicated? Will stories of family romance be different, characteristic of their culture? More specifically, if we look at early modern

American culture, will it differ from the English culture of the same period in how incest behavior is coded?

Toward the end of Chateaubriand's *René*, the eponymic protagonist sets out to the new world full of melancholy hope that he may find temporary palliative for his suicidal depression. He has fallen in love with his sister, Amelia, who has been locked away forever in a convent. René heads westward to the land of starting over, the land of dreams, the land where everything can be forgiven, and almost everything forgotten, the land where there is no personal, national, or racial past. He heads off into the American wilderness. And what does he find? He finds Chactas, an Indian chief, as natural a man as Rousseau could ever have imagined, living as pastoral a life as any poet could have desired, and Father Souel, a missionary who has come to the Mississippi lands to teach the Indians how to live the European way. René tells the old chief and the wise Father his story of woe. Instead of comforting the lad, these wise men scold him, tell him he has been a fool, and assure him he will find no comfort here. Father Souel makes it clear to his young countryman that this land of manifold opportunities is not the land of infinite alternatives. He tells René to pack his things and go home:

> Nothing in your story deserves the pity you are now being shown. I see a young man infatuated with illusions, satisfied with nothing, withdrawn from the burdens of society, and wrapped up in idle dreams. . . . Your sister has atoned for her sin, but if I must speak frankly, I fear that through some terrible justice, that confession, emerging from the depths of the tomb, has in turn stirred up your own soul. What do you do all alone in the woods using up your days and neglecting all your duties? You will tell me that saints have retired to the wilderness. Yes, but they were there weeping and subduing their passions, while you seem to be wasting your time inflaming your own. . . . Whoever has been endowed with talent must devote it to serving his fellow men, for if he does not make use of it, he is first punished by an inner misery, and sooner or later Heaven visits on him a fearful retribution.

The wise chief tells the young European the mixed message of the new world: its tolerance is matched only by its abomination of aberration.

> My son, he [Father Souel] speaks severely to both of us; he is reprimanding the old man and the young, and he is right. Yes, you must give up this strange life, which holds nothing but care. Happiness can be found only in the common paths. (pp. 112–113)

René returns home to France and to his wife and unhappiness. Thus, the literary work that introduced incest as a subject of romantic inquiry into Europe ends with the final American response, "You can't do that on our shores."

It may be ironic, but not unpredictable, that American culture, which for the better part of two hundred years has prided itself, even boasted, of its independence from oppressive ancestral traditions, has been in many instances the most supportive of the traditional forms it spurned. Nowhere is this better seen than in family matters. American concepts of domestic relations are often contradictory and short-lived. On the one hand we have stressed the importance of individual choice, of "breaking away," of each generation bettering the previous, of melting-pot diversity. On the other hand we have enforced role behavior, prolonged adolescence, partially abetted the generation gap, fueled xenophobia, and tolerated, at times encouraged, racial and religious barriers we professed to have abolished. The paradox of the last few decades in which beatniks, hippies, and now punks live side by side with "togetherness," the Jesus movement, and jingoism, characterized nineteenth-century culture as well. All Western heterogeneous societies have such diversities and contradictions. The degrees, however, are different.

American domestic boundaries may have occasioned such concern both to maintain and to violate because, with no past and with the clear and present danger of the wilderness before us, we were tempted to exaggerate what we had and did not have. At first this struggle took the form of the bizarre confrontation between Roger Williams and John Cotton over, among other things, family patterns and rights. It would later unfold in the movement west, in race relations, and now in our sense of the nuclear family. As long as there was plenty of room to go around, if you disapproved of your neighbor's conduct, or your own family's, you could move on. By the nineteenth century, however, new land east of the Appalachians had run out. The Renés were sent home, or far across the Mississippi.

For the most part, the struggle over social boundaries had less to do with inherited patterns or with ecclesiastical polity than with economic necessity. The financial panic of 1837 and the transformation from an agrarian to an industrial state had dislocated families, forcing them west or back into population centers. The political upheaval of Jacksonian democracy was extending the concept of nation over state over family and was having profound implications, as we see in the reactionary prose of Thoreau, Emerson, and even Cooper. The industrial revolution was having its impact on what held families together. Separation anxiety, parental love, habit, tradition, and mutual fears were now joined by the possibility of economic gain. American families were different. Those who were not born to wealth could *become* rich.

In a sense, the promise of organizing the family anew in order to achieve wealth continued the debate between Salem and Provincetown, except that economics replaced religion and the geography of conflict had moved. By the 1830s the literal confrontation was between the axis of Boston and southern New England on the one hand, and, on the other, familylike communities scattered on the near frontier of Pennsylvania and Ohio to the west, and upper New York and southern Vermont to the north. Not by happenstance did Coleridge and Robert Southey intend to head to the banks of the Susquehanna River in Pennsylvania to start their Pantisocracy based on the communal ownership of everything including each other, for they knew of the experiments in family living that were occurring on the near frontier. As the California coast has become to us today, so the rolling hills of the upper New England states and the eastern Midwest were to the early nineteenth century—a place sufficiently far away to be safe, yet close enough to be noticed.[1] With the exception of the Mormons, experimental American communities rarely headed out into the real wilderness. What they did was best done *almost* in private. They did, after all, have a point to make, and that point almost always had to do with showing both their financial success and the corruption of their neighbors.[2]

A two-day trek north of Boston in the early nineteenth century would have taken you close to one of the most interesting attempts to deal with the domestic and economic problems of the disease of modern life—an attempt to literally establish the fictional family designs of English romanticism. Of all the utopian communities that sprang up along the periphery, such as the Shakers, Amish, and Hutterites, none was more important in reconfiguring the modern family than the Putney, Vermont, commune of John Humphrey Noyes. Noyes had seen the problem of the fracturing family and he proposed the obvious return to pure forms. If God was the father of man, and if we were all his precious children, then our relationships should be those of siblings—all our relationships. Noyes was one of the few to confront the specific sexual ramifications of the argument, which has the elegance of the Elizabethan world picture, that our little human world reflects His larger and perfect one.

The Perfectionists, as Noyes humbly called his group, were not the first to learn that propagation à la the angels was difficult. His immediate predecessors in resolving this prickly matter, the Shakers, had already learned what reproductive problems were engendered by *literally* being in the family of God. Celibacy was their answer, not so much as the result of logic as of the sexual phobias and inhibitions of their founder, Ann Lee. Still, it was clear that for any "little family" to evolve it somehow would have to gain members. The conjugal bed might be "made of embers," as Mrs. Lee reported of her own, but in the frontier commune the alternative to embers was to be frozen forever in one nonreproducing family.

So, literally like the angels, the Shakers added to their family horizontally. They adopted family members, be they orphans or converts. As many modern communes have discovered, the family hierarchy is too strong to subvert, so it must be built upon. Mother was Mrs. Lee, still called "Mother Ann," and "Father" was her own brother William—a substitution that was in no literal way sexual, but nevertheless must have posed a psychological problem. For all the members were their "children." Mixed into this was the mythic older brother, temporarily missing in the flesh but alive in the spirit, Jesus Christ, whose relationship to Mother Ann must have given the family, as both followers and children, another moment of confusion.

It was just this kind of confusion that John Humphrey Noyes wanted to resolve. From the romantics he found inspiration, from Christianity he drew the outlines, and from the Shakers he observed an invaluable example. Noyes adopted many of their organizational practices. After all, he was going to apply the most modern methods of efficiency to communal life and would not make the Shaker mistake of planned anachronism. When it came to the problem of siblings breeding, he resolved the dilemma by fiat.[3] He proposed "universal marriage"—all men henceforth would be married to all women, and, it should be stressed, all women married to all men, at least initially. Charmingly, he called the process "omnigamy." Noyes explains:

> In a holy community there is no more reason why sexual intercourse should be restrained by love, than why eating and drinking should be, and there is as little occasion for shame in the one case as in the other. . . . The guests of the marriage supper may have each his favourite dish, each a dish of his own procuring, and that without the jealousy of exclusiveness. I call a certain woman my wife; she is yours; she is Christ's; and in Him she is the bride of all saints. She is dear in the hands of a stranger, and according to my promise to her I rejoice.[4]

Having Christ as the buffering agent intellectually detoxified any threat of forbidden encounters, but Noyes was sensitive enough to realize that intellectual explanations only satisfy intellectuals. What happens when thinking turns to doing? His method of deflecting the psychological inhibitions as well as the physical threat of inbreeding was accomplished by his self-touted system of "male continence." Males would be allowed to treat all women like sisters, and all sisters like women, only after they had proved themselves able to treat no woman as a wife. In other words, he proposed sex without orgasm. Although Noyes claimed his success was achieved by the conscious constriction of the seminal ducts, it seems more likely that coitus interruptus was simply given new emphasis.

Whether or not sibling incest occurred within the intrepid band that Noyes collected in the southern Vermont woods is now beside the point. At the time, however, this was the only point. One of the reasons the people around Putney were so eager to rid themselves of the Perfectionists was that they could not countenance such sexual deviance so close by. In the first small commune of some twenty people were Noyes's own brother and two sisters, and two brothers-in-law. The probabilities of inbreeding were too great to be overlooked. Noyes's explanation of "complex marriage," of "omnigamy," and of "male continence" may have satisfied commune members. They may have believed him when he said: "The only plausible objection to amative intercourse between near relations, founded on the supposed law of nature that 'breeding in and in' deteriorates offspring [thus had been] removed."[5] But the neighbors needed convincing. The Noyes Bible Group was driven out—the proffered charge was adultery; the implied charge was incest.

The Perfectionists went deeper into the hinterlands, into upstate New York, where in relative peace they turned their prodigious energies away from explaining to others and to themselves, and started to behave like Americans. They first manufactured animal traps and then formed a joint stock company to produce flat silverware. How ironic that today we should remember them only by the trade name of the flatware (Oneida) we usually give to celebrate the one institution Noyes abhorred above all—marriage.

Whatever their differences, the romantic movement and

fundamental Christianity were similar in almost demanding adult mimicry of childlike relationships. Both stressed the model of idealized childhood as the centerpiece of faith. The success, limited as it now seems, both of the Shakers and the Perfectionists testifies to the profound desire of people under stress to return to simpler states of familial interaction. Here in nineteenth-century America the spirit of Shelleyan romanticism was made flesh. Not only was the language of recognition full of "brothers" and "sisters," but the dress (bloomers, frocks, pantalets) as well as the diurnal habits of sleeping and eating separately, imitated the idealized family of childhood memories. To a psychohistorian these may seem regressionary methods of coping, but to an economist they can be remarkably efficient. If only sex had not become mixed up in family relationships Noyes's vision might have proved prophetic. Even now his words retain their peculiar logic:

> Love between the children of God, is exalted and developed by a motive similar to that which produces ordinary *family affection* . . . the exciting cause is not sexuality . . . but the fact that the parties have one Father. . . . The sons and daughters of God, must have even a stronger sense of blood-relationship than ordinary brothers and sisters, because the Spirit of the Father . . . is always renewing their consciousness of unity with him and with each other. Marriage, in the world, requires a man to "leave father and mother and cleave unto his wife." But the sons and daughters of God can never leave *their* Father and Mother. Of course, the paramount sexual affection, required by the law of marriage, can have no place among them. They live as children with their Father forever, and the paramount affection of the household is . . . *brotherly* love, an affection that grows directly out of the common relationship to the Father, and of course is as universal as that relationship. . . . This affection as it exists between the different sexes is necessarily unlimited as to number. A brother may love ten sisters, or a sister ten brothers, according to the customs of the world. The exclusiveness of marriage does not enter the family circle. But heaven is a family circle; and . . . brotherly love . . . takes the place of supremacy which their matrimonial affection occupies in this world.[6]

But sex did become involved; incest was a threat, and, when confronted, Noyes had to admit its clear and present danger. Pressed, as he was in his *Essay on Scientific Propagation*, he attempted to transform this supposed weakness into a strength. Noyes argued, almost forgetting his vaunted prophylactic method of "male continence," that although

> it must be conceded that, in the present state of human passions and institutions, there are many and great difficulties in the way of our going back to the natural simplicity of the Hebrew fathers or forward to the scientific simplicity of the cattle-breeders, yet it is important to know and remember that these difficulties are not physiological, but sentimental . . . in the pure races, such as the European aristocracies and the Jews . . . vital power and beauty have been the result of close inter-breeding.[7]

Argue as he might, the threat still remained. And that threat, together with encroaching "civilization," forced these utopians (numbering now about two hundred) to once again disband. If Noyes had followed his fellow Vermonter Joseph Smith out into the real wilderness of Utah, he might have been able to stabilize his community and perhaps to survive. However, the Latter Day Saints never restructured the family in such a way as to make sibling intercourse a possibility. Polygamy is tame compared to the "complex families" envisioned by Percy Bysshe Shelley and John Humphrey Noyes.

If Noyes had had to depend on the American intellectual community for support of his "errand into the wilderness," he would have been in still more desperate straits—quite possibly he never would have made it out of Vermont. Had his "city upon the hill," his American Eden, been outside Boston, he most probably would have been arrested. Note that Brook Farm was almost closed down by its neighbors, even though the Institute for Agriculture and Education had presented no sexual ambiguities; in fact, there was little sexual activity at all. Although the more intense battle of individual versus state freedoms was to be fought throughout the century, the battle over family organization was short-lived. The patriarchs clearly won.

As with their English counterparts, the radical spokesmen of American romanticism—Thoreau, Whitman, and Emerson—were men who had little or no family of their own. It is of more than passing interest that the American intellectuals who advocated the most sweeping rearrangement of the family were a self-advertised recluse, a homosexual, and a man who was an extremely passive parent and distant husband. In revolutionizing family matters often those with the least family were the most confident in deciding how others should live. They spoke with the confidence of inexperience.[8]

The American artists who did indeed concentrate on family interactions were not philosophers, not the transcendental stockholders of the "Brook Farm Institute for Agriculture and Culture," but were rather the emotional and intellectual descendants of John Cotton—modern Puritans. For them the family was the anchor of self and thus the center of their fiction. The introspective impulse was vitalized in the fiction of the first American novelist, William Hill Brown; it continued through the first important early gothicist, Charles Brockden Brown, and then unfolded in the central works of nineteenth-century American literature—works by Poe, Hawthorne, and Melville. These Americans were all family men and they all took the family as a central subject of their fiction. In their make-believe families it is clear that they would tolerate little aberrant behavior. If experimentation did occur, it would be quickly supressed. Fundamental codes would be enforced at the expense of individual freedom. In an economic sense, good business practices would prevail. The "new man," the corporate man, backed by a stable family, would make sure that the John Humphrey Noyeses of the world would stay not just on the frontier, but far off in the deepest woods.

To see how this strain of American Puritanism energized, subverted, and finally repressed family romance, I will return to the central prohibition of family life, incest, and trace how it functions from the first native novel, William Hill Brown's *The Power of Sympathy*, through the *Schauerromans*, to temporarily play itself out in the works of Hawthorne, Poe, and Melville. Although I will only briefly discuss the incest theme in modern American literature, I do not argue that this is *the* dominant theme of American letters, but it certainly is one of the most dynamic and, until recently, one of the most neglected. To a considerable extent the frisson of incest inspired many of the greatest works of American romanticism as well as some of the most awkward.

The transformation of the European romance tradition first into the gothic, and then into the hybrid of the American gothic, was of degree rather than kind. The story remained the same—young people under sexual stress. Viewpoints, participants, and conclusions were just shifted by crucial degrees. Although many critics have argued that "the American experience" led to a unique view of family life more informed by capitalism, or the frontier, or puritanism, or narcissism, than by biology, such singularity is not borne out.[9] These are mitigating factors, to be sure, but the peculiar shade cast on the family romance by the "dark" introspective American romantics from Brown to O'Neill was not as much the result of their personal perceptions as it was the gradual evolution in Western culture toward greater concentration on intrafamilial dynamics. One need only read the works of Schiller, De Sade, Müllner, Tieck, Alfieri, and later Wagner, to realize that the situation on the Continent was in many respects like that in America. The industrial revolution that allowed a quick economic escape from family often produced just the opposite result. Families needed to stay close together to consolidate their gains, but not too close. Literature, both serious and popular, reflected this need. The sentimental tradition gave way to the budding gothic, which in turn carried the macabre. The family matrix, cemented for generations by the inability of members to get loose, now risked collapsing in upon itself.

Montague Summers, one of the first catalogers of the gothic, once slyly commented that to make a sentimental tale gothic, all an author need do was substitute a castle for a house, a snarling baron for a father, a knight for a boyfriend, a ghost for an attorney, a witch for a housekeeper, and a midnight murder for marriage. A slight exaggeration here, a minor change there, and tears could be changed into shivers. The only constant was the role of the central protagonist—the young female. The heroine remains forever the center of concentration, for it is always the violation of her privacy that charges our response.[10] In the transformation of the sentimental into the "low" gothic, the violator need only be changed from boyfriend to baron to brother. However, for the macabre, the "high" gothic, the shift must be made from brother to father.

What the Americans did to this story line was to compress the nuclear family and excise all the satellite characters. The witch/housekeeper, ghost/attorney, and all the supernumeraries are removed to lesser, or nonexistent roles. The "home" or castle is isolated by surrounding wilderness, and the internal pressure is increased until matters, and occasionally even characters, spontaneously combust. Call it Mettingen, Saddle Meadows, Usher, Yoknapatawpha, the centrifugal forces placed on a usually motherless family as the male sexual violation of daughter/sister is no longer threatened, but often realized, caused a catastrophe so complete that finally nothing of the family remains. Let the English mythologize incest as did Byron, or metaphysicalize it as did Shelley, the nineteenth-century American experience is uniformly horrible, irrepressibly gothic, maybe even characteristically pragmatic.

But not always. Because the exception, while not always proving the rule, at least shows where the rule is supposed to apply, I should like to examine first an overlooked work by a central nineteenth-century American artist—a short story by Edgar Allan Poe, *The Spectacles*. Although ostensibly *The Spectacles* satirizes the sentimental tradition of "love at first sight," it shows as well those aspects of human behavior usually only exposed under the dark cloud of the gothic. The plot of *The Spectacles* was not original with Poe; it had a history as an American tall tale. Clearly, Poe was drawn to expanding its salty humor as a potboiler for the Philadelphia *Dollar Newspaper*. Just as clearly, judging from his lengthy revisions, once he became involved, he could not let it go until he had touched a nerve, a rather particular nerve.

The Spectacles is told to us by a foppish man-about-town who
is attempting to enter fashionable society. First, he has changed
his name in order to inherit a small fortune from a distant
relative. Once "Napoleon Buonaparte Froissart," a respectable
enough French name even in the Colonies, he has become
simply Mr. "Simpson."[11] Still, the exchange was certainly worth
it, for what he might have sacrificed in presumptuous name,
he more than made up for not just in his current bank account, but in future economic expectations as well. After all,
in this country money makes money.

All Mr. Simpson now lacks is the proper lady friend to help
him consolidate the gain via matrimony and, at the opera, he
thinks he has found one. He spies the aristocratic Eugenie Lalande sitting off at a distance; it is love at first sight. She is the
very essence of polite society, complete with sequined gown,
a young female companion and opera glasses. Both Simpson
and Mme. Lalande are terribly nearsighted. Mme. Lalande
solves her problem by bringing her opera glasses; he is too
proud to do so. As their myopic eyes meet, he is enraptured:
"This was my *first* love—so I felt it to be. It was love su-
preme—indescribable. It was 'love at first sight'; and at first
sight too, it had been appreciated and *returned*" (p. 895). What
is returned, of course, is only her dim vision of him, but like
a Platonic lover gone berserk, that is all the encouragement he
needs. Simpson has become "possessed" and is as monoman-
iacal in his devotion to her vision as his brother narrators in
Morella, *Bernice*, and *Ligeia* would be toward their inamoratas.

Unlike his other fictional incarnations, however, Simpson
keeps his distance, first from diffidence and then from bash-
fulness. Finally when Eugenie takes a trip out of town he is
convinced he must act. After loving her from afar, he approaches and gushes a proposal of marriage. She is literally
aghast, asks him to please reconsider, to step back and have
another look, but he will have none of it. He will not be restrained:

"My sweetest Eugenie," I cried, "what is all this about which
you are discoursing? Your years surpass in some measure my

own. But what then? The customs of the world are so many
conventional follies. To those who love as ourselves, in what
respect differs a year from an hour? I am twenty-two, you say;
granted: indeed you may as well call me, at once twenty-three.
Now you yourself, my dearest Eugenie, can have numbered no
more than—can have numbered no more than—no more than—
than—than—than—." (p. 903)

Simpson obviously hopes she will interrupt to tell him her
age, but she doesn't. Instead, she only asks if he will please
use her opera glasses, her "little ocular assistant," to be sure
his vision is clear. But no, his vision is clear enough. Again,
she entreats; he refuses. Rather like the narrator of *The Cask of
Amontillado* leading dumb Fortunato down the stairs asking
him at every landing if he wishes to continue, Mme. Lalande
repeats her offer. In desperation she forces him to take the
glasses. He puts them aside until too late.

Almost too late; after all, this is not a horror story but a tall
tale. Simpson waits until his wedding day to use the glasses
and only then when almost at the altar does he realize his
fiancée is an elderly matron. The sight is, in his own words,
"*horrific*": " 'You wretch!' said I catching my breath—'you—
you—you villainous old hag!' " To which she exclaims that
she may be old (in fact, 82 years old), but "hag" she is not.
She is the grand dame of a prestigious family, the Froissarts.
Dumbfounded, Simpson, aka Froissart, screams hysterically,
as he now realizes that he has married his great-great-grand-
mother!

The marriage is mysteriously annulled. The materfamilias is
understanding if not forgiving, and offers him instead the hand
of her lovely young consort: "a distant and exceedingly lovely
relative of her second husband's—a Madame Stephanie Lalande" (p. 914). This is the marriage to be consummated with
the complete blessing of the family. Any possible horror has
been dissipated and the sentimental resolution has carried the
day. Or has it? Look again, for as Daniel Hoffman noted Fois-
sart

doesn't have to marry his great, great, grandmother. He married his cousin. Even if we smile at Poe's impostor, aren't we struck by the consanguinity which afflicts his suitor? How curious that his faulty vision leads so precipitously toward incest! And the happy resolution only mitigates somewhat the closeness of the attachment of his heart for a member of his mother's blood.[12]

Even keeping in mind that Stephanie is not really consanguineous because she is from the great, great, grandmother's *husband's* family, the point is still well taken. For all the posturing and punning, for all the folderol and foppery, the focus of the story returns us again to the magnetic attraction, the blind attraction, of a young man and his love of/at first sight, his mother, or, in this case, his barely displaced mother. Yes, he will "marry" Stephanie, but his heart is elsewhere. Admittedly, he finally ends with his cousin, his "mother's" consort, in a sense, his sister. Little wonder that Poe should have revised and diluted the relationships, but for all the sublimation and effacement, certain family relationships cannot be erased. After all, it is just these currents that provide the frisson, that excite our interest. *The Spectacles* concludes when our Hero accepts both his proper Leander, as well as his proper economic and social place in the family—the Froissart family:

Nevertheless I am *not* the husband of my great, great, grandmother; and this is a reflection which affords me infinite relief;—but I *am* the husband of Madame Lalande—of Madame Stephanie Lalande—with whom my good old relative, besides making me her sole heir when she dies—if she ever does—has been at the trouble of concocting me a match. In conclusion: I am done forever with *billets doux*, and am never to be met without SPECTACLES. (p. 916)

When Poe wrote this *jeu d'esprit* in the 1840s, he was well aware of the melodrama that lurked within his subject especially when the tale was played out in the New World. The mistake of a newly minted American of distinct European background, who allows his ardor to settle on a member of his own family, would be told again and again. It would be told more than a century later in a work Poe himself would surely have been proud of—Vladimir Nabokov's *Lolita*. Although we usually think that this theme was only exploited after Poe, actually, other American writers had already pulled back the curtains of family life. What they saw was always shocking. In fact, in the first extended American novel, William Hill Brown's *The Power of Sympathy; or the Triumph of Nature*, published in 1789 just at the appearance of English gothicism, there is a sibling relationship that ushers in what, with Poe, will become the most famous family implosion.

At the commencement of American prose fiction, William Hill Brown inadvertently shows how much of the nascent American gothic was informed by Richardsonian romance. The central subplot of *The Power of Sympathy* traces the ill-fated love of a Lovelacean Harrington and his almost-Clarissa, Harriot. Harrington is a rogue whose plan is "to take this beautiful sprig [Harriot], and transplant it to a more favorable soil, where it shall flourish and blossom under my own auspices. In a word, I mean to remove this fine girl into an elegant apartment, of which she herself is to be the sole mistress"(1, letter #3, p. 17).[13] However well laid his plans of sexual exploitation may have been, her beauty soon transforms his sexual lust into domestic desire. He proposes marriage—the conqueror has been conquered, the victimizer has become victim. Although she is an orphan and destitute, he will make her a place in the world, give her a name, father her a family.

But just as the happy couple are about to stroll altarward, they meet plot complication number three, which turns the sentimental into the gothic. They learn that, because of a paternal indiscretion, they are brother and sister. Drawn together by "the Power of Sympathy" they are now split asunder by "the Triumph of Nature." Although Harriot had earlier assured us that the *"link of Nature"* had drawn them together, they now learn that Nature will not tolerate this particular "link" (2, letter #50, p. 113). They should have known what they could not have known. Too late Harrington blurts: " 'Had I

THE

POWER of SYMPATHY:

OR, THE

TRIUMPH of NATURE.

FOUNDED in *TRUTH.*

IN *TWO* VOLUMES.

VOL. II.

FAIN would he ftrew Life's thorny Way with Flowers;
And open to your View Elyfian Bowers ;
Catch the warm Paffions of the tender Youth,
And win the Mind to Sentiment and Truth.

PRINTED at *BOSTON,*
by ISAIAH THOMAS and COMPANY.
Sold at their Bookftore, No. 45, Newbury Street.
And at faid Thomas's Bookftore in Worcester.
MDCCLXXXIX.

(Boston: Isaiah Thomas)

Title Page/vol. 11, *The Power of Sympathy,* 1789

known her to be my sister, my love would have been more
regular—I should have loved her as a sister—I should have
marked her beauty—I should have delighted in protecting it' "
(2, letter #55, p. 127). And too late Harriot confesses, " 'O! I
sink, I die, when I reflect—when I find in my Harrington a
brother—I am penetrated with inexpressible grief—I experi-

ence uncommon sensations—I start with horror at the idea of incest—of ruin—of perdition' " (2, letter #50, pp. 109–110). The curtain has fallen: Harriot dies from shock; Harrington by his own hand.

Viewed in the context of the burgeoning English tradition of the gothic novel, *The Power of Sympathy* is notable primarily for the artlessness of its prose style, the desultory manipulation of events, and the surplus of extraneous plot. But viewed from the perspective of the particular treatment of incest in early modern American culture, *The Power of Sympathy* is important for just those deficiencies. Its very flatness becomes its importance. No chances are taken with the plot or with the style, no "let's just try it once," no experimentation or titillation as in the English novel. To spin this roulette wheel is to invite disaster. Note that *both* parties must die rather than be forgiven for ignorance. William Hill Brown took his task with utmost seriousness. He told just what he announced on the original title page.

This same dispassionate tone and stern voice is echoed in the eight or so subsequent works before the 1830s in which, with only one exception, incest is actual, not implied, and the penalty is not diffused but final. When the incestuous act, or its threat, occurs in the sentimental works of mid-century as it did in the now almost forgotten, but once vastly popular writers like Susanna Rowson or Sara Wood, it is severely countered with death, exile, or permanent stigma.[14] As opposed to what was happening to René and his Amelia, Laon and his Cythna, or even Manfred and his Astarte, American fictional siblings were finding not temporary solace, or purposeful inspiration, but destruction and death. "Do it and die" is the clear American message. In this respect the early American gothic more nearly resembles the austerity of the folk ballad than the tender mercy of the English novel. If this part of American culture had to be aligned with a Western tradition, it would not be with the English or the French, but with the German.[15]

Perhaps as a tribute to its Northern European counterparts, Charles Brockden Brown's *Wieland* specifically emphasizes

Germanic ancestry to supply badly needed motivation. To make incest properly gothic much must be made of family background—witness the familial patterns established in *Otranto*, *The Monk*, *Melmoth*, or *Frankenstein*. In *Wieland* the circle is even more elaborately spun out and then more abruptly contracted. Early on we are introduced to the mysterious old prophet Wieland who has left his fatherland, Germany, to expunge some unexplained sin. As an apostle of some mysterious truth, he is compelled to minister to the heathen Indians not so much to save them as to save himself. From what he flees we don't know, but we do know the escape drives him insane. If we are to believe the cloyingly semi-omniscient narrator, the pressure of the nameless sin builds inside the elder Wieland until he literally explodes; he spontaneously combusts; he burns up from within. The curse, however, is not destroyed; it is passed on to his son Theodore. Here, for all practical purposes, the novel really begins, but that Brown should think it necessary to provide the European causality may intimate his need to tie his bizarre tale into an appropriate context.

We are never told the exact nature of the curse carried out of Germany to the New World. Probably it is, as Fred Lewis Patee and others have contended, "the destruction of the family."[16] But how and why? What kind of behavior can cause a family to be blown apart from within? Is it the same process that spontaneously combusted the family father? Are these the sins of the father that are literally visited upon the son? Judging from what little has preceded *Wieland* in American cultural history, we may already be able to guess. In this almost classic tale of nineteenth-century family tragedy, the destruction proceeds apace with mechanical rigor. What is striking in Brown's version is that there is so much hesitating and rethinking as the awful denouement approaches, even though we are continually told that inevitable disaster looms ahead.[17]

After the elder Wieland's death the mother dies, leaving Theodore and his sister Clara alone, orphaned in the New World with no one to keep them company or to trust. They soon find another sibling pair (Henry and Catherine), as well as a "mysterious" older man, Carwin. As expected, the youngsters fall in love with their counterparts of the opposite sex. This is a configuration common enough in the English and German novels of the time in which sibling pairs multiply the prospects for pathos. We are assured that all would be well except that this Carwin insinuates himself so completely into the mind of Theodore that the young man has no idea what any of the relationships mean. Are they brothers and sisters, future in-laws, or lovers? He is not the only one who has lost control of role placement in this little family drama. During her parallel love affair, sister Clara dreams such interpretively helpful dreams as:

> I at length imagined myself walking, in the evening twilight, to my brother's habitation. A pit, methought, had been dug in the path I had taken, of which I was not aware. As I carelessly pursued my walk, I thought I saw my brother, standing at some distance before me, beckoning and calling me to make haste. He stood on the opposite edge of the gulf. I mended my pace, and one step more would have plunged me into this abyss."
> (p. 62)

Theodore does marry Catherine, but his sister's marriage to Henry is postponed; Henry happens to have a German fiancée. If we think we are confused, poor Theodore has so confounded the roles of the women surrounding him that he imagines his sister to have been sexually tainted and settles the "punishment" of her on his *wife*. In a crescendo of chaos, he literally drags his wife to his sister's house, kills her in his sister's bed, and then leaves her corpse there ostensibly as his sister's. Brown exercises no subtlety in this *Doppelgänger* transference; it is presented almost without affect. Now that Theodore has removed any impediment to his "real" sister, now that he has removed the surrogate, can he confront the real personage of repressed desire? No, not at all. Rather like Victor Frankenstein, or even like Dr. Jekyll, he can approach only just so close and then the realization of his real repressed sexual interest causes him to replay the father's finale. He ends his life, not in spontaneous combustion as did his father, but in a self-inflicted destruction reminiscent of the folk ballad. He stabs himself to death with his sister's penknife.

Clara now safely finishes the sublimated exchange by returning to Germany and marrying Henry, who has conveniently settled affairs with his fiancée. As with the seemingly unconscious social coda at the end of *The Spectacles*, in which a proper family member (a cousin for a "mother") is substituted, Clara marries her brother-in-law, her barely displaced "brother." What distinguishes her behavior from her brother's, from what her father possibly had been cursed for, is that the displacement is removed two layers from reality. In addition, her action occurs far from the boundaries of the New World. Remember that Clara leaves America, and its acute sensitivity and swift punishment, for the Old World of Northern Europe. Little wonder that *Wieland* was subtitled *The Transformation*, for what we have seen are the changes wrought by a frontier family who wishes to, or is cursed to, rearrange their roles. The further sub-subtitle even specifies where such a price will be paid—it is *An American Tale*.

Although I have earlier (Chapter 2) discussed the sibling incest in Edgar Allan Poe's *Fall of the House of Usher*, it should be noted that one of its more perplexing aspects is that the eerie *mise en scène* is probably *not* in America. As a matter of fact, the House of Usher seems to be located in the Stygian lands of Annabel Lee or in some distant Ulalume which, if anything, is Germanic in the pictorial mode of Von Schwind, Richter, Friedrich, or Runge. All we know of its geography is that the house is surrounded not by a swamp, which might have given a misty air of the American South, but by a "tarn," which usually refers to an Alpine lake. Poe was not haphazard with descriptive terms, and he may well have chosen "tarn" very carefully. As contrasted with swamp, bog, fen or, better yet for the Ushers, quagmire, a tarn is specifically "a body of water that does not participate in the exchange of waters and keeps itself to itself."[18] Just as the tarn allows no entry or exit of itself, so the Ushers, brother and sister, are hermetically sealed in the cocoon of family. For them there can be no sexual excursions beyond the family border and so they must collapse in on themselves.

This geographic isolation seems a peculiarly American treatment of incest. The Wielands are sealed off in Mettingen, Pierre Glendinning and Isabel are initially confined to Saddle Meadows, the crazed Poe narrators are stuck in manor houses with their Morellas or Ligeias. Even the Faulkner and O'Neill families are mired in the South or frozen in New England. As opposed to the English tradition where incest may "open up" relationships with the proximate world, in the American milieu incest almost invariably closes it down. The family circle constricts until, as in the case of the Ushers, it consumes what is left of the family. Although critics such as Leslie Fiedler claim that this collapse into the self represents Poe's real-life focus on his nubile cousin, whom he called "Sis," and hence that "incest in Poe is too personal and pathological to shed much light on the general meaning of the latter theme in American literature and life," such is not the case.[19] The incest motif is so pervasive in Poe's other works, as well as so embedded in the American nineteenth-century *Zeitgeist*, that one suspects it is more closely tied to cultural anxieties than to personal eccentricities.

In *Berenice* and *Eleanora*, for instance, crazed narrators attempt to explain away the forbidden attraction of a cousin. In the more dense *Morella* and *Ligeia* the same libidinous energies are directed first to a seemingly proper exogamous mate but then swung back to concentrate on the tabooed issue of their sexual union. Daughter is confused with mother, who, in turn, is confused with wife. Within this core father-daughter relationship, the now fully berserk narrator proposes a physical closeness that generates palpable horror. In *The Living Dead*, I argued that to generate this frisson Poe superimposed the vampire myth on the incestuous interaction so that the forbidden transfer of sexual energy from narrator to proper mate, then to improper mate, is mythologized and thus distanced from our conscious understanding.

The one activity that is conspicuously missing from Poe's

fictional father-daughter dyad is the one activity that creates their relationship and the one behavior that horrifies us in the audience: sex. Sex is never mentioned, never even directly implied; instead we know only that certain women are enervated by the narrator's presence and that when one is mysteriously pushed aside, he commences courtship in earnest with her younger, innocent double. In contradistinction to *Usher*, where the participants are coevals, in these other tales the male narrator is first a child suitor to an older woman, then is a father to the child of their mysterious union, then suitor to this child.

The collision of these intrafamilial roles and relationships is the magnet that first holds fictional chaos together and then lets it fly apart. In each retelling, the price of these pseudo-sexual liaisons is first the unbalancing of a once attractive, but now totally maniacal, narrator, and then the collapse of his fledgling family. This demise is not simply the result of concentric narcissism or class struggle. It is a more generalized, a more sociobiological description of how human consciousness, if you will, refuses to countenance certain reproductive strategies.[20]

With this more generalized interpretation in mind, we might well conclude with Fiedler that there is nothing particularly *American* about Poe's treatment. But then notice how Hawthorne develops the same motif at approximately the same time.[21] In *Alice Doane's Appeal*, written just as Poe was starting his series of incest tales, Hawthorne set the specifically American stage for his own rendition of sibling entanglement:

On a pleasant afternoon of June, it was my good fortune to be the companion of two young ladies in a walk. The direction of our course being left to me, I led them neither to Legge's Hill, nor to the Cold Spring, nor to the rude shores and old batteries of the Neck nor yet to Paradise; though if the latter place were rightly named, my fair friends would have been at home there. We reached the outskirts of the town, and turning aside from a street of tanners and curriers, began to ascend a hill . . . [upon which] the curious wanderer . . . will perceive that all the grass, and every thing that should nourish man, or beast, has been destroyed by this vile and ineradicable weed: its tufted roots make the soil their own, and permit nothing else to vegetate among them; so that a physical curse may be said to have blasted the spot, where guilt and phrenzy consummated the most execrable scene, that our history blushes to record. For this was the field where superstition won her darkest triumph; the high place where our fathers set up their shame, to the mournful gaze of generations far remote. (pp. 266–67)

This specifically New England locale is "curst" by Nature in a typically romantic way. Its barrenness is a singularly Wordsworthean image. Think only of the "curse poems" like *Hart Leap Well, Peter Bell, The Thorn, The Danish Boy,* or even *Michael,* in which a sentient Nature, Mother Nature, has refused to share her bounty with man because of some particularly loathsome act of natural subversion. As with Wordsworth, in Hawthorne and Poe natural infecundity is also the result of a human act of atrocity. Beneath this dirt lies the body of a man whose story will explain why this patch of ground on Gallows Hill has been, and shall always be, barren. Even in America there is a force stronger than the force that drives up the green grass, a force so powerful that it can never be removed or overcome.

Many years ago, during the Puritan sway, a young man, Leonard Doane, "characterized by a diseased imagination and morbid feelings . . . with a deep taint of his nature," lived alone with his "beautiful and virtuous" sister. They were the last of their family save for a phantasmagoric brother, Walter, who mysteriously has been separated from them and whose surname is "Brome." All we know about this darkly enigmatic sibling is what we glean from Leonard's notebooks. It seems that Leonard suspects some "secret sympathy" has developed between his sister and Walter, for he writes:

Searching into the breast of Walter Brome, I at length found a cause why Alice must inevitably love him. For he was my very counterpart! I compared his mind by each individual portion, and as a whole, with mine. There was a resemblance from which I shrank with sickness, and loathing, and horror, as if my own features had come and stared upon me in a solitary place, or had met me in struggling through a crowd. Nay! the very same thoughts would often express themselves in the same words from our lips, proving a hateful sympathy in our secret souls. (p. 271)

The doubling motif, so much a staple of barely sublimated incestuous desire, is invoked. A man just like Leonard loves Alice in a forbidden way, in a way a brother should not love his sister. The narrator now enters to help explain:

Leonard Doane went on to describe the insane hatred that had kindled his heart into a volume of hellish flame. It appeared, indeed, that his jealousy had grounds, so far as that Walter Brome had actually sought the love of Alice, who also had betrayed an undefinable, but powerful interest in the unknown youth. The latter, in spite of his passion for Alice, seemed to return the loathful antipathy of her brother; the similarity of their dispositions made them like joint possessors of an individual nature, which could not become wholly the property of one, unless by the extinction of the other. At last, with the same devil in each bosom, they chanced to meet, they two on a lonely road. (p. 272)

Indeed they meet, and rather like Victor Frankenstein and his monster, or Dr. Jekyll and his Mr. Hyde, or a host of other *Doppelgängers* driven by the self-destructive nature of a buried desire to do what should not be done, Leonard throttles his alter ego, Walter. Almost immediately Leonard regresses into childhood and now, for the first time, the inner dynamics are played out on the surface. In Leonard's own words:

Methought I stood a weeping infant by my father's hearth; by the cold and blood-stained hearth where he lay dead. I heard the childish wail of Alice, and my own cry arose with hers, as we beheld the features of our parent, fierce with the strife and distorted with the pain, in which his spirit had passed away. As I gazed, a cold wind whistled by, and waved my father's hair. Immediately, I stood again in the lonesome road, no more a sinless child but a man of blood, whose tears were falling fast over the face of his dead enemy. But the delusion was not wholly gone; that face still wore a likeness of my father; and because my soul shrank from the fixed glare of the eyes, I bore the body [of Walter] to the lake. . . . (p. 273)

Did Walter really exist? Did Leonard really kill him? Was Walter the violator of his sister's virtue? Or was it Leonard? As if to make sure we never quite phrase, let alone answer, these questions, Hawthorne has the inner story of Leonard being told to a wizard. The function of this sorcerer is clearly to sidetrack us away from the Leonard-Walter-father triad. All we know for sure from the story's frame is that under a patch of barren ground lies the body of someone who did something so horrible that Nature herself is repulsed and will issue forth no new life.

The narrator, really a wizard manqué, now continues the game, but raises the stakes.

I dare not give the remainder of the scene, except in a very brief epitome. This company of devils and condemned souls had come on a holiday, to revel in the discovery of a complicated crime; as foul a one as ever was imagined in their dreadful abode. In the course of the tale, the reader had been permitted to discover, that all the incidents were results of the machinations of the wizard, who had cunningly devised that Walter Brome should tempt his unknown sister to guilt and shame, and himself perish by the hand of his twin-brother. I described the glee of the fiends, at this hideous conception, and their eagerness to know if it were consummated. The story concluded with the Appeal of Alice to the spectre of Walter Brome; his reply, absolving her from every stain; and the trembling awe with which ghost and evil fled, as from the sinless presence of an angel. (p. 277)

As Byron reportedly said of Coleridge's metaphysics, "I wish he would explain this explanation," for this gloss serves both to deflect still further the hideous act, while at the same time to categorize the crime. For most readers the distance now is simply too much. We have been deceived too often. However, the fact that Hawthorne should feel the need of still another buffer shows how cautious most authors, especially American bourgeois authors, thought they should be if they were to describe familial interactions that their English brethren, admittedly aristocratic brethern, were enacting with comparative impunity. The lessons of Oneida had to be remembered. To approach the subject of incest in *this* country, at least in front of *this* audience of young women, Hawthorne has had to adopt a fairy-tale "once upon a time" format; tell the story by word of mouth many times removed from the "here and now"; quote copiously from Leonard's diary; and, finally, turn his back on the verifiability of the tale and claim it was caused by the machinations of a wizard. All that we finally know for certain is that whatever happened here in New England, whatever the "black horror and deep woe," it has left Nature unwilling to bring forth new life. The outer tale finally concludes as the narrator and his young lady friends leave the barren and infertile patch and return to the world of community.

> We slowly descended, watching the lights as they twinkled gradually through the town, and listening to the distant mirth of boys at play, and to the voice of a young girl, warbling somewhere in the dusk, a pleasant sound to wanderers from old witch times. Yet ere we left the hill, we could not but regret, that there is nothing on its barren summit, no relic of old, nor lettered stone of later days, to assist the imagination in appealing to the heart. We build the memorial column on the height which our fathers made sacred with their blood, poured out in a holy cause. And here in dark, funereal stone, should rise another monument, sadly commemorative of the errors of an earlier race, and not to be cast down, while the human heart has one infirmity that may result in crime. (p. 280)

". . . the human heart has one infirmity that may result in crime"—hardly are the words read than one wonders about all the other equally mysterious crimes in the Hawthorne canon that have stubbornly remained cloaked in the mist of uncertain explanations. I would not venture to assume an overly incestuous relationship between Rappachini and his daughter, or in the deflected adultery of *The Scarlet Letter*, or even such a reading of the strangely childlike interaction of Holgrave and Phoebe in *The House of Seven Gables*. I do believe, however, and some critics have also suggested, that the possibility of incestuous relationships was one of the recurring subjects of Hawthorne's art.[22] Granted that such sexual constellations of family members may simply be an occupational hazard if a writer is going to deal with "the secrets of the human heart," as Hawthorne contended. But if the self-same heart holds the "one infirmity that is criminal," then the subject of incest seems destined to be overtly, or covertly, exposed. What separates Hawthorne's treatment is not just that he needs to distance himself from expressly acknowledging incest, but that it seems so irredeemable an act on American soil. The stigma of incest is a brand not worn like the "A," but instead burned into the everlasting soul of Nature.

There is never anything titillating about incest in Hawthorne's work—it is sad, irredeemable, and tragic. Not so, however, in the sensationalist fiction of the mid-century. Here, in pulp novels, incest became one of the staples, the mentionable unmentionable, the *almost*-consummated forbidden act. By 1850 the increasing stability of the family, thanks to the clustering of population centers, the rise of large-scale industry, and the receding of the frontier with all its attendant physical and psychological demands, not only allowed family introspection, but occasionally demanded it. Women who read at home and men who read on the railroad wanted more than thrills, they wanted to know specifically who they were and where they were going. Cheap pulp, massive steam-driven presses, permanent ink, and the likes of Maria Susannah Cummins, Augusta Jane Evans, Miriam Coles Harris, Mary Jane Holmes, Mrs. E. D. E. N. Southworth, Harriet Beecher Stowe, and Susan Warner were as ready to inform women as were Emerson Bennett, Osgood Bradbury, "Ned Buntline," F. A. Durivage, Henri Foster, Joseph Holt Ingraham, George Lippard, and George Thompson were to inform their husbands.[23]

Whether the setting be city life or country habitat, the titillation caused by brothers who treat wives as sisters and sisters as wives (which, after all, was the Victorian ideal taken literally) formed the donnée of inappropriate seduction. No longer were these dynamics only embedded in the gothic where trembling was sanctioned by the genre. A literary format was being revived here as it was in England, where the trembling was an end in itself. The gothic romance was recharged as it now told of the middle-class family under specific and identifiable sexual pressure. This form is still popular, as a glance at any best seller list or a trip to the drug store book display will attest. A curious audience eager to witness the excitement and horrors of "home sweet home" is still in place.

The bourgeois American audience, financially able and irrepressibly eager for this scenario of families run amok, was so powerful a force in the literary marketplace that by mid-century it was demanding reams of its own sentimental pulp. Reader-response critics, who contend that audiences create works of art by forcing artists to address specific topics, will find no better situation to observe how economic and social pressures were brought to bear on storytellers. Readers make writers write, just as movie viewers make moviemakers make movies.

Melville, whose greatest novel, *Moby-Dick*, was written at roughly the same time as his *Pierre*, demonstrates the struggle both for and against the market. *Moby-Dick* is an intricate, dense, intellectually turbid vision of the world as seen by men without families. It took, even at Melville's prodigious speed, years to write and almost as long to publish. It found no market and, I daresay, without academics who provide a scholarly market, this book would still not be widely read. However, while waiting for *Moby-Dick* to appear in print, Melville started the first draft of *Pierre*, finished it, found a publisher who rushed it to print just as *Moby-Dick* was slowly being introduced. *Pierre* had middling success, but at least it had good prospects. Melville was optimistic about *Pierre*; he knew what would happen to *Moby-Dick*. Yet, *Pierre* is a careless work, sloppily written, about a sentimental protagonist and the maudlin destruction of his family which results from specific sexual confusion. Ironically, in spite of all the artistic blunders, we can learn much about survival on the high seas of family life from the landlocked *Pierre*.

I suppose the kindest comment made by critics about *Pierre* is that it is a parody, a send-up of the hundreds of fictional genealogies that were spewed forth from the maw of the steam presses and avidly consumed by newly literate Americans.[24] Indeed, it is clear in the first fifty pages that Melville is scoffing at the pomposity of his little fictional family, the Glendinnings, as they play out the fantasies of silver-fork fiction. Secluded in the edenic world of Saddle Meadows, the foppish Pierre lives with his doting mother in nectarine innocence. The father/husband has long since died, leaving only his fortune and two portraits behind. Pierre calls his mother "sister" and "sis"; she calls him "love": it is clearly a hothouse of family romance deep in the Berkshires. Here is a sample:

> This romantic filial love of Pierre seemed fully returned by the triumphant maternal pride of the widow, who in the clearcut lineaments and noble air of the son, saw her own graces strangely translated into the opposite sex. There was a striking personal resemblance between them; and as the mother seemed to have long stood still in her beauty, heedless of the passing years; so Pierre seemed to meet her half-way, and by a splendid precocity of form and feature, almost advanced himself to that mature stand-point in Time, where his pedestaled mother so long had stood. In the playfulness of their unclouded love, and with that strange license which a perfect confidence and mutual understanding at all points, had long bred between them, they were wont to call each other brother and sister. Both in public and private this was their usage; not when thrown among strangers, was this mode of address ever suspected for a sportful assumption; since the amaranthiness of Mrs. Glendinning fully sustained this youthful pretension.—Thus freely and lightsomely for mother and son flowed on the pure joined current of life. But as yet the fair river had not borne its waves to those sideways rebelling rocks, where it was thenceforth destined to be forever divided into two unmixing streams. (p. 25)

At the age of sixteen Pierre all but "marries" his mother; they partake of the holy sacrament of communion not so much with Christ as with each other. What is missing in the little Glendinning family, we are repeatedly told, is a sister/daughter. The bemused narrator opines, "So perfect to Pierre had long seemed the illuminated scroll of his life so far, that only one hiatus was discoverable by him in that sweetly-writ manuscript. A sister had been omitted from the text" (p. 27). To which Pierre blurts out, "Oh, had my father but had a daughter! . . . someone whom I might love, and protect, and fight for, if need be. It must be a glorious thing to engage in a mortal quarrel on a real sweet sister's behalf! Now, of all things, would to heaven, I had a sister" (p. 27)!

Sisters were, after all, central in chivalric romance because they could be fought for without the embarrassment and debasement of sexual desire. No sooner is a sister requested than she is delivered. Into this dwindling family the sister *must* come, and indeed she does in the person of Lucy Tartan. Bright, vivacious, the only daughter of a "most cherished friend of Pierre's father," also now conveniently deceased, also raised by a widowed mother, Lucy is the "light" the Glendinnings need to find their way to familial happiness. Pierre will make this girl his wife and then make his wife a sister, then make this sister his mother's daughter, and then all will live happily ever after. The circle will be closed. Eden will be reconstituted in upstate Massachusetts just across the state line from the Oneida community, which was also plodding toward perfection by condensing the family.

Dull black clouds swag across the heavenly skies of Saddle Meadows, or, in the novel's terms, ocean waves foam over the cliffs of Glendinning harbor. Both Lucy and Pierre feel "some nameless sadness" coming on. "Foretaste I feel of endless dreariness," says Lucy, and Pierre counters, "God help thee, and God help me, Lucy. I can not think that in this most mild and dulcet air, the invisible agencies are plotting treasons against our loves" (p. 61). As might be expected, neither Pierre nor Lucy can understand their sense of unease, this mysterious harbinger of the sad irreconcilability of ordinary life. We do not have to wait long to find out, for who should appear but the "real" sister, Isabel Glendinning, natural child of Pierre's father's youthful indiscretion, a child who, above all else, is the single object of Pierre's eternal quest. Why should he treat his mother like a sister when he has Lucy, and now why should he treat Lucy like a sister when he has his very own sister or, at least, his very own half-sister?

The introduction of the image of actual incest is laid on with a sticky hand, and yet, for all the sentimental parody, one senses that halfway through this inevitable plot development Melville realized that for all its ridiculousness there was a real story struggling to get out. Critics who have been able to trudge through the first half of *Pierre* have been quick to comment that once the constellation of mother-son and brother-pretend sister links with real brother-real sister, it sets up a vibration that even Melville couldn't slow down.[25] The novel now takes hold as the real sister replaces imagined sister who has replaced mother-as-sister. In the process we come to realize that the subtitle of *Pierre, or the Ambiguities* is indeed about liberating family characters from predefined family roles. No one knows who is who, especially not Pierre and, even more important, not the reader.

For these sins of confusion, not for his misplaced ardor, Pierre is cast out of the family. His mother disinherits him and in doing so she pushes him still closer to the only family he has left—into the waiting arms of his sister. As his vision of controlling the family fades, Pierre is forced to recognize that this is the result of the other side of paternalism: you cannot be a master unless you have servants. This knowledge comes too late to stop the fall from grace, yet Pierre wants to sanctify all he can. Ostensibly to assure Isabel her place in the family, Pierre proposes marriage. A marriage, mind you, Pierre proudly asserts, without sex. Isabel responds to this "glorious ideal" by

lean[ing] closer to him, with an inexpressible strangeness of intense love, new and inexplicable. Over the face of Pierre there shot a terrible self-revelation; he imprinted repeated burning kisses upon her; pressed hard her hand; would not let go her sweet and awful passiveness.

Then they changed; they coiled together and entangledly stood mute. (pp. 225–226)

Asexual relationships, as Pierre will discover, are best left to parthenogenetic species. Exiled from Eden, Pierre goes to the city with Isabel, still determined to make her not only a part of the family but part of his intimate life. He has already lost his mother; losing his sister would destroy him.

Meanwhile his mother, who has already disowned Pierre, dies, leaving the Glendinning fortune to a priggish cousin, who having inherited Pierre's lands, also wants to acquire his erstwhile fiancée, Lucy. Slowly it dawns on Pierre that his charity for Isabel is really only mistaken Eros; altruistic aims disguising carnal desire; vice parading as virtue. In one of the book's more extraordinary passages, Pierre, who has earlier seen himself as the martyred Christ, now dreams of himself as the withered Titan Enceladus, who in ancient times propagated his family through the body of his mother and sister. Pierre wakes in horror as he realizes he is living out that myth. Here the narrator, no longer bemused by his posturing protagonist, enters the text to make certain the point is well taken, although in slightly muddied form:

Old Titan's self was the son of incestuous Coelus and Terra, the son of incestuous Heaven and Earth. And Titan married his mother Terra, another and accumulatively incestuous match. And thereof Enceladus was one issue. So Enceladus was both the son and grandson of incest; and even thus, there had been born from the organic blended heavenliness and earthliness of Pierre, another mixed, uncertain, heaven-aspiring, but still not wholly earth-emancipated mood; which again, by its terrestrial taint held down to its terrestrial mother, generated there the present doubly incestuous Enceladus within him; so that the present mood of Pierre—that reckless sky-assaulting mood of his, was nevertheless on the side the grandson of the sky.

Recovered somewhat from the after-spell of this wild vision
folded in his trance, Pierre composed his front as best he might,
and straightway left his fatal closet. Concentrating all the remaining stuff in him, he resolved by an entire and violent
change, and by a willful act against his own most habitual in-
clinations, to wrestle with the strange malady of his eyes, this
new death-fiend of the trance, and this Inferno of his Titanic
vision. (pp. 388–389)

Knowing what he now knows about the mythic past, Pierre
realizes his demise is close at hand. He has, after all, been
raised in the sentimental tradition, nurtured on its myths, has
even attempted to write out its truths in an abortive Melvil-
lean novel. Now he has to be, like Enceladus, consumed in its
foregone conclusion. Having undermined all authority of roles,
having placed the Glendinning family at the edge of destruction, Pierre is reunited in the last scenes with his Lucy and
his Isabel. Pierre, now destitute in prison, is finally visited by
the sister who is a sister, and the sister who just pretends to
be a sister. As these "sisters" enter his cell, Pierre cries out:

"Ye two pale ghosts, were this the other world, ye were not
welcome. Away!—Good Angel and Bad Angel both!—For Pierre
is neuter now!" . . .
At these wailed words from Isabel, Lucy shrunk up like a
scroll, and noiselessly fell at the feet of Pierre.
He touched her heart.—"Dead!—Girl! wife or sister, saint or
fiend!"—seizing Isabel in his grasp—"in thy breasts, life for infants lodgeth not, but death-milk for thee and me!—The drug!"
and tearing her bosom loose, he seized the secret vial nestling
there. (p. 403)

Pierre dies, poisoned, drinking the metaphoric death from her
breast. To complete the triad, Lucy drains what is left, and
the novel ends, ". . . her whole form sloped sideways, and
she fell upon Pierre's heart, and her long hair ran over him,
and arbored him in ebon vines" (p. 405).
In a sense, Pierre's death ends the romanticizing of family
sexual relations. As Shelley had been for English romantic po-

etry, Melville was now for American romantic prose. No one could, or really wanted to, rewrite their texts. The first unfolding of family sexual dynamics was over. What had begun with the zealous transportation of revolution over the very doorstep of the bourgeoisie, what had energized some of the greatest poetry of romanticism, what had stimulated prose fiction almost to the point of supporting the gothic as the dominant genre, what had occasioned some of the most adventuresome utopian experiments in the wilderness as well as some of the most repressive American responses, had here run out of steam. The first of the modern conversations, so to speak, on the subject of forbidden relations was over. The taboo was firmly in place and interests, literary and other, moved elsewhere.

We are now entering the second of these conversations, a revival of interest. As I mentioned in the first chapter, this has often become a strident and shrill debate as certain interests have turned into supposed advocacy just as happened in the first blush of romanticism. Exactly how our current discourse will end is anyone's guess. Perhaps our interests will lead us to the desultory plottings of another Pierre, or maybe to the sublime rejoicings of another Laon. Perhaps the family knot will be untied as kinship patterns are reevaluated and reformed. In any case, I hope I have shown that we are not the first to address these secret anxieties, and not the first to be confused and startled and upset when they are made public. Although all scholars dream of resolving such confusion in an eleventh-hour conclusion, let me venture into the current thicket still attempting to follow the same trail, albeit now unmarked and unbeaten, of more current literary fictions and speculations. For if artists are indeed the first apprehenders of unarticulated truths, it may prove that we are indeed revising the taboo in ways as yet unknown to most of us.

Conclusion

A FTER MELVILLE, the focus of American literary interest turned elsewhere, turned outward toward realism and naturalism, overlooking the relatively narrow confines of the nuclear family under stress. This is not to say that intrafamilial sexual configurations were no longer scrutinized. Writers such as James, Howells, and Wharton continued to explore them. However, the demands of decorum made such exaggeration of family dynamics as we have witnessed in Poe, Hawthorne, and Melville less likely.[1] Novels of manners refined the gothic interactions to the nth degree and, in so doing, deflected sexuality into social conduct. The experimental novelists, the new generation who could have dissected family dynamics with scientific precision, such as Dreiser, Lewis, Norris, and especially Crane, had other concerns. On the one hand, they were choosing subjects of national and international magnitude such as economics or class struggle. On the other hand, they were detailing with cold precision the flat, singularly unromantic, unfeeling, nonsexual family life of the Babbitts, Cowperwoods, or Griffiths. They were trying to get outside the individual family to something bigger, something substantive, something different, something really important.

In a sense this was analogous to what was happening in English literature. The rise of the detached observer with his dispassionate delivery, as well as an interest in family affairs as it relates more to ancestry and social position than to specific interactions, made the sagas of the Pallisers, the Newcomes, and the Forsytes of particular interest. Whereas a generation before "intricate carving on ivory," as Jane Austen had said,

was the object of artistic endeavor, the later Victorians attempted to paint canvases of Constablean size. Late nineteenth century English society, realizing its responsibility as a
world force, endeavored to spread its best influence abroad.
And that was the influence of the moneyed middle class. Literature followed. Artist and audience accepted the fact that
family tradition was not only the private property of the aristocracy but was as well the purifying agent of the status-con-
scious middle class. This audience had bloodlines too, and they
were not about to portray them tangled in such aberrations as
incest. This burgeoning class not only bought books, it wrote
most of them. Thackeray, Meredith, Trollope, Kingsley, and
even Dickens became upwardly mobile by writing about upwardly mobile families. One might further argue, together with
the Marxists, that as money replaced blood as a metaphor of
family power, interest in polluted fortunes became more a
source of audience interest than poisoned bloodlines.

What separates the fin de siècle American and English traditions is that while the Americans seem to have passed family romance by, the English exhibited an almost prurient curiosity in off-center family sexual balance. Appropriately, perhaps,
this period was misnamed (usually by the Americans) "decadence." At the end of the century, in the 1880s and 1890s, the
English romantic tradition, at least in this important aspect,
reasserted itself and flowered in the high gothic works of Ste-
venson, Stoker, Wilde and, to a lesser degree, Wells. In the
works of these authors, most specifically in Stoker's *Dracula*,
family romance is played out with a minimum of conscious
censorship and we all know the result. By the early twentieth
century the myths of Dracula and Jekyll/Hyde were added to
the Frankenstein saga to become the stalwarts of romantic,
and now of contemporary, horror.[2]

This is not to say that the incest prohibition and all its attendant social ramifications were no longer subjects of American
literary concern. They certainly were, but in the early twentieth century we were rather like the English of the 1870s. The
most obvious exception is William Faulkner's Stupen and
Compson families in which intermarriage and tabooed sexual-

ity permeate family patterns both as a means to explain heritage and as a way to plumb character. The most notable of all the Yoknapatawpha relationships is between Quentin Compson and his sister Caddy in *The Sound and the Fury*. Faulkner himself clarifies in the Appendix what is not so clear in the text:

> QUENTIN III. Who loved not his sister's body but some concept of Compson honor precariously and (he knew well) only temporarily supported by the minute fragile membrane of her maidenhead as a miniature replica of all the whole vast globy earth may be poised on the nose of a trained seal. Who loved not the idea of the incest which he would not commit, but some presbyterian concept of its eternal punishment: he, not God, could by that means cast himself and his sister both into hell, where he could guard her forever and keep her forevermore intact amid the eternal fires. (p. 411)

But as John Irwin, *Doubling and Incest/Repetition and Revenge*, and Constance Hall, *Incest in Faulkner*, have argued, the incest taboo in Faulkner's works seems more in the service of narrative demands, of character development, of consciousness itself, than in unfolding social concerns or generating shocks. True, Faulkner did revitalize the moribund tradition of American dark romanticism as it relates to family structure (*Absalom, Absalom*), but, more to the point, he revived the traditional gothic which was floundering in the weird tales and bloody pulps of mass culture.

There can be no gainsaying that Faulkner not only made Southern gothic fashionable, he also cleared the way for others from O'Neill (*Desire Under the Elms*, *The Two-Character Play*) to V. C. Andrews (the Dollangangers series: *Flowers in the Attic*, *Petals on the Wind*, *If There be Thorns*, *Seeds of Yesterday*) to unfold the subject of family transgressions in a medium other than that of the police-story magazine. I don't argue that the influence was direct—in fact, the curiosity was clearly bubbling beneath the surface, as movies of the period suggest. However, Faulkner was in many ways the most important influence because he was recognized as *the* American modernist. That Faulkner would treat this subject made it, if not fashionable, at least acceptable. Again, this is not to say that twentieth-century authors had not returned to inappropriate sexual designs in order to drive plot, or to develop character, or to make social comment. Consider e. e. cummings':

> annie died the other day
> never was there such a lay—
> whom, among her dollies, dad
> first ("don't tell your mother") had;
> making annie slightly mad
> but very wonderful in bed
> —saints and satyrs, go your way
> youths and maidens; let us pray

or the barely sublimated relationship of Fitzgerald's Dick Diver and Nicole in *Tender is the Night*, or his *Daddy's Girl*.[3] It is clear that the father-daughter dyad as well as sibling relationships were still configurations of tremendous force. Still, whatever their power, these relationships were more often a concern of popular, rather than artistic, culture.

As we look back on the last three generations, we can see that our present concerns with family matters did not incubate ab ovo in the 1970s, as we often assume, but were instead the issue of a gradual unfolding of middle-class sensitivities. With the rise of the bourgeoisie on one hand and the avant garde on the other, anxiety about role stability encouraged artists first to subvert and then to affirm sexual boundaries. To be sure, this experimentation reflected changing demographics, political orders, territoriality, industrialism, feminism, and the like, but it also progressively made manifest the most deep-seated fears of socialized humans. After looking at how these fears have been preserved and conducted in print media for the last two hundred years, is there any reason to believe that we are any different in our current response? Is there any reason to believe the future will be any different? Will the incest taboo change?

To speculate on an answer, we might conclude by looking

at a work that seemed to promise a significant departure from the past. It seemed to articulate a new image of the female child which, in turn, implied a reformation of family interactions. If the assumption I have been accepting about the lagging relationship between culture and taboo is valid, then this work may possibly signal a subtle shift in sensibilities. The work is *Lolita* by Vladimir Nabokov. Since its French publication in 1955 and its American debut three years later it has achieved such recognition that the name itself, "Lolita," has became a description of a stage of maturation, an eponym for the preadolescent female, and implicitly, a mode of sexual behavior inside a family.[4]

To say that the publication of *Lolita* took American culture by storm is no dust-jacket contention. The book traveled a most circuitous publishing route from Maurice Girodias' Olympia Press to an *Anchor Review* excerpt, until finally G. P. Putnam's had the courage to publish it as a trade hardcover. One need only look at the reviews of 1957–58, as the novel was just beginning to find its way first into English and then into American reviews, and you will see that we were at a cultural bend in the road. Rarely has reaction been so vehement and so conflicting. Described as "sickening," "obscene," "perverse," to "tour de force," "hilarious parody," and "a great American novel," *Lolita*, for better or worse, cleared a path that had been closed for over a century. Here, in a sense, was Byronism revisited. *Lolita* made reviewers react, readers pause and, what was more important, it quickly filtered into popular consciousness. Here was a book you knew about *without* reading. Such recognition was partly because Stanley Kubrick, then one of the most popular and daring directors, was to make a movie of the book, but it was also because everyone knew, or thought they knew, what this book was about. What is culturally still more interesting is the fact that the other blockbuster, *Doctor Zhivago*, which appeared almost simultaneously and was by another Russian, Boris Pasternak, essentially affirmed all the family values that *Lolita* subverted. There is no doubt which novel has endured, and no doubt which will continue to be revived.

From the point of view of cultural history *Lolita* is both at the confluence of the Anglo-American stream which first bubbled forth in the early nineteenth century, and then slowed to a trickle, and as well at the headwaters of what is now a torrent of social, political, and legal concern about incest. Let me take first things first and try to fit *Lolita* into the English and American romantic traditions and then to discuss its subsequent influence.

Although the fact is of no literary importance, Nabokov himself was a curious mixture of English (he was educated at Cambridge) and American (while writing *Lolita* he was a professor of literature at Cornell). He clearly understood both literary traditions and just as clearly knew how to turn them inside out. In *Lolita*, Humbert, the confessing child molester, repeatedly refers to Byron's liaisons with his half-sister Augusta (a relationship expanded in *Ada* which was published a few years after *Lolita*). He quotes lines, sympathizes with the poet's ostracism, and even befriends his namesake, a Dr. Byron, who has a daughter of his own. The allusions to Poe are far more frequent and textually important. Lolita is Humbert's Annabel (a reference to Poe's *Annabel Lee*); Humbert often registers himself as "Edgar A. Humbert" or refers to himself as "Monsieur Poe, Poe"; Pavor Manor (where Humbert confronts his double à la William Wilson) is clearly modeled on the House of Usher. In fact, there are far more references to Poe in *Lolita* than to any other author or work.[5] This is not only because Nabokov considered Poe the most important American nineteenth-century writer, or relied on the reader's knowledge of Poe's relationship with his "nymphet" cousin Virginia Clem or even on our reading of the fictional family romances of *Morella, Ligeia*, or *Berenice*, but rather because Nabokov wanted to place *Lolita* squarely in the tradition of American romanticism.[6] Nabokov, who can be cloying at times, wants to pay homage to Poe and also, rather like the English "decadents" of the 1890s, wants even more to subvert the cultural tradition of middle-class sensibilities.

Of all the sacred subjects *Lolita* parodies (American education, psychiatry, motel culture, fast food, law, adolescence etc.)

none is more central than the concept of family. While *The Ladies' Home Journal* was heaping praise on the post-Korean War American family, Nabokov was assailing it. Although critics have claimed that here in *Lolita* Old Europe is debauching Young America, or conversely that Young America is debauching Old Europe, it is clear that the stable nuclear family of the West is being systematically undermined. What is not so clear is why this subversion does not evoke the horror we expect. This lack of frisson is part of what is scandalous about *Lolita*. To see how it is evaded we need look at both sides of the family sexual collision: what happens to Humbert, and especially what happens, or does not happen, to the child victim Lolita.

First the obvious should be noted. Whereas the usual American configuration is sibling incest, *Lolita* describes father-daughter incest. The character of Humbert is picked up, almost in toto, from its place in the gothic novel where he played the part of paternal oppressor of countless ingenues from Radcliffe's Schedoni to Stoker's Dracula. He is then turned upside down, inside out, and deposited in a picturesque New England town (elms, white church). Humbert is a force rarely seen in democratic, pluralistic, egalitarian America. He is the Duke of the castle, the evil Baron. He is now moving among us as the bespectacled college professor, but his methods have not changed a bit since his earlier days of skulking through darkness. Humbert ingratiates himself into a weakened household, plays first the role of husband, then father, then violator and spoiler. At times the gothic claptrap becomes mixed with an almost academic case study of family dissolution, as in chapter 31. In these pages Humbert pauses to detail the state statutes and laws on incest as if to show that there really is a recognizable social disorder, but such information is introduced only to make sure we don't misplace Humbert's actions. He is real and he poses a threat. But does he do any damage?

Lest we miss how close Humbert's "Confessions of an Unjustified Sinner" is to mainline gothic, we need only be reminded of the central positioning of Clare Quilty (Clearly

Guilty), who appears in one cameo after another as Humbert's double. So here is Quilty coming out of Humbert's Hyding as a dentist, a playwright, a tennis player, a psychologist—all the time pursuing Humbert from one continent to another in the mysterious manner of the Frankenstein monster and Victor, or, better yet, Mr. Hide and Dr. Seek.[7] At the end, in Pavor Manor, the two half-selves meet in a furious crescendo of action. *Doppelgängers* wrestle each other into reunion:

> We fell to wrestling again. We rolled all over the floor, in each other's arms, like two huge helpless children. He was naked and goatish under his robe, and I felt suffocated as he rolled over me. I rolled over him. We rolled over me. They rolled over him. We rolled over us. (p. 300–301)

What is noteworthy about both the function of incest, and the splitting of narrative personalities is that, for all its wit and parody, *Lolita* really is a gothic story, although the shock has been displaced into black humor. Again and again, as Humbert's mask slips, we catch sight of a pathetically obsessed consciousness, a man driven beyond the social pale into a never-never land of sexual obsession. Humbert is the romantic solipsist nonpareil, the protean impersonator, who is so desperate to fix forever the forbidden object of desire that he slips over the brink into madness. Humbert has no self other than the one he manufactures through his relationship with Lolita, and when she grows past him, he is left helplessly stranded.

What makes *Lolita* scandalous is not only the violation of taboo; it is that the participants shatter our expectations of what should happen next. We have been assured by folklore, by the gothic, by melodrama, that the victim will be forever ruined. But while we are witnessing the gradual atrophy of Humbert, we are catching sight of Lolita, not shriveling up, but, in the lepidopterous terms of her characterization, entering chrysalis. She may not emerge a butterfly, but neither is she consumed in the flames of sin and degradation. Our culture warns us this cannot be so, but it is. Lolita is not permanently scarred. She does not have to commit suicide or enter a convent; in fact, she seems to leave the now decimated family in rather good shape. I dare say this aspect of the novel more than any other proved *Lolita* unwholesome, pornographic, and indecent. Lolita violates our picture of the stereotype: she survives, a coquette who is not punished, a "bad" girl who does not fall.

In American literature of the nineteenth and early twentieth centuries, "bad girls" are not allowed to grow up. In English literature as well this has been true, especially in the genre most closely tied to popular culture—the sentimental novel. On one hand there are books like Richardson's *Clarissa* and *Pamela*, which are not *Bildungsromans* as much as they are books of etiquette, novels of manners. They are not stories of good girls maturing into womanhood, but of good girls striving for ladyhood. These girls will succeed only if they can be nonsexual. At the other extreme are books about girls who "fall," usually because of specific sexual experience. Here again the protagonist is "initiated," yes, not into womanhood, but rather into ruin. In works from Defoe's *Moll Flanders* and *Roxana* onward, good girls go bad, thanks in large measure to violating the incest taboo. Although these girls themselves may not be overly concerned about the violation, there is no doubt that the reader is supposed to interpret their actions as moral turpitude.

The split in the English novel between the Defoe and Richardson heroines continued throughout the eighteenth century. By and large one had a choice between a Roxana ("The Fortunate Mistress") and a Clarissa ("The History of a Young Lady"), between a Molly Seagrim or a Sophia, between a novel by Fanny Burney or one about Fanny Hill. For the Victorians the choice was still the same, except that both heroines were often included between the covers of the same book so that comparisons could be more efficiently made. So Thackeray gives us both Amelia Sedley and Becky Sharp, both Rebecca and Rowena. But take your pick—either way you end up with extremes. And these extremes are carried on through the Brontës, Dickens, Meredith, Hardy, and Galsworthy, almost to the present time.

For most of the early twentieth century the Hobson's choice of an Edith Wharton heroine or a Maggie, Girl of the Street, Isabella Fletcher or Sister Carrie, Mrs. Dalloway or Caddie Compson, remains in place. The same choice Thackeray presented in *Vanity Fair* was still with us in the early twentieth century: either a heroine ravished into sex or one ravished away from it, either a bawd or a bluestocking, a whore or a nun. It may be that there have been so few effective women's *Bildungsromans* written by men because the male almost unconsciously accepts the cultural assumption that the specific act of female maturation is sexual and that is the one act he is forbidden to treat sympathetically. He has been so conditioned, and women writers, until rather recently, have too. Although men write about girls growing up in almost always implicitly sexual terms—rarely is there a girl who matures because of changes in psyche—almost always maturation results from changes in her social status. She gets married and suddenly is a woman.

But what is the connection with incest? Possibly this. The novel in which a woman overtly "falls" into sexuality and hence out of social favor has been the basis of a subculture of "underground" novels. From *Fanny Hill* to *Candy*, they are considered pornographic novels, not only because of the blatant sexual content but also because of the apparent unconcern of the ingenue involved. Note that incest is almost inevitable as one of the threshold experiences. Perhaps these novels, and the social codes they imply, tainted the subject of female maturation to such a degree that the woman writer as well as the male may unconsciously have assumed that to write honestly will somehow necessitate confronting the anxiety of "the daughter's seduction" and the complexities that entails.

Admittedly, there are novels about maturing girls that don't concentrate on the loss of virginity at home as being the gateway to adulthood, but they do something perhaps as inappropriate. In novels by women such as Jane Austen or by men such as Henry James, the adolescent female usually runs the risk of being too good to be true, of being rarified out of reality. The heroine leaves childhood to enter into ladyhood without the intermediate stage of womanhood—without sex. I suppose the historical exception is George Eliot, who did take her heroine downstairs but was still cautious about having her leave the house perhaps because sexuality awaits. Sexuality is conspicuous by its absence. Think only of the relationships of Dorothea and Casaubon in *Middlemarch*, Gwendolen and Grandcourt in *Daniel Deronda*, Hetty and Adam in *Adam Bede*, Romola and Tito Melema in *Romola*, even Eppie and Silas in *Silas Marner*. If these relationships are implicitly erotic, then the eroticism is between a stern, harsh older man and a young, eager woman. Are these intrafamilial tensions acted out through surrogates? Or is this simply the nature of love between an older man and a young woman? As I mentioned in the previous chapter, a deflection of the parent-child configuration may be implied in the fate of Maggie Tulliver, where the incestuous configuration is worked out between siblings. In either case the alternatives are confusing—stay protected within the family and risk being drowned in its sexual flood, or leave the nest and work out your role with an older, domineering male. Until the last decade no one in America seriously picked up where Eliot left off, although Willa Cather (*My Antonia*, 1918), Ruth Suckow (*The Odyssey of a Nice Girl*, 1925) and Carson McCullers (*The Member of the Wedding*, 1946) have certainly tried.[8]

The women's movement has increased awareness that other alternatives are possible, and literary treatments have changed markedly. The poems of Sylvia Plath, the novels of Doris Lessing and the recent work of writers such as Maya Angelou, Alice Walker, and Lisa Alther portend not just a new woman's view of self, but a new placement within the family. It also seems clear that men's willingness to confront sexual stereotypes and forbidden interactions, emanating from the womens' movement, will have ramifications almost as profound. As kinship roles change there may well be an increase in both the incidence of and taboos on intrafamilial encounters. It is less clear, but I think the future may bear this out, that in some degree modern temperaments first started to shift as a result of the furor caused thirty years ago by the book, and then by the film, *Lolita*.

At first it seems ironic that one of the first modern attempts to create a female *Bildungsroman* should be a book that focuses on what traditionally has been the province of either the gothic or the pornographic: namely, family romance gone awry—more specifically, incest itself. To write about the unmentionable, Nabokov had to fuse the genres and, if you look at the central scene of Lolita's sexual transition, you will see how subtly it is achieved. From Humbert's point of view the "growing up" of Lolita occurs during the night in The Enchanted Hunters motel where Lolita is "made a woman." But what Humbert is unwilling to admit, until years later while writing his confessional memoirs, is that it was Lolita who seduced him, not he her. What we may overlook is that the central event in the gothic is simply turned around. Humbert admits on the eve of the trial: "Frigid gentlewomen of the jury! . . . I am going to tell you something very strange: it was she who seduced me" (p. 134).

This is often the hidden male view of rape, but the irony is, of course, that Humbert was deflowered and turns out to be the moral stinkweed, not Lolita. In fact, we learn that sexual intercourse has remarkably little to do with Lolita's growth into womanhood. Not only did she "have sex" long before Humbert, her relationship with him was more the result of curiosity and convenience than of coercion. The trauma of incest seems avoided as Lolita has had no cultural conditioning other than her chocolates, comics, and chewing gum. Even after she breaks loose from the crumbling family she has little knowledge and less guilt. We witness her final transformation in scenes overlooked by critics and readers alike who have gotten bogged down in the overlong transcontinental chase. Humbert visits Lolita, convinced that she will have gone the way of all fleshly girls in literature who have been "sexually ravished" by men, let alone ravished by their fathers. He is taken aback by what he finds. In an almost clinical observation, Humbert reports on Lolita, now Mrs. Schiller:

> Couple of inches taller. Pink-rimmed glasses. New, heaped-up
> hairdo, new ears. How simple! The moment, the death I had

kept conjuring up for three years was as simple as a bit of dry wood. She was frankly and hugely pregnant. Her head looked smaller (only two seconds had passed really, but let me give them as much wooden duration as life can stand), and her pale freckled cheeks were hollowed, and her bare shins and arms had lost all their tan, so that the little hairs showed. She wore a brown, sleeveless cotton dress and sloppy felt slippers. (p. 271)

Lolita is no longer a nymph; the downy pubescence is gone. But what he can't see is that his "girl-child" has become a woman. In the novel's lepidopterous terms the pupa is now a butterfly.[9]

Against the splintery deadwood of the door, Dolly Schiller [Lolita's married name] flattened herself as best she could (even rising on tiptoe a little) to let me pass, and was crucified for a moment, looking down, smiling down at the threshold, hollow-cheeked with round *pommettes*, her watered-milk-white arms outspread on the wood. I passed without touching her bulging babe. Dolly-smell, with a faint fried addition. My teeth chattered like an idiot's. (p. 272)

Here she is spread out like a butterfly pinned to a collector's cork, only she is not dead. She is enthusiastically alive. Humbert is losing all control, for, although she has matured (pregnancy equals maturity), she is neither slut nor saint. She is, in fact—and this is what galls Humbert and upsets our conditioned expectations—happily independent, worse yet, happily married.

In the scene with her husband Humbert is flabbergasted that Lolita, considering all her experiences with him, could be content with another man. This was not the way it was supposed to be. Sex, especially the kind of forbidden sex Lolita has encountered, was supposed to stain her forever. She was supposed to wither away. As much as Humbert wants to believe this (after all, such implied consequences are the basis of his oppressive paternalism) he realizes that no such thing has happened. She has grown away from him into womanhood.

He is powerless—no longer father. Humbert is profoundly shaken when Dick, Lolita's husband, tells him "Lo" will make a "swell mother" (p. 276). How can this be—Lolita a swell mother, indeed!

Humbert accepts the unacceptable. As he stares at her he comes to realize ". . . that I loved her more than anything I had ever seen or imagined on earth, or hoped for anywhere else" (p. 279). Backed into a corner, Humbert has to admit that Lolita is human and that she is a woman and that she is no longer his.

> And it struck me, as my automaton knees went up and down, that I simply did not know a thing about my darling's mind and that quite possibly, behind the awful juvenile clichés, there was in her garden a twilight, and a palace gate—dim and adorable regions which happened to be lucidly and absolutely forbidden to me, in my polluted rags and miserable convulsions; for I often noticed that living as we did, she and I, in a world of total evil, we would become strangely embarrassed whenever I tried to discuss something she and an older friend, she and a parent, she and a real healthy sweetheart, I and Annabel, Lolita and a sublime, purified, analyzed, deified Harold Haze [her natural father], might have discussed—an abstract idea, a painting, stippled Hopkins or shorn Baudelaire, God or Shakespeare, anything of a genuine kind. Good will! She would mail her vulnerability in trite brashness and boredom, whereas I, using for my desperately detached comments an artificial tone of voice that set my own teeth on edge, provoked my audience to such outbursts of rudeness as made any further conversation impossible, oh my poor, bruised child.
>
> I loved you. I was a pentapod monster, but I loved you. I was despicable and brutal, and turpid, and everything, *mais je t'aimais, je t'aimais!* And there were times when I knew how you felt, and it was hell to know it, my little one. Lolita girl, brave Dolly Schiller. (p. 286–87)

This is one of the rare moments when Humbert is "so tired of being cynical" that he lets the facade fall. For a second he admits that Lolita is a person with depth, with feeling, with ideas and hopes, and with a life of her own. And he admits as well, that although he loves her, he has been a monster to her. He has molested her. She has survived. He has withered. She has not.

The Anglo-American tradition of father-daughter sexual interactions was controverted not only by the text, but by what happened next. In 1961 Stanley Kubrick made the film version. As is often the case the social impact was more in the fact that such a subject would, and could, be filmed by a major studio (MGM), than that it was actually exhibited. In fact, the Kubrick film is a rather cautious, even timid to the point of tedious, transposition which does the novel little service, but shows much about the prohibition in our culture. The film is worth looking at if only because it shows how cautiously we treated this subject only twenty years ago and, by extension, how much our social consciousness has changed. It is also of interest because the lollipop-sucking seducer of older men has become one of our burgeoning cinematic images as Nastassia Kinski, Tatum O'Neal, Brooke Shields, Jodie Foster, and current centerfold culture attest.

Although Nabokov is listed as the sole author of the screenplay, he repudiated the credit, claiming that most of his script was neglected, or too radically revised to be considered his. The unpublished scenario bears him out.[10] However, clever dialogue and wry topicality were not what the audience had come to see. Like the reading audience, the viewing audience wanted, first, the titillation of seeing the prohibition disrupted, second, the story, and, a distant third, the social commentary. Here was an audience that had only been informed by a tradition of censure and horror, the tradition of Hawthorne, Poe, and Melville. The film, however, is *not* an American film. Kubrick made the movie in England, a culture (as we have seen) with a different bias. Everything American was carefully tempered. For instance, there are no external scenes of American highway life, thereby bypassing much of the novel's humor. More interesting still is that the film was purposefully miscast. Although Peter Sellers was a grand Quilty and Shelley Winters a marginal Mrs. Haze, James Mason, an American's idea of an English aristocrat, was Humbert. Only the vacuous Sue Lyon as Lolita and the Nelson Riddle "thousand and one strings" orchestration were as inappropriate. Mason is serious, even tortured, totally without any of Humbert's awkward tenderness and stumbling brutality. In the film Humbert is hard-edged, controlled, sinister, even cruel. Nothing is made of his lighthearted, although manic, print personality. It is almost as if anything sensitive was removed and replaced with a cardboard outline. Equally disappointing is that Sue Lyon has no personality. One can understand the need to cast an older, vapid, Lolita because neither the American audience nor the studio censor would tolerate a real pubescent. The advertising image of "Lo" in heart-shaped sunglasses sucking a lollipop notwithstanding, Miss Lyon's "Lo" spends most of the film looking as if she is trying to fit into clothing one size too small, and acting mildly annoyed and confused by the mechanical advances of the dour Mr. Mason.

All the film's crudities—pulsating soundtrack, miscasting, inappropriate dialogue, predictable dissolves before supposed forbidden sexual encounters, abrupt cutting, and scene transposition via innuendo—tell as much about the sensitivities of the 1960s as they do about moviemaking. They also tell a cultural history. Incest is un-American. It doesn't happen here. René go home. It is revealing of how Hollywood pictures the family that, although Kubrick knew that Peter Sellers would and could play the parts of Humbert and Quilty, the "front office" second guessed him by arguing the need to have a Montgomery Clift or Lawrence Harvey type. After all, the one genre *Lolita* must not become is the one genre it is as a novel: a gothic farce. In addition, as Kubrick told Gene Phillips in 1970:

> I would fault myself in one area of the film, however; because of all the pressure over the Production Code and the Catholic Legion of Decency at the time, I wasn't able to give any weight at all to the erotic aspect of Humbert's relationship with Lolita; and because his sexual obsession was only barely hinted at, it was assumed too quickly that Humbert was in love. Whereas in the novel this comes as a discovery at the end, when she is

(M-G-M)

James Mason and Sue Lyon, *Lolita*, 1961

no longer a nymphet but a dowdy, pregnant suburban house-
wife; and it's this encounter, and the sudden realization of his
love, that is one of the most poignant elements of the story.[11]

What Kubrick blames on the Production Code and the Legion
of Decency were as well vestiges of a world formed by the
Puritans, described by the romantics, and maintained by the
rising middle class. It is a world ordered by specific and repeatable family myth.

Kubrick knew as well that Nabokov's literate, albeit ba-
roque, script would more nearly capture the novel's exuberant
tone, yet such a tone would antagonize the censor and possibly the audience. So the movie version of *Lolita* is played out
in the genre Hollywood producers (not directors) first developed and clearly felt more comfortable with—the film noir. At

the beginning of the film Quilty is killed, and the rest of the story is essentially played out as a murky who-done-it, not a why-did-he-do-it. The theme of incest is suppressed presumably because any mention would frighten away the audience. "Better a killer than a pervert," the studio seems to have said, and this is reinforced by the euphemistic and totally misleading epilogue which appears just before the final credit "creep": "Humbert Humbert died of coronary thrombosis in prison awaiting a trial for the murder of Clare Quilty."

By the 1960s the story of a specific Lolita had ceased to be important. What galvanized public attention was the portrayal of a nymphet who supposedly was, at least, a co-conspirator in her own defloration and, at most, the seducer of her stepfather. Was this characterization a symptom of a new hostility toward children, a hostility that can also be seen in such films as *The Bad Seed, Rosemary's Baby, The Innocents,* or *The Exorcist,* all of which appeared between the late '50s and the early '70s? Ask anyone who a "Lolita" is and you will find the latent resentment of a culture which both appeases and deplores what it imagines to be innocence. "Lolita" has become an eponym for the sexually manipulative child, not because this was her role in the novel or in the film (the advertising told a different story), but because that is the role we seem to *want* her to perform.[12] Or, in contradistinction, do we see here the demythologizing of innocence which implies sexual independence?

An additional legacy left by *Lolita* is not to be found either in print or celluloid. Its influence is that it refocused popular attention on the dark corners of family life and held the light there long enough for us to realize how much has been hidden away. Are our attics filled with the secrets of the House of Seven Gables? Do our basement vaults still hide the mysteries of the House of Usher? Probably so. To be sure we have become more candid about admitting the darkness, and we certainly have become conscious that this darkness has been with us for generations. The American family has changed, and is changing, and with it our assumptions not just of the present but of the past have been called into question. We do have a different history from the English and the French and the Germans, but we share a fundamental anxiety about family instability.

As I tried to point out in the first chapter, while it *seems* that the family is going through profound changes, such sensations have been with us before, and they have been shared by Western cultures. The major difference is that now the social sciences have verified the family dynamics implied by the artists. In a sense the gothic has been proved to be the realistic. There can be no doubting that we know much more now about family life than ever before and no doubting that what we know is not always comforting. We seem destined to know even more. But will our awareness translate into different family behavior? Will our cultural traditions be reformed? Will our roles change? Will the women's movement, media exploitation, academic study, marital habits, and demographic changes make any noticeable change in the function or application of the incest prohibition? And vice versa? Perhaps.

If literature, seen in its broadest sense as an externalized communal psyche, can be trusted as a predictor, we will have to conclude that we are still very much in the wash of nineteenth-century concerns. It is not happenstance that while the arts have found incest an energizing force, no all-encompassing theory has yet been forthcoming from the social sciences. The attraction theories of Freud have proven as incomplete as the repulsion theories of Westermarck. There is, however, promise in interdisciplinary theories which are supple enough to grant vast exceptions. What is clear is that the mix-up of the taboo, the act, the inhibition, and the institution of exogamy is symptomatic of deep-seated anxieties not only about sex, but about the family structure itself. Although the balance between license and restraint may shift, a dynamic tension has endured. However much we may want to acclaim ourselves free of the fears of our Victorian foreparents, we will have to realize that their apprehensions and our own are remarkably similar. We have better statistics, but we have every bit as much disquietude.

As we enter the second stage of modern concern, knowing that we are not the first may make us less apprehensive, or perhaps less threatened by what we often take as the ultimate breakdown of order. The nuclear family is probably not going through meltdown. The prohibition on incest has proved one of the most pervasive and influential organizing patterns in human life. It has also proved one of the most resistant to change. The enigma of incest draws its energy from so deep within the human psyche that it seems almost instinctive. It is not, yet our anxiety has such far-reaching effects. From our deep-seated consternation roles, behavior, families, and culture have been established. This unease will not markedly change overnight, or over a generation, or even over a century, but it will change. It has in the past.

The shock and horror of incest have excited each new generation, none more so than our own. We are not the first generation to be confused and uneasy. We will not be the last. Whether the anxiety of incest be unfolded in the ballad, the art poem, the gothic novel, the pornographic novel, the philosophical treatise, the scientific monograph, the sentimental novel, the romance, the etiquette/advice column, the movies, television, or in advertising, it has been a powerful stimulus to our individual and collective imaginations. It has made us shiver and wonder. It has made us imagine and create.

For whatever reasons, the human unease at contemplating, much less violating, this prohibition has inspired some of the most lasting works of modern literature and popular culture— as well as some of the most ephemeral. For however virulent the force of the taboo, we seem to need reminding, and we will take this reminding in whatever format and genre we can find. This force, and our need to communicate its intensity, have infiltrated every medium of communication. No mode of communal memory is exempt. While we may be naturally incest-averse, our culture has taken no chances and probably will continue to do so. While we may be able both to subvert and to enforce the prohibition, we are not able to break free of its influence. That the taboo is often violated in real life and in fictional life, that we exact consequences no matter where the violation occurs, tells us that whatever resides in the prohibition is something we cannot articulate and hence must continue to reiterate. We may think we are different from generations past, and in important ways we may be, but if the culture of the last two hundred years tells us anything, it is that in the most fundamental ways we are not.

Appendix: A Synopsis of the Biological, Psychological, and Sociological Approaches to Incest

S INCE THE CONCENTRATION of my thesis is on how art and popular culture carry the incest prohibition, these explanations (biological, psychological, sociological, economic) may have more heuristic than practical relevance. I have left out much, and oversimplified, and have done these interpretations an injustice in being be so reductive. I mention them here primarily to show how the concepts of incest as an act, as a taboo, as a double standard, as a sublimated desire, as an inefficient reproductive strategy, as a buttress of marriage, as an assumption of family in a wider society, are all interpenetrating explanations. And they are all reflections of the cultures that produced them. Although often seemingly contradictory, they are indicative of our abiding modern concern with an enigma—the scientific circumscription of the same subject we have seen articulated by the artists and the folk.

The biological explanation of the incest taboo has had a long and complex history, full of contradiction, paradox, and opposing conclusions. Essentially, biological conjecture rests on two interrelated premises: 1) incest increases the possibility of genetic deformities that lead, consciously or unconsciously, to 2) a "natural" aversion to the act. Until the mid-nineteenth century this was the dominant academic, as well as popular, explanation for the taboo. There may be some truth to it, for harmful recessive alleles will occur with more frequency in an inbred population. It does not necessarily follow, however, that genetic degeneration caused the taboo to be established. First, for any important "inbreeding depression" to be achieved, the breeding population must be kept small and a sufficient number of generations must pass without genetic cleansing so that the deformity may be set. Ironically, in the short term the opposite effect may be achieved, namely, the strain may improve its fitness by close inbreeding. Jeffrey Burnham recently argued in "Incest Avoidance and Social Evolution" that inbreeding in small groups with "low genetic loads" was the rule, not the exception, with hominids and so eliminated many of the lethal homozygotes early in mankind's evolutionary process. After all, we inbreed dairy cows for increased milk production, beef cows for meat, race horses for stamina and even bloodhounds for olfactory acuity. What the few field studies of incestuous humans in Middle Europe and Appalachia have shown is that along with increased incidence of epilepsy, lower birth rates, nervous system disorders, and minimal mental retardation, there were also offspring of above average intelligence and of far above average body size. Additionally, anthropologists have concluded from the carefully preserved and exhumed bodies of Incan rulers that no morphological or physiological peculiarities occurred even though their blood lines had not been "cleansed" for over fourteen generations.

The fact of the matter is that too much inbreeding is potentially as harmful as too much outbreeding—somewhere in between is optimal. In humans this seems to be about the level of second cousins. Extremes are easily tolerated as long as they are short-lived. As L. A. White observed more than three decades ago, long before the genetic argument was scientifically debunked:

> If the offspring of a union of brother and sister are inferior it is because the parents were of inferior stock, not because they were brother and sister. But superior traits as well as inferior ones can be intensified by inbreeding, and plant and animal breeders frequently resort to this device to improve their strains. If the children of brother-sister or father-daughter unions in

our own society are frequently feeble-minded or otherwise inferior it is because feeble-minded individuals are more likely to
break the powerful incest taboo than are normal men and women
and hence more likely to beget degenerate offspring. (pp. 416–
17)

The real problem with the biological explanation is not that
mild consequences outweigh the fierce taboo, but that societies pay no attention to biology when applying Procrustean
sexual standards. Why should relatives by marriage be forbidden sex partners? Even more perplexing: why, in some societies, should sexual relationships between parallel cousins (persons whose parents are siblings of the same sex) be abhorred,
but sexual relations with cross-cousins (for instance, offspring
of father's sister and mother's brother) not only be allowed,
but mandated? The cousins may well carry different genetic
packages (for instance, parallel cousins are more likely to be
closely related), yet cousin incest is forbidden by nongenetic
criteria. (For a clear-headed discussion of the biological and
legal contradictions inherent in *our* current jurisprudential system, see Carolyn Bratt, "Incest Statutes and the Fundamental
Right of Marriage: Is Oedipus Free to Marry?" We are no exception to general human inconsistencies on this subject.)

Perhaps incest aversion is biological, yes, but not in the sense
of an instinct, rather as a genetic message stored between the
genes and human consciousness. In other words, it is like operating instructions embedded into a computer program,
understood by the processor but never appearing on the screen.
In fact, biologists seem to have located just such a reproductive program in Japanese quail, who can sense who their siblings are even when they have been raised apart. The quail
seem to maintain a balance between inbreeding and outbreeding which, although not instinctual because it is sometimes
violated, suggests an innate inclination for avoidance. Patrick
Bateson, "Preferences for Cousins in Japanese Quail," suggests that humans may maintain a similar balance by choosing
mates "who differ but not to a large extent, from well-known,
closely related members of the family."

Here we have to be careful not to argue that there is a natural incest aversion, as Edward Westermarck was misinterpreted as having done at the end of the nineteenth century in his *History of Human Marriage* (1891). For as James Frazer and others quickly pointed out, if there is a *natural* aversion there will be no taboo. There is no taboo against eating bark or howling at the moon because most of us simply have no interest in these actions. Natural aversion does not mandate complete aversion, however. We may, and often do, prohibit certain behavior in others precisely because *we* are averse to it.

Conversely then, could the taboo on incest imply that we must subconsciously desire it? Not likely. Incest inhibition and/or phobia may instead be one of those imponderables that, as Kant said, can only be understood like the starry heavens above. It may simply be part of the unfathomable moral universe we carry within ourselves. Contemporary biologists prefer DNA to categorical imperatives of inner law, and in their search for what unites all aspects of species behavior, they may have found new proof of a degree of innate incest avoidance. The primary imperative of human behavior is reproduction. Before all else, above all else, do only this: reproduce. Even the incest phobia pales before this commandment. There is no doubt that if you put a fecund female into prolonged isolation with a postpubescent consanguineous male, they will almost certainly commit incest. But here is a situation far more interesting. If you put prepubescent children together and raise them in proximity they will tend to spurn each other as sexual partners. In other words, we will copulate with proximate relatives if we have to, but we will not copulate with playmates if we don't have to. From the *sim-pua* societies in northern Taiwan, where the practice of importing a bride to be raised from childhood with the preadolescent groom produces a disproportionate percentage of infertile, as well as unhappy, marriages, to the Israeli kibbutzim, where no marriage has been reported to have resulted from nonconsanguineous individuals who have been raised together, the human response is clear. There is little sex interest between early childhood friends and little sex interest leads to minimal reproduction. Familiarity does not breed contempt; it simply does not breed at all. Yet, as we have learned from isolated human communities from Scandinavia to Brazil to Micronesia, if we have to be incestuous to breed, we will.

Have we been programmed to discard early companions for some biological purpose, or is it simply more efficient not to confuse playmate with sexmate? Since animals cannot "know" relatives they must depend on mechanisms like proximity, color, taste, and territory, but since humans have language we have a second line of defense, as it were, through the naming function. The misreading of genetic coding might account for the short-circuiting of nonconsanguineous partners such as in-laws, but it might also signal a weak reception of linguistic messages. There are a number of language-associated traits common to every human society, traits like kin selection, law-making, class and age grading, which add to social stability but do not seem in themselves crucial. Perhaps incest avoidance is one of these: a biologically encouraged cultural mandate which is consciously and unconsciously transmitted among members of a society. The mildly tone deaf sociobiologists call this a "culturgene."

Sociobiologists have conjectured that intense, although unconscious, competition may account for the fact that father-daughter incest is far more common in all human societies than mother-son incest. For the father "realizes" that his genetic packet will be untied by allowing his son and wife to reproduce, but it will be tightened by his own copulation with his daughter. But will the child issuing from father-daughter incest be cared for within the family? Probably not, for the daughter is not a "mother," and the family mother (husband's wife) will not tend genetic issue only partially hers. The biologist J. B. S. Haldane was once asked if he would give up his life for his brother and he humorously replied no, but that he would for three brothers or nine cousins. His point was that, while he might be gone, his genetic posterity would be preserved.

So the sociobiological answer to the riddle of incest is essen-

tially that incest is prohibited because it is genetically inefficient—inefficient because of the negative imprinting of proximity, inefficient because outbreeding has the cultural
advantages of stability and cohesion, inefficient because of
possible genetic defects, but especially inefficient because the
offspring of an incestuous union would not be expedient mul-
tipliers. (Pierre Van den Berghe, "Incest and Exogamy: A
Sociobiological Reconsideration," and Ray Bixler, "Incest
Avoidance as a Function of Environment and Heredity," detail the arguments from a sociobiological bias.) In the words
of the most famous exponent of this view, Edward O. Wilson:

> The biological hypothesis states that individuals with a genetic
> predisposition for bond exclusion and incest avoidance contrib-
> ute more genes to the next generation. Natural selection has
> probably ground away along these lines for thousands of gen-
> erations, and for that reason human beings intuitively avoid
> incest through the simple, automatic rule of bond exclusion. To
> put the idea in its starkest form, one that acknowledges but
> temporarily bypasses the intervening developmental process,
> human beings are guided by an instinct based on genes. Such
> a process is indicated in the case of brother-sister intercourse,
> and it is a strong possibility in the other categories of incest
> taboo." (pp. 39–40)

So just as we have genetically "learned" to fear snakes, spi-
ders, rats, heights, and close spaces that were real dangers in
our ancient environment, we have slowly but inexorably come
to fear and avoid incest. Wilson and his student Charles
Lumsden argue in *Promethean Fire: Reflections on the Origin of
the Mind* that the evolution of the human species has been
vastly aided by our peculiar ability to transform cultural experience into the genetic design. As Wilson has speculated
from the same premises, all other things being equal, if we
were now able to breed in place for a hundred or so generations we might find that we would develop genetic phobias
for guns, electrical outlets, fast-moving automobiles, nuclear
fission, and even politicians.

The traditional psychoanalytic interpretation reverses the

premise of the natural aversion theory favored by some biologists and contends instead that there is a natural propensity not for inbreeding, but for intrafamilial sex. The distinction must be made between incest avoidance (biological) and the incest taboo (psychological). That incestuous desire animates the "family romance" between son and mother (oedipal) and daughter and father (Electral) is accepted by traditional psychoanalysts as a given of the human condition. Not much is said about sibling incest, which is more common, other than that it is a deflection of the parent-child yearning. The suppression of this desire and the establishment of the incest taboo is thus the central developmental core of all human life. Unless this desire is quickly sublimated or repressed, "reaction formation" neurosis will develop and the family will disintegrate. Ironically, the family is strengthened by the taboo, for the potentially explosive incest desire is translated into socially stabilizing parental and filial love. Only vestiges of incestuous designs remain tangled in the individual and communal fantasies of dreams, literature, myth, and madness.

But why did this incest desire have to be repressed? Why couldn't it be enacted, or cathected, safely in less obscure forms? Why must there be so much displacement that we cannot even entertain incest as a conversation topic, let alone an active image in the imagination? To explain the origin as well as the ferocity of this repression Freud posited, in *Totem and Taboo*, the theory of the primal horde. He hypothesized that back at the dawn of history and language, families lived in small tribes and bred incestuously. Incest was accepted because kinship was so vague. In fact, while mothers knew who their sons were, fathers did not know whose daughters were whose. As in bands of chimpanzees and gibbons, and even baboons and some gorillas, a strong male often took over the group and refused to allow the younger males sexual access to any of the females. As the sociobiologists attest, humans will countenance any prohibition sooner then sexual denial. Reproduction is not a right or duty; it is *the* categorical imperative. The strong male forbade the boy cubs to come close. These women were his, they were "taken," and the boys were driven out.

Patriarchy begins. The young males were doubtless enraged by this sexual denial and bound together to fight the oppressor, their father. Freud continues the story:

> One day the brothers who had been driven out came together, killed and devoured their father and so made an end of the patriarchal horde. United, they had the courage to do and succeed in doing what would have been impossible for them individually (some cultural advance, perhaps, command over some new weapon, had given them a sense of superior strength). Cannibal savages as they were, it goes without saying that they devoured their victim as well as killing him. The violent primal father had doubtless been the feared and envied model of the company of brothers; and in the act of devouring him they accomplished their act of identification with him, and each of them acquired a portion of his strength. The totem meal, which is perhaps mankind's earliest festival, would thus be a repetition and a commemoration of this memorable and criminal deed, which was the beginning of so many things—of social organization, of moral restrictions and of religion. (pp. 141–142)

It is important to stress (as Freud really didn't, if only because there was no way for him to realize how he was to be misread) that the boys did not want *just* to copulate with their mother or their sisters, even if they could have known who they were. They simply wanted to copulate, to release the pressures of their sexuality. But once the act was done, once they had destroyed, literally consumed, the father-oppressor and then had satisfied their sexual desire, they were intelligent enough to realize that they were now fated to assume his role and would now have to battle among themselves as well as against a new generation of youngsters. And so over generations of inter- and intrafamilial turmoil a social contract, the first cultural bargain, was struck: certain universally recognizable women were "put aside," made off-limits to the males of the family; they were tabooed. They were tabooed because they were objects of stronger desire, and because relationships with *these* women would rend the fabric of the only society known, the clan. If there was an original sin in human culture, here it was.

Successive generations felt the guilt of the patricide and, to a lesser degree, of the incest and, fearful that they might be next, saw to it that their young learned the rules before it was too late for both of them. Freud's story continues:

> The tumultuous mob of brothers were filled with the same contradictory feelings which we can see at work in the ambivalent father-complexes of our children and of our neurotic patients. They hated their father, who presented such a formidable obstacle to their craving for power and their sexual desires; but they loved and admired him too. After they had got rid of him, had satisfied their hatred and had put into effect their wish to identify themselves with him, the affection which had all this time been pushed under was bound to make itself felt. It did so in the form of remorse. A sense of guilt made its appearance, which in this instance coincided with the remorse felt by the whole group. The dead father became stronger than the living one had been—for events took the course we so often see them follow in human affairs to this day. What had up to then been prevented by his actual existence was thenceforward prohibited by the sons themselves, in accordance with the psychological procedure so familiar to us in psychoanalysis under the name of "deferred obedience." They revoked their deed by forbidding the killing of the totem, the substitute for their father, and they renounced its fruits by resigning their claim to the women who had now been set free. (p. 143)

From this first communal renunciation came the sublimation of psychic energy that has, in a sense, separated us from animals, giving us what they lack: religion, art, culture, books on incest, history, politics, and neuroses.

Freud did not really believe that the primal horde "scenario" had to take place; it did not have to, for we act as if it did. (Here, as elsewhwere on this subject, he vacillated throughout his life.) The "omnipotence of thoughts," our imaginations, our dream lives, can produce effects every bit as real as any "reality." And these "thoughts," as Freud found—and modern anthropologists and psychologists have at least concurred with Freud here—are especially accessible in the fantasy life of neurotics, children, and "savages." Often individuals in these groups even believe the scenario to be true, while the rest of us simply act *as if* it happened. We act as if certain females really are forbidden. We act as if the fate of Oedipus would be ours if the taboo were violated. So we make sure the information is not lost on the next generation even if it means, as it often does, that they are frightened, even horrified, by the mere contemplation of this forbidden act.

The "universal horror of incest," as Freud called it, is therefore a way of deflecting the anxiety of sexual ambivalence. While we may be curious in childhood about sex with a parent or sibling, we unconsciously recall the hopeless tangle of patricide and cannibalism and suppress the desire. Freud had read James Frazer. We had overthrown the king and we had better make sure our fate was not his. So we "celebrate" the grisly act by repeating the scenes through totems and myths as if to confess our own hostile desires while repressing those of our children. This celebration eventually becomes one of the central events in the rites of passage through latency, for the young must be led across the mine field of sexuality not only for their own sakes, but for ours as well. They must be taught not just "when," but especially "with whom," or they will send us all back into the bush. The town is better than the jungle; linen sheets are better than leaves. So conscience was born; so culture began.

Freud did not come away with his "hypothesis . . . of such a monstrous air" (p. 142) unscathed, for every cultural anthropologist from Marrett to Lévi-Strauss has had to first push the primal horde conjecture aside. Freud's grand theory has usually been attacked for its stark simplicity and inattention to field data. Here the critics were correct. Most of Freud's psychological proof came from neurotic patients, while most of his anthropology came from Westermarck, Frazer, McLennan, Smith, and especially from studies of Australian aborigines which were popular around the turn of the century and soon became suspect. Additionally, what really damaged this explanation was Freud's unorthodox style of presentation. He probably should not have presented the primal horde theory as a horror story, but that, of course, is exactly what it was. It is interesting to note that a quarter of a century later in *Moses and Monotheism*, Freud flattened the tone, but to no avail. "Real scientists," as A. L. Kroeber, the dean of American anthropologists, reportedly said of Freud's elaborate conjecture, do not tell "Just-So Stories," whatever the tone.

Freud's extrapolations from the primal horde to the psychopathology of everyday life have always met with considerable skepticism, never more so than today. Thanks to the opening up of the Freud letters (Harvard University Press has just started to publish them), it is clear that originally Freud considered actual sexual violation the wellspring (the *"caput Nili"* or source of the Nile, as he called it in an 1896 speech to the Vienna Psychiatric and Neurological Society) of much individual neurosis. His early female patients, as we know from the Anna O. episode and others, complained of paternal sexual molestation, but Freud, for any number of reasons ranging from his prudery to his observation of his father's sexual behavior to his own possible affair with his sister-in-law, did not want to believe that literal incest was common.

Freud's renunciation of the "seduction theory," which essentially was a theory of literal incest, in favor of a view that woman fantasized early memories of intrafamilial sex, is the basis of Jeffrey Masson's controversial *The Assault on Truth: Freud's Suppression of the Seduction Theory* (itself the basis of Janet Malcolm's *In the Freud Archives*, an account of the Freud industry and the men who profit by its existence and/or overthrow). In letters Freud wrote to William Fliess from 1887 to 1902 we can see his seduction theory change from actual incest to incest illusion, from physical violation to the metaphoric reconstitution of oedipal and Electral fantasies. Although Freud's abandonment of the seduction theory has proved to be grist for the anti-Freudian mill, he inspired a generation of analysts who, for better or worse, have made incest an analogy rather than a reality.

One of the most provocative of the modern Freudians is Jacques Lacan, who has coupled modern French structuralism with classical psychoanalysis. For Lacan, as for Lévi-Strauss and Michel Foucault, the prohibition of incest is the fulcrum, what he called the "subjective pivot," upon which family and language and society and sexual maturation all balance. Like Freud, Lacan contends that incest is imagined, not enacted, yet without this imaginary line in the social dust, the whole concept of relationships and preferences would be profoundly altered. In human societies, this taboo defines the "forbidden" and as such sets all future limits of desire and sacrifice. That the taboo should be culturally coded with enigma (witness our own connection between Oedipus and the riddle) is because this primordial "law" is the immutable nucleus around which the constellation of human culture is spun. It is at the intersection of nature and language, in the buffer between consciousness and unconsciousness. Lacan's contemporary reaffirmation of Freud's thesis shows that the psychoanalytic concern with the taboo is still very much alive and still very controversial.

What Freud was to psychoanalysis, Talcott Parsons was to sociology. Incest was the keystone in both of their often contradictory explanations of human behavior. Where Freud found that the incest taboo sexually separates the young from the old and from each other, Parsons, following the lead of Tylor, Seligman, and others, found that the taboo ultimately unites them all into a greater cohesive social unit. Parsons was not the first to argue this point, but he was one of the most persuasive and the timing for his argument was right. In the 1950s Parsons emphasized that the control of erotic impulses is an indispensable element in socialization, not alienation. In "The Incest Taboo in Relation to Social Structure and the Socialization of the Child," he claimed that efficient sexual reproduction and clear descent lines are only part of the taboo's function. The incest prohibition also forces the child outside the family to form new alliances, rather than risk the implosion of the family directed back on itself. In other words, the taboo is the centrifugal force that not only establishes different families, but also stabilizes certain roles inside the family. As the sociobiologists argue for the gene, the sociologists argue for the family. The successful family is the efficient family and the efficient family, like the efficient gene, inherits the future. To be effective, family roles are exclusive; one cannot be father and spouse, son and father, at the same time inside the same nuclear unit. To do so would be to create a "self-liquidating" group. Human groups are most efficacious when there is a shared sense of the unit and of each member's role in the unit.

Within each family there are in reality two families: one is formal, created by function, and the other is experiential, formed around feelings. There are male and female roles, and there are mother and father roles. To be successful a family needs to avoid any threat to these roles, not to deny pleasure, but to ensure cohesion. If this means the repression of the erotically experiential family, then so be it. The regulation of choices thus leads to the establishment and continual reaffirmation of, first, individual roles (father-daughter is not man-woman, but husband-wife is), then of families and finally of societies. Kinship is not biological; it is learned, and the impetus to learn the social structure is the prohibition on incest. The reward of extending kinship is social stability; the penalty is collapse of roles, sibling rivalry, intrafamilial strife, and a crumbling society. What makes these sexual lessons especially important for the human being is that our period of parental dependence is so long, and our socialization so complex, that much time is needed for the elaborate indoctrination. The "transfamilial" roles are not the natural results of biology, but of slow and often repetitive acculturation. It takes time, and the incest prohibition essentially "buys" that time.

Whereas the biological explanation of incest centers on incest avoidance, and the psychoanalytic explanation revolves around the relation between taboo and redirected libido, the sociological explanation ultimately focuses on the institution of exogamy. For in order to force young family members to forge links with others, certain inner links are removed. In Parsons' words, it

is not so much the prohibition of incest in its negative aspect which is important as the positive obligation to perform functions for the sub-unit and the larger society by marrying out.

> Incest is a withdrawal from this obligation to contribute to the
> formation and maintenance of suprafamilial bonds on which
> major economic, political and religious functions of the society
> are dependent. (p. 108)

We see the opposite, of course, when we examine the case of
royalty in which exogamy is discouraged in order to isolate
and consolidate the ruling class. Endogamy, for many modern
sociologists, explains the inherent instability of historic blood-
line royalties, but this is still debated. Recently, for instance,
Pierre Van den Berghe and Gene Mesher, "Royal Incest and
Inclusive Fitness," and Roy Wagner, "Incest and Identity: A
Critique and Theory on the Subject of Exogamy and Incest
Prohibition," have argued the "fitness maximizing strategies"
of endogamy and conjectured as to how they are effected.

Currently some of the most popular and provocative theories of the incest taboo are being generated from Claude Lévi-
Strauss's extrapolation of exchange alliances. Like the Freud-
ian psychoanalysts and the Parsonian sociologists, Lévi-Strauss
believed that the incest taboo straddled the bounds of nature
and culture, emanating from neither yet belonging to both.
The taboo on incest constitutes a "rule" that is exaggerated in
human societies for nonbiological reasons. Here is yet another
argument that starts by positing the connection between exogamy and the incest taboo. Lévi-Strauss assumes that there is
a primary relationship between intrafamilial sex and extrafam-
ilial marriage. However, he contends in *The Elementary Structures of Kinship*:

> The prohibition of incest is less a rule prohibiting marriage with
> the mother, sister, or daughter, than a rule obliging the mother,
> sister, or daughter to be given to others. It is the supreme rule
> of the gift, and it is clearly this aspect, too often un-recognized,
> which allows its nature to be understood. (p. 481)

In all societies, not only in patriarchies, women are "frozen"
within a family so that their distribution can be controlled within
a system of alliances. Daughters are held back until a proper

gift exchange can be effected. The men, by predesignated alliances, "strike the bargain" by allotting a scarce quantity for
social stability.

Lévi-Strauss quotes an anecdote told by Margaret Mead that
is a favorite of anthropologists, especially of the structuralists.
Professor Mead was questioning the Arapesh of Polynesia on
the subject of incest. She asked a tribal elder what he thought
of a brother and sister marrying and he responded with indig-
nation: "What? You want to marry your sister? Are you not
quite right in the head? Don't you want any in-laws? Can't
you see that you can gain at least two in-laws if you marry
another man's sister and another man marries your sister? With
whom will you go hunting and till the fields, and who can
you visit?" If the story is not literally true, it ought to be, for
it tells an enduring human truth. In order to maximize the
social, political, and especially the economic benefits, human
societies must establish rigorous parameters. The exchange of
females accomplishes this by interlocking discrete families into
a network. With Lévi-Strauss, the "marry out, or be killed out"
theories of Edward Tylor are provided with a rationale: give
or starve. Tribes that do not exchange do not reproduce.

Such arguments of alliance have been currently carried forward by the feminists, who take the next logical step. The
analogy of "giving" however is transformed into "trading."
The feminist explanation is clearly provocative for it implies
economic exploitation, and possibly will prove the most productive in understanding the past, present, and future of the
taboo in Western patriarchies. Elizabeth Janeway, "Incest: A
Rational Look at the Oldest Taboo," Florence Rush, *The Best
Kept Secret*, and Judith Lewis Herman, *Father-Daughter Incest*,
have extrapolated role behavior from socioeconomic theory.
The father protects his rights to the mother by denying her to
the son, the mother maintains her relationship with her husband by excluding her daughter, and they both forbid sibling
incest to solidify their positions. But their positions are not
equal. Thus, while the father may deny the daughter to the
son, and the son to the wife, he does not always deny himself
the daughter. In a patriarchy, possessions, and hence power,

pass through the male line and thus the taboo on father-daughter incest is less severe than that of mother-son. The issue of the father's incest is his, while the issue of mother-son or sibling incest is claimed by no one. Hence our extraordinary concern with female, not male, virginity. The father guarantees the virginity of his daughters in order to assure equitable reciprocity, much as the producer of a commodity protects his future entry into the market as a consumer by delivering his goods according to a common standard. For trade to be efficient, an ounce of gold must always be bought and sold as the same quantity of the same commodity even though it be in the form of, say, a bar of gold or a necklace. The gold has no intrinsic value but to facilitate its use as a standard we pretend it is worth so much an ounce and never stop to question the attribution. The analogy may seem inappropriate in isolation but trade alliances depend on such common analogies, on symbols, that eventually require a language to communicate them, and ritual friendships and alliances to stabilize them.

Male exploitation of women as economic commodities also explains traditions common to Hebrew, Christian, Greek, and Roman cultures which granted the male a legal right to the females, especially to female children. The Hebraic tradition of the "Zona" or outcast female whose only "sin" was to remain with her own kin (this term later took on the pejorative meaning of "whore") implies that the woman who refused to be traded out of the family was to be an object of scorn. We carry the same bias in terms like "old maid," "maiden aunt," or "spinster" for females who have passed the common age for marriage, but there is no linguistic counterpart for males. Or what of the legal tradition of excluding the concept of marital rape because a man cannot abuse what he owns? Or the modern vestige of property rights when the father "gives" his daughter in marriage; or the implication of the dowry which so clearly implies an economic transaction? In each case the economics of patriarchy "puts woman in her place" and her place is clearly that of a commodity to be exchanged.

What is similar about all these explanations is that they very much reflect the times of their promulgation. As with the literary and folk concern which we have examined, these theories show a society struggling to make intellectual, political, economic, moral, psychological, and especially scientific, sense out of the enigma of incest. That no scientific or literary work has untangled the various threads is a tribute not just to the tightness of the knot of incest, but, perhaps more importantly, to our enduring curiosity about how it was tied.

Notes

---

1. "Judge Sentences Brother and Sister for Marrying," *New York Times*, August 2, 1979, p. 12; "Touch of Incest," *Time*, July 2, 1979, p. 76; Peter Bonventre and Marsha Zabarsky. " 'I Married My Sister,' " *Newsweek*, July 2, 1979, p. 36; and Joe Mullins and Ken Potter, "Our Only Crime Was to Fall in Love." *National Enquirer*, July 10, 1979, p. 26.

2. Lord Byron, *Complete Works: Letters and Journals*, 1: 19–22.

3. Byron, *Letters and Journals*, 2: 229–230.

4. As quoted by Leslie Marchand, *Byron: A Biography*, 1: 503.

5. Recently scholars, among whom Marchand is the most eminent, have conjectured that Byron had to flee because he had forced anal sex upon his wife—a capital charge at the time. Clearly all these scandals made continued life in England insupportable. They also profoundly influenced the critical reception of his work, a reception which, until the middle part of this century, was more concerned to test Byron's poetry by his morality than to divorce critical judgment from moral censorship. Central to this controversy was Harriet Beecher Stowe's *Lady Byron Vindicated*, which argued that Byron suffered disintegration of the brain and was spared a life of total evil only by happenstance.

6. In 1984 the popular press found another sensational story of incest, this time between mother and son. As the story first broke in early September, Mary Ann Bass, 46 years old, married her 26 year old son, Danny James Sullivan, because "she did not want any other woman to have him." Mother and son had been separated since he was 3 years old and reunited when he was 18. They dated, fell in love, and married in 1978. Apparently, she only told him about their relationship some months after their marriage, but she was so obsessed she would still "not let him go." His natural father then claimed that Danny knew Mary Ann was his mother, and that he had known for thirteen years. The marriage voided, a few days later Danny married another, and a month later (October 23) was indicted on incest charges by a grand jury. His mother was also charged with bigamy (Danny was her fifth husband). The two finally pleaded "no contest" to incest and were

given suspended five-year sentences on the condition they seek "psychiatric and other counseling." Appropriately for all the stereotypes, these events occurred in the hill country of Tennessee.

7. Here is just a sampling of Anglo-American legal study and/or interpretation in the last few years: T. C. N. Gibbens, "Sibling and Parent-Child Incest Offenders: A Long-term Follow-up"; L. J. Kirkwood, and M. E. Mihaila, "Incest and the Legal System"; Anthony Manchester, "The Law of Incest in England and Wales"; Morris Paulson, "Incest and Sexual Molestation: Clinical and Legal Issues"; David Royce and Anthony Watts, "The Crime of Incest"; Ronald Sklar, "The Criminal Law and the Incest Offender"; Ralph Slovenko, "Incest"; Harold Traver, "Offender Reaction, Professional Opinion, and Sentencing"; Carolyn Bratt, "Incest Statutes and the Fundamental Right of Marriage"; and Phyllis Coleman, "Incest: A Proper Distinction Reveals the Need for a Different Legal Response." The concluding chapter of Judith Herman's *Father-Daughter Incest* has a state-by-state synopsis of incest statutes.

8. This argument is detailed in M. J. Weich, "The Terms of 'Mother' and 'Father' as a Defense Against Incest."

9. It is surely important that the more technologically and linguistically advanced a culture is, the more well-defined the immediate family becomes, and the narrower the incest range will be. The vaguer the definition of family members, the more encompassing the taboo. Yehudi Cohen, "The Disappearance of the Incest Taboo," argues that the only restrictions that seem to prevent incest are not legal, but social. The more technological and dependent on legal prohibitions we become, the more we think we can organize incest out of existence. What is really happening is that, as the family constricts, the taboo is enforced over a smaller range.

10. Alfred Messer, "The 'Phaedra' Complex," makes the case that to inhibit the stepfather-stepchild interaction the father should legally adopt the child, the natural father should be released from child support, and the child should be encouraged to refer to the parents as "mother" and "father." In other words, once the family is identified as such, the social stigmas will reassert themselves. I must say that as a language teacher I wish some other term had been coined because in mythology Aphrodite rebuked Hippolytus, a youth who prided himself on his chastity, by making his mother, Phaedra, lust for him—not quite the etymology implied in the current use.

11. For the pros and cons of this biological argument made in the last few years see: Morton Adams, "Incest: Genetic Considerations" as well as his "Children of Incest," co-authored with James Neel; Joseph Bashi, "Effects of Inbreeding on Cognitive Performance"; Ray Bixler, "The Incest Controversy"; Gardner Lindzey, "Some Remarks Concerning Incest"; Frank Livingstone, "Genetics, Ecology and the Origins of Incest and Exogamy"; Leon Kamin, "Inbreeding Depression and I. Q."; R. D. Murray, "The Evolution and Functional Significance of Incest Avoidance"; Eva Seemanova, "A Study

of Children of Incestuous Matings," which was reported on in the popular press, for instance in "Children of Incest," *Newsweek*, October 9, 1972; Victor Siskind, "Bias in Estimating the Frequency of Incest" and "Incest and 'Vulnerable' Children," *Science News*, October 3, 1979.

12. The Attorney General's Task Force on Family Violence (formed in September 1983) will produce reliable national figures, but until their findings are made public we have only the conjectures and extrapolations from individual studies. For example, see Judith Lewis Herman, *Father-Daughter Incest*; David Finkelhor, *Sexually Victimized Children* and his "Sex Among Siblings"; Susan Forward and Craig Buck, *Betrayal of Innocence*; Robert Geiser, *Hidden Victims*; Linda Muldoon, ed., *Incest: Confronting the Silent Crime*; Georgia Simari and David Baskin, *Incest: No Longer a Family Affair*; Alvin Rosenfeld, "Incidence of a History of Incest"; Ida Nakashima and Gloria Zakus, "Incest: Review and Clinical Experience"; Joyce Spencer, "Father-Daughter Incest: A Clinical View"; Victor Siskind, "Bias in Estimating the Frequency of Incest"; Jane Brody, "The Incidence of Incest is Far More Common Than Most People Realize"; Joel Greenburg, "Incest: Out of Hiding"; and Aric Press, Holly Morris and Richard Sandza, "An Epidemic of Incest."

13. As reported by A. O. Sulzberger, Jr., "Conferees Heard a Controversial View of Incest."

14. For more on child resilience to trauma, see Daniel Goleman, "Traumatic Beginnings: Most Children Seem Able to Recover," and Nadine Brozan, "Helping to Heal the Scars Left by Incest."

15. One of the more revealing movie genres currently in vogue is the time-travel science-fiction story. This tale can exploit the possibity of equalizing ages, thereby making parent-child incest less toxic. Time-travel films, of which *Back to the Future* is the most popular, have increased manyfold in the last decade. These films play out a fascination which can also be seen in such prose works from H. G. Wells' *The Time Machine* to Robert A. Heinlein's *All You Zombies* and *The Door into Summer*, as well as Robert Silverberg's *Up the Line*.

16. Daniel Goleman, "Sexual Fantasies: What Are Their Hidden Meanings?" discusses the current research on this subject, which has become especially important in sex therapy since the innovations and discoveries of Masters and Johnson. Although incest fantasies do not seem to occur with much currency in the individual imagination, they do appear in literature and popular culture; see Chapter 8 of Drs. Phyllis and Eberhard Kronhausen's *Erotic Fantasies: A Study of the Sexual Imagination*, which is a general survey, and my chapter 4, which details the fantasy in the gothic and pornographic nineteenth-century novel. It is noteworthy, however, that incest scenarios are not present in fantasy prose designed especially for women. Tania Modleski, *Loving with a Vengeance: Mass-Produced Fantasies for Women*, tells me that this plot configuration is entirely missing from the Harlequin romances. The gothic tells quite a different story.

17. The general speculation is that about ten percent of most mammal

populations will move to the extremes in choosing mates. There is no reason to suppose that if left alone humans would be an exception. Most human reproduction occurs at the degree of second and third cousins.

18. Here, for instance, is Michel Foucault in *The History of Sexuality*: "This
interpenetration of the deployment of alliance and that of sexuality in the
form of the family allows us to understand a number of facts: that since the
eighteenth century the family has become an obligatory locus of affects,
feelings, love; that sexuality has its privileged point of development in the
family; that for this reason sexuality is 'incestuous' from the start. It may
be that in societies where the mechanisms of alliance predominate, prohibition of incest is a functionally indispensable rule. But in a society such as
ours where the family is the most active site of sexuality, and where it is
doubtless the exigencies of the latter which maintain and prolong its existence, incest—for different reasons altogether and in a completely different
way—occupies a central place; it is constantly being solicited and refused; it
is an object of obsession and attraction, a dreadful secret and an indispensable pivot." (p. 108–109)

19. Miriam Slater, "Ecological Factors in the Origin of Incest," was one of
the first to draw critical attention to the demographic argument for all of its
ramifications. E. A. Hammel, C. K. McDaniel, and K. W. Wachter, "Demographic Consequences of Incest Tabus" and Yehudi Cohen, "The Disappearance of the Incest Taboo," explain the demographic restrictions and
the demographic projection for human populations. It may be that computer microsimulations may determine rather precisely the effects of incest
taboos on the availability of "fertile marriageable partners" and thus help
explain the taboo's inconsistent history and application.

2. THE HORROR OF INCEST

1. For a thorough etymological interpretation, see Herbert Maisch, *Incest*,
pp. 11–13 and Joseph Shepher, *Incest: A Biosocial View*, pp. 25–29.

2. It might be noted that when continental writers like Schiller, Verdi,
Goethe, and especially Wagner retold their myths, they inserted horror, guilt
and often punishment where it had not been in folklore. After Milton's Sin
and Death, the Anglo-American response was to create the family anew—
distinct and different from the gods. Hence the taboo often unfolds as a
mortal strives to be a god and in so doing is first elevated and then crushed
for his overreaching.

3. Although the focus of this study is on modern culture, it should be
noted that one of the most popular subjects of Renaissance art was the portrayal of Lot and his daughters. In the biblical story, after the destruction of
Sodom and Gomorrah, the only survivors left, Lot and his virgin daughters,
lived in a cave. After getting their father drunk on wine, the two daughters
seduced the father on consecutive nights in order to "preserve the seed of

the father." Lot's stupor renders him unable to remember, but the race survived. Variations of this scene were portrayed by such masters as Albrecht Altodorfer, Albrecht Dürer, Frans Floris, Lucas van Leyden, Christoph Pandiss, Joseph Vien, Simon Vouet, Guido Reni, and many others. The scene became a touchstone of sensibility. By the eighteenth century interests had shifted to less voluptuous and more restrained scenes, but by the nineteenth century, continental artists, especially Gustave Courbet, revived the once popular archetype. But modern interest has never returned with such vigor to what was once almost a standard of painterly control: the forbidden act held in balance with social necessity. Lot's daughters may in fact represent a situation that often occurred in evolution—breed in or die out.

4. Lieberman, *Edvard Munch*, p. 8.

5. See Legman, *Rationale of the Dirty Joke*, pp. 91–97.

6. True, dread of incest is not *always* present, but it usually is. Clyde Kluckhohn, "Recurrent Themes in Myths and Mythmaking," includes incest motifs among the six most prevalent themes in the folklore of all races. Having surveyed the massive Human Relations Area Files at Harvard, as well as the standard indices, he concludes: "Although there are cases where I have as yet no positive evidence for the presence of the incest theme, there is no corpus of mythology that I have searched carefully where this motif does not turn up. Even if, however, incest could be demonstrated as a theme present in all mythologies, there would still be an important difference between mythologies preoccupied with incest and those where it occurs only incidentally and infrequently" (p. 47). And, "The mere recurrence of certain motifs in varied areas separated geographically and historically tells us something about the human psyche. It suggests that the interaction of a certain kind of biological apparatus in a certain kind of physical world with some inevitables of the human condition (the helplessness of infants, two parents of different sex, etc.) bring about some regularities in the formation of imaginative productions, of powerful images" (p. 49).

7. Jack Zipes has collected many of the past and present variations in *The Trials and Tribulations of Little Red Riding Hood*. The academic interest in this particular tale has been nothing short of passionate. In March 1984, a conference entitled "Fairy Tales and Society: Illusion, Allusion and Paradigm" was held at Princeton University. The focus was on *Little Red Riding Hood*. Feminists, Freudians, Marxists, literary critics, social historians, and even architects (concerned about the design flaw of the lock on grandmother's door) had their say. All agreed on one matter—whatever is buried in the text is something momentous which we have yet to outgrow our need to tell, hear, and explain.

8. Robert Darnton in *The Great Cat Massacre* claims that the oldest versions of *Little Red Riding Hood* address the problems of starvation and hunger. If this is so it is interesting how the concerns have shifted—concerns not just of the tale, but of the critics.

9. Herman, *Father-Daughter Incest*, pp. 1–2.

10. In Christian martyrology Dympna was first the center of a cult of young women, and was then sainted; she is remembered today with a hospital in Gheel named in her honor. She is the patron of ill and homeless and abused young girls.

11. Spiers, "The Scottish Ballads," p. 45.

12. While I try to argue this case with the English folk ballad, it is made for the Western continental folksong by Paul G. Brewster, *The Incest Theme in Folksong*.

13. I attempt to substantiate this point in "The Incest Theme and the Authenticity of the Percy Version of 'Edward.'"

14. Maurice Richardson, "The Psychoanalysis of Ghost Stories," first made this assertion and it has since become almost a given in literary and popular interpretation of the myth; see my "Psychoanalysis of the Vampire Myth," pp. 83–92, and *The Living Dead*, chapter 4.

15. This point (along with all of its sexual connotations) as well as many others is made in C. F. Bentley's excellent study, "The Monster in the Bedroom: Sexual Symbolism in Bram Stoker's *Dracula*." On various other aspects of the book's sublimated sexuality, especially as it relates to the incest taboo, see Joseph Bierman, "*Dracula*: Prolonged Childhood Illness," Phyllis Roth, "Suddenly Sexual Women in Bram Stoker's *Dracula*," and Carrol Fry, "Fictional Connections and Sexuality in *Dracula*."

16. Although modern commentators such as Sandra Butler, *Conspiracy of Silence*; Susan Forward and Craig Buck, *Betrayal of Innocence*; Robert Geiser, *Hidden Victims*; Judith Herman, *Father-Daughter Incest*; Blair and Rita Justice, *The Broken Taboo*; Florence Rush, *The Best Kept Secret*; Karin Meiselman, *Incest: A Psychological Study*; and Linda Sanford, *The Silent Children*, would agree with Brownmiller, it is probably best to keep in mind that there is a considerable body of psychological thought, also from a feminist view, that would disagree, and not slightly. These views are clearly dated, but possibly still important if only for historical reasons. See, for instance, Helene Deutsch, "The Psychology of the Sexual Act," in *The Psychology of Women*, pp. 77–105, and Karen Horney, "The Problem of Feminine Masochism," in *Feminine Psychology*, pp. 214–233; *The Neurotic Personality of Our Time*, p. 280; and *New Ways in Psychoanalysis*, pp. 113–117. For Horney on young girls' "instinctive" rape dreams, see "The Denial of the Vagina," *Feminine Psychology*, pp. 154-155. The legacy of women's masochism still lingers in popular culture as Natalie Shainess's *Sweet Suffering: Woman as Victim* attests.

3. "STRANGE FITS OF PASSION": INCEST IN ROMANTIC ART

1. Although this is by no means a comprehensive listing, some of the important general preromantic studies of incest in English literature can be found in Luciano Santiago, *The Children of Oedipus*; Florence Rush, *The Best Kept Secret*; R. E. L. Masters, *Patterns of Incest*; and Jean Hagstrum, *Sex and*

Sensibility. Recently, there have been a number of more concentrated full-scale studies of incest in the works of individual artists, for instance, Mark Taylor's *Shakespeare's Darker Purpose*, but this is a field of study that for obvious academic and social reasons has not been throughly plowed. This is especially true of eighteenth-century literature where the plays of Dryden (*Don Sebastian, Oedipus, Love Triumphant*) have gone largely unstudied with respect to the incest prohibition as has the nascent novel (*Moll Flanders, Joseph Andrews, Tom Jones, Evelina, The Man of the World*). An interesting case might be made for the scholarly neglect of incest in terms of class and professional aspirations. Until recently it was tacitly assumed by scholars that the study of "the best that has been known and thought in the world" did not include the subject of sexual behavior.

2. Although incest in Shakespeare's plays has been covered (Barbara Melchiori, "Incest in Shakespeare's Late Plays"), the subject of incest in Jacobean tragedy seems to appeal more to graduate students than to established scholars. See, for instance, George Schore, "'Incest? Tush!' Jacobean Incest Tragedy and Jacobean England," and Paul Smith, "The Incest Motif and the Question of the Decadence of English Drama, 1603–1632." It is clear that incest was viewed more ambivalently in Jacobean times than it is now. Incest tragedy is a rich and fascinating subgenre and it tells much about Jacobean popular culture. More important, in this transitional era between medieval and modern the moral judgments about incest were being formulated. As I hope to show in chapter 4, the rise of the middle class carried with it fears about family dysfunction and hence the necessity of intrafamilial interdictions. Incest, which is an element of scandal on the Jacobean stage, is rarely punished as such; by the mid-nineteenth century it is always punished.

3. For more on the incest theme in Milton, see Noam Flinker, "Cinyras, Myrrha, and Adonis: Father-Daughter Incest from Ovid to Milton," and his "Father-Daughter Incest in *Paradise Lost*."

4. Marcia Pointon, *Milton and English Art*, chapter 2.

5. Tompkins, *The Popular Novel in England*, p. 66. Tompkins' concern is also with the continental tradition, to which Peter Thorslev's "Incest as Romantic Symbol" remains the best general introduction. For a general survey of sibling incest in English romantic poetry see, Allen Richardson, "The Dangers of Sympathy."

6. Byron, *Complete Works*, 4: 157.

7. It should be noted that in the first draft of *The Bride of Abydos* (1813) Selim and Zuleika were siblings. As events turned out Byron found it necessary to change the relationship to that of cousins, but even a cursory reading shows his original intent has not been covered up by the more distant family relationship.

8. This is not the view of Errol Durbach, "The *Geschwister-Komplex*: Romantic Attitudes to Brother-Sister Incest in Ibsen, Byron and Emily Brontë," who contends that incest is used by Byron to give "pseudo-religious signif-

icance" to human love. This view makes sense only if you consider *Cain* outside the context of Byron's other work.

9. This trend in Shelley scholarship is mirrored in such recent works as Nathaniel Brown's *Sexuality and Feminism in Shelley* (1979), in the sympathetic tenor of the collected articles in *Essays on Shelley* (1982) edited by Miriam Allott, as well as in Jean Hall's *The Transforming Image: A Study of Shelley's Major Poetry* (1980).

10. After the second edition of the Bateson biography, Alethea Hayter wrote the *Times Literary Supplement* (August 9, 1974) to refute the attribution of incest longings to Wordsworth, pointing out that sibling relationships were quite different in the nineteenth century. On September 13, 1974 Donald Reiman, a prominent literary scholar and now librarian at the Carl H. Pforzheimer Library, responded by asserting that Wordsworth seemed closer to Dorothy than "normal," even Victorian normal, and pointed to poems like "'Tis said that some have died for love" to prove it. Reiman contended William was "consciously in love with Dorothy in a way he considered potentially dangerous," and that he therefore "feared their affection could possibly lead either himself to suicide or Dorothy to a death for which he would feel responsible" (980). A month later (October 4, 1974) Mary Moorman, one of the biographers of Wordsworth, joined the fray, contending that Reiman misread "'Tis said that some have died for love," and that the Wordsworths' relationship was characterized by what Dorothy herself called "fraternal love" (1079). Not willing to rest so soon, Professor Reiman countered (November 1, 1974) that "incest" and "incestuous feelings" were different and loaded terms, and he believed that the feeling, not the act, characterized the Wordsworths. Molly Lefebure, author of *Samuel Taylor Coleridge: A Bondage of Opium*, now entered the epistolary exchange (November 8, 1974) saying that the probabilities point to the fact that the relationship was indeed incestuous not in thought but deed. She pointed to proof in Dorothy's *Journals* and in Coleridge's description of the Wordsworths, but within a week Mary Moorman was back (November 15, 1974) to say that Miss Lefebure had misread both the *Journal* and Coleridge's jaundiced words. Professor Reiman had the last word (December 27, 1974) as *TLS* seemed exhausted by the whole affair, reasserting that feelings and acts are separate, and that we'll never know for certain about acts, but the poetry betrays the feelings.

11. Reiman, "Letter to *Times Literary Supplement*" November 8, 1974, p. 1261.

12. In her *Journals* Dorothy speaks of her brother thus: "William's head bad . . . I petted him on the carpet . . . after dinner we made a pillow of my shoulder, I read to him and my Beloved slept. . . ." Dorothy is in her early 30s, so it may be strained to consider this the effusions of a youngster. But could it be anything else? My colleague Richard Brantley has pointed out to me that far more may be gleaned from a careful reading of how Dorothy responded years later on her brother's wedding day: "On Monday 4th October 1802, my Brother William was married to Mary Hutchinson. I

slept a good deal of the night and rose fresh and well in the morning. At a little after 8 o'clock I saw them go down the avenue towards the Church. William had parted from me upstairs. I gave him the wedding ring—with how deep a blessing! I took it from my forefinger where I had worn it the whole of the night before—he slipped it again onto my finger and blessed me fervently. When they were absent my dear little Sara prepared the breakfast. I kept myself as quiet as I could, but when I saw two men running up the walk, coming to tell us it was over, I could stand it no longer and threw myself on the bed where I lay in stillness, neither hearing or seeing anything, till Sara came upstairs to me and said 'They are coming.' This forced me from the bed where I lay and I moved I knew not how straight forward, faster than my strength could carry me till I met my beloved William and fell upon his bosom. He and John Hutchinson led me to the house and there I stayed to welcome my dear Mary" (p. 154). An important note: the line from "I gave" to "fervently" is erased in the MS.

13. From a letter to Coleridge we know of Wordsworth's cancelled last stanza: "I told her this; her laughter light/Is ringing in my ears/And when I think upon that night/My eyes are dim with tears."

14. Moorman, "Letter to *Times Literary Supplement*" December 27, 1974, p. 1467.

15. I attempted to detail this argument and explain the interpretive importance in "'Desire With Loathing Strangely Mix'd': The Dreamwork of *Christabel.*"

16. While the incest configuration postponed the acting of Shelley's *Cenci* until the end of the century, it also postponed the production of Shaw's *Mrs. Warren's Profession* until 1924. Mrs. Warren's profession did not upset the censor as much as the implied relationship between Vivie and Frank.

17. Although many nineteenth-century artists used the Cenci episode, notably Walter Savage Landor and Robert Browning in England, Stendhal and Dumas (père) in France, Francesco Guerrrazzi and Alberto Moravia in Italy, only Shelley and the American romantics (Hawthorne's (*The Marble Faun* and Melville's *Pierre*) really exploited the dramatic possibilities of incest as a way to get to the inner dynamic of family life; see Diane Hoeveler, "La Cenci: The Incest Motif in Hawthorne and Melville," and my chapter 5.

18. This speculation continues to spill over from popular into scholarly imagination as witnessed still in numerous "psychological" interpretations of Shelley's oeuvre. Such speculation can be found in Thomas Moore, "Percy Bysshe Shelley: An Introduction to the Study of Character"; Arthur Wormhoudt, *The Demon Lover*, pp. 88–111, and John Hagopian, "A Psychological Approach to Shelley's Poetry."

19. E. B. Murray, "Elective Affinity in *The Revolt of Islam*," has argued that Laon cannot be the child's biological father since lovemaking occurred after Cythna's abduction and thus paternity must belong to the tyrant. Such may be the case, but to make it Murray has to overlook such textual evidence as Laon's first greeting of the child "with a father's kiss" (l. 1934) as

well as the general implication of the work itself as being a family romance free from the constraints of society.

20. *Memoirs of Shelley*, 2: 364. For more on the rewriting of *Laon and Cythna* to dilute the incest, see Fredrick Jones, "The Revision of *Laon and Cythna*"; Ben Griffith, "The Removal of Incest from *Laon and Cythna*"; and Nathaniel Brown, *Sexuality and Feminism in Shelley*, pp. 212–213.

21. I am indebted to the sensitive reading of *Laon and Cyntha* by Nathaniel Brown, "The Detestable Distinctions" in *Sexuality and Feminism*, pp. 212–228, which essentially argues for the understanding of incest in its poetic context as well as in the spirit of the times. Brown contends that the incest is not metaphoric as much as speculative and Shelley's concerns are more with the concepts of personality and sexuality than with scandal and taboo.

22. *Letters of Percy Bysshe Shelley*, 2: 154.

4. "I SHALL BE WITH YOU ON YOUR WEDDING NIGHT": INCEST IN NINE-
TEENTH-CENTURY POPULAR CULTURE

1. Or such is the contention of Jack Goody, "A Comparative Approach to Incest and Adultery."

2. Donald Cory and R. E. L. Masters, *Violation of Taboo*, p. 5.

3. Although many scholars have discussed the occurrence of incest in the Bible, Florence Rush, *The Best Kept Secret*, Chapter 2, is one of the most concise and perceptive.

4. Diamond, *The Evolution of Law and Order*, p. 21.

5. As quoted by Luciano Santiago, *The Children of Oedipus*, p. 76. Other recapitulations of the Henry/Anne divorce, as well as the court's delibera-tions, can be found in Marvin Albert, *The Divorce*; John Bagley, *Henry VIII and His Times*; Francis Hackett, *The Personal History of Henry VIII*; and Philip Sergeant, *The Life of Anne Boleyn*.

6. *Blackstone's Commentaries on the Law*, p. 778.

7. I am indebted in the following paragraphs to an excellent overview of eighteenth-century assumptions concerning incest: Alfred Aldridge, "The Meaning of Incest from Hutcheson to Gibbon."

8. Mandeville, *The Fable of the Bees*, 1: 330–331.

9. Bolingbroke, *Collected Works*, 8: 495.

10. As quoted, but not glossed, by Aldridge, "The Meaning of Incest," p. 311.

11. *Ibid.*.

12. Michaelis, *Commentaries on the Laws of Moses*, 2: 56–58.

13. Stone's *The Family, Sex and Marriage in England* is a crucial work in this new field of historical study; also of note are: Peter Laslett, ed. *Household and Family in Past Time* as well as his *Family Life and Illicit Love in Earlier Generations*, Brian Strong, "Sex and Incest in the Nineteenth-Century Fam-ily"; Anthony Wohl, "Sex and the Single Room: Incest Among the Victorian

Working Classes"; Michael Anderson, *Family Structure in Nineteenth-Century Lancashire*; and Steven Ozment, *When Fathers Ruled: Family Life in Reformation Europe*. Most of these studies make use of the pioneering works in early modern industrial life: James Kay-Shuttleworth, *The Moral and Physical Condition of the Working Classes* (1832); P. Gaskell, *The Manufacturing Population of England* (1833); Henry Mayhew, *London Labour and the London Poor* (1844); and, of course, Friedrich Engels, *The Condition of the Working Class in England* (1844).

14. Webb, *My Apprenticeship*, p. 310*n*.

15. Lord Shaftesbury, "Address on Public Health," as quoted in Anthony Wohl, "Sex and the Single Room," p. 204.

16. What social studies there were supported this; for instance, P. Gaskell in *The Manufacturing Population of England* (p. 137) contended that overcrowding was the reason the sexes "mingled in wild carouse, and crimes of all shades are perpetrated, blasphemy, fornication, adultery, incest, child-murder."

17. Shaftesbury's speech is reprinted in John Hollingshead, *Ragged London in 1861*, p. 233.

18. These testimonies are recounted in Anthony Wohl, "Sex and the Single Room," pp. 207–209.

19. At the same time that the English Laureate is bemoaning the closeness of cousins in the country, the Prince Consort—Prince Albert of Saxe-Coburg-Gotha—is setting up royal house in London with his cousin Queen Victoria. More ironic still, it was their uncle, King Leopold I of Belgium, who engineered the match between the not-very-smitten 17-year-olds.

20. Tennyson may have been hesitant for more reasons than worry over his poetic standing. His brother Frederick had fallen in love with his cousin Julia, supposedly proposed to her, and a family scandal had ensued.

21. For more detail on the subject of girls growing up in fiction, see my comments on *Lolita* in the Conclusion.

22. For examples of implied or actual mother-son incest see Francis Lathom, *Astonishment!!!* (1802) and Selina Davenport, *An Angel's Form and a Devil's Heart* (1818); while for the more common cousin-cousin incest, see, among many, Mrs. Carver, *The Horrors of Oakdale Abbey* (1797), Mrs. Patrick, *More Ghosts!* (1798), T. J. Horsley Curties, *The Watch Tower* (1804) and, by far the most famous example, the last part of Charles Maturin, *Melmoth the Wanderer* (1820).

23. Although there have been many recent interpretations of this aspect of romanticism, the first, and still the best in many respects, is Mario Praz, *The Romantic Agony*.

24. I recall this story in more detail in *The Living Dead*, pp. 103–105.

25. Here is what Mary Shelley reports of Polidori's contribution to the wager in her Preface to *Frankenstein* (p. ix): "Poor Polidori had some terrible idea about a skull-headed lady who was so punished for peeping through a key-hole—what to see I forget: something very shocking and wrong of course;

but when she was reduced to a worse condition than the renowned Tom of Coventry, he did not know what to do with her and was obliged to dispatch her to the tomb of the Capulets, the only place for which she was fitted." Was what the old lady saw the liaison of individuals she knew were really siblings?

26. Whereas Emily Brontë concentrates on the dynamics of sibling incest in *Wuthering Heights*, her sister Charlotte seems just as interested in the father-daughter dyad in *Jane Eyre*. The "red room" episode, Jane's initial role as caretaker of Rochester's children, the father-daughter relationship that even Mrs. Fairfax observes developing, the displaced evil wife/mother in the attic who must be removed, as well as the modification of fatherhood fulfilled by metaphoric castration (blind in one eye, loss of one limb)—all this suggests that there is a subtext to *Jane Eyre* which centers around what must be done to circumvent the incest taboo. This thesis is first put forward by David Smith, "Incest Patterns in Two Victorian Novels," and reaffirmed in a number of recent readings, most notably John Maynard's *Charlotte Brontë and Sexuality*, pp. 100–105.

27. Already by the time of Sterne's *Tristram Shandy* (1759-1767) the folk-loric jokes about incest are finding a place in the novel. One of Sterne's characters declares that, "since there is no prohibition in nature, though there is in the Levitical law—but that a man may beget a child upon his grandmother." This provides the context for Stern to tell one of his many bawdy jokes (vol. 2, chap. 32) which at least shows the currency of the noninstinctual interpretation of the taboo.

28. This argument is detailed in Sylvia Manning, "Incest and the Structure of *Henry Esmond*."

29. See Smith, "Incest Patterns in Two Victorian Novels," pp. 144–162. This view is also shared by Mark Spilka, *Dickens and Kafka*, and Robert Penn Warren, in whose 1963 novel *Flood* a brother and sister named Maggie and Brad have similar feelings and meet a similar fate.

30. Both parodies are reprinted in Patricia Skarda and Nora Jaffe, *The Evil Image*, respectively, pp. 29–31 and pp. 23–25.

31. George Levine, "Review of Recent *Frankenstein* Criticism," p. 205. Also of interest in this context is his *The Realistic Imagination*. For a brief but concise summary of scholarship on *Frankenstein*, see David Ketterer, *Frankenstein's Creation: The Book, the Monster, and Human Reality*, and my article on "The Horror of *Frankenstein*."

32. The problem of an authoritative text is a complicated one because we really do not know Mary Shelley's intentions. For those who like the 1818 text there is James Rieger's edition of *Frankenstein*, which gives the variant readings; and for those who don't really care there is a spate of popular reprints of the 1831 book. The most important shift, for my purposes, is that in the 1818 text Elizabeth is cast as Victor's first cousin, while in 1831, to avoid any hint of consanguinity, she is cast as an aristocratic foundling. I will be glossing quotations from Harold Bloom's Signet Edition which not

only is the most popular current edition, but also includes Bloom's provocative Afterword. My major complaint about this edition is that for some reason the publisher "normalized" the spelling of "daemon" to "demon" thereby destroying an important distinction. Bloom is of course aware of the distinction for in the Afterword he refers to the creature the way Victor does, as a "daemon." For more, see the next note.

33. Victor's creature, which, since the movies, we automatically refer to as a "monster," is most often referred to by Victor as a "daemon." In the M. K. Joseph edition of the 1831 *Frankenstein* the spelling "daemon" properly indicates Mary Shelley's intention that the creature represent life that is "other" than human. Unfortunately, the Signet Edition, with the Afterword by Harold Bloom, changes it to "demon," and hence does real damage to the intended characterization of both protagonist and his creation. The daemon becomes a demon, but this is, in part, because of the way he is treated as well as the task he is called upon to perform within the Frankenstein family.

34. I suppose all the secondary female characters like Justine are really weak doubles of Elizabeth—that is to say, fantasy sisters to Victor. For more on this aspect of Justine in particular, see J. M. Hill,"*Frankenstein* and the Physiognomy of Desire," pp. 335–358.

35. Although the *Doppelgänger* has been much discussed in literary criticism, the best discussion of its importance in *Frankenstein* is in Morton Kaplan, "Fantasy of Paternity and the *Doppelgänger*: Mary Shelley's *Frankenstein*" and Robert Kiely, *The Romantic Novel in England*.

36. For more on this aspect of the novel, see Gordon D. Hirsch, "The Monster Was a Lady: On the Psychology of Mary Shelley's *Frankenstein*," and Susan Harris Smith, "*Frankenstein*: Mary Shelley's Psychic Divisiveness."

37. Since most of the texts Miles consults are rare and unreprinted, all future parenthetical page numbers will not be from mentioned works, but from Miles' own compendiously quoted, not glossed, *Forbidden Fruit*.

38. It is of singular importance, however, that not only is incest portrayed in pornography as an upper-middle class activity, it almost always involves intelligent young adults who are sexually curious before their induction. Never, that I know of, is an unwilling or ignorant child made part of the family dynamics.

39. It is noteworthy that forbidden partner scenarios are infrequent in X-rated videotapes. Of the more than a thousand "sexvids" surveyed by Robert H. Rimmer in *The X-Rated Videotape Guide*, less than ten concern themselves with incestuous configurations. Although titles like "Unnatural Family" and "Wicked Sensations" hint of forbidden partners, they instead detail a family involved in lots of sexual activity, rather than in taboo-violating behavior. In the handful of cases where the incest taboo is breached, the treatment duplicates prose pornography by exploiting the fall of a social interdiction with self-conscious enthusiasm. But, while the ban is temporar-

ily subverted, the final message affirms its necessity. The "sexvids" go a step farther than their prose counterparts by portraying one of the partners as finally traumatized or reprehensible to begin with. So in "Like Mother Like Daughter," a long-separated father returns from the Orient to be seduced by his daughter. When he discovers the relationship he is so upset that he leaves the country for good. Or in "That's My Daughter," long-separated dad and daughter do indeed consummate the act, but do it in the roles of "John" and prostitute. Although the father is excited, the daughter is portrayed as a "rather slimy person" who doesn't care what she does as long as she's paid.

The two "Taboo" films deserve a closer look, or, at least, a précis. In "Taboo" (1980), a married couple is having sexual troubles. As usual it is the wife's fault—after all, in adult films the audience is male—and the couple split up. The son, 19-year-old Paul, stays with Mom. One night she hears him groaning in bed and fellates him to climax and to sleep. In many non-western cultures this act, when performed by hand, is a common way of putting preadolescent boys to sleep and so may have no incest overtones. Mom, however, knows she had ulterior motives, and leaves Paul a note apologizing. Paul is not upset and tells her: "It happened and I want it to happen again." Here the tape stops: the story is over. Rimmer comments (p. 142) that "the real story of mother-son incest has yet to be told." One wonders what that "real" story is.

"Taboo II," made three years later, promises that answer, but does not deliver. Now Paul is living with Dad and the story centers around another family in the neighborhood. In this family Mom, Dad, Junior, and Sis all frolic in bed together, but not sexually. Junior has made a play for Paul's mother, but decides he likes Sis better. The happy family takes a turn for the worse after Mom finds Dad is having an affair at work. She mopes around the house and happens on Junior and Sis in bed, this time not frolicking. She is horrified and is about to telephone Dad when Junior confesses his guilt and is contrite. Mom now feels pity for Junior and soon they are in bed together. Mom feels guilty, but enjoys it. Later, at bedtime, Mom confesses to Dad, puts on her sleeping mask, and falls asleep. What should Dad do but seduce Sis that very night in that very bed. Mom is a sound sleeper. Now Dad has bad feelings about what he has done and makes tender love to Mom. It is clear as this video ends that Mom and Dad are reconciled and have no further need of Junior and Sis. In other words, their incest has been gratuitous, resulting not from desire but from hurt feelings.

5. "THE DISEASE OF THE LAST OF THE USHERS": INCEST IN NINETEENTH-CENTURY AMERICAN CULTURE

1. Whatever it is in the American culture that prompts this behavior, has yet to be resolved. Witness the Rajneeshpurham in Oregon, a settlement on

what is left of our frontier based on the subversion of contemporary capitalistic culture. It is clearly important to parade the Bhagwan Shree Rajneesh about in one of his forty-six Rolls-Royces to show how decadence itself can be perverted and just as important to show how much more compassionate to the poor they can be than the "outside" world is. Also of interest is their rearrangement of the family under "father" Bhagwan and "mother" Ma Anand Sheela, for, we are told, the incest taboo has been "set aside." Honest sex needs no "complications." It may not be happenstance that the commune fell apart after Ma Anand left the family.

2. In the last two decades the frontier community has been a subject of considerable academic interest; see, for a general view, A. N. Kaul, *The American Vision*. There are a plethora of specific studies, for instance, Laurence Foster, *Religion and Sexuality: Three American Communal Experiments of the Nineteenth Century*; Diane Barthel, *Amana: From Pietist Sect to American Community*; Raymond Muncy, *Sex and Marriage in Utopian Communities*; Arthur Bestor, *Backwoods Utopias*; John Chandler, "The Communitarian Quest for Perfection"; and William Bridges, "Family Patterns and Social Values in America 1825–1875." I am particularly indebted to Anne Dalke, "'Had I Known Her to be my Sister': Incest in Nineteenth-Century American Fiction" for making many provocative connections between the literary establishment of the nineteenth century, the reading public, and the frontier experiments.

3. Noyes himself came from a family known for their inability to effectively breed out; in fact, according to the family biography, *A Yankee Saint*, by Robert Allerton Parker, the Atkinson/Noyes family was "said to be so bashful that they could not pop the question to anybody but cousins. This became known as the 'Atkinson difficulty.'"

4. Noyes to David Harrison, January 15, 1837. In Dixon, *Spiritual Wives*, 2: 55–56.

5. Oneida Association, *Bible Communism*, p. 53.

6. *Ibid.*, pp. 27–28.

7. Noyes, *Essay on Scientific Propagation*, p. 17, 21.

8. The Transcendentalists were clearly in the avant garde in these matters, of which they knew little, even though they had an experimental family at Brook Farm near Boston. Recent study of this commune questions the Transcendental Club's high social concerns as Hawthorne's *Blithedale Romance* first intimated. The "brotherly co-operation" of the farm was more to ensure George Ripley's leisure than to revolutionize family dynamics. Although Brook Farm was primarily an economic experiment, the fact that the institution of marriage was never really discussed gives some indication of a dedication to matters other than to concepts of family life. When the Farm disbanded in the mid–1840s, it was not because of dissension from the nearby citizens of West Roxbury but from within the group.

9. For example, Henri Petter, *The Early American Novel*, believes that "near incest" was an American imitation of an English "fashion"; Alexander Cowie,

The Rise of the American Novel, contends that incest appears as a desire to edify the young; Edward Wagenknecht, *Calvalcade of the American Novel*, and Leslie Fiedler, *Love and Death in the American Novel*, see it as a reaction to Puritanism; Anne Dalke, " 'Had I Known Her to Be My Sister . . .' " interprets incest as an outgrowth of paternalism, and James Wilson, "Incest and American Romantic Fiction," sees it as the extension of romantic solipsism. I am oversimplifying, to be sure, but I do it to show the range of possible interpretations. I think it is clear that all apply in varying degrees.

10. Summers, *The Gothic Quest*, p. 35.

11. Poe may well have been aware of the nineteenth-century belief that Napoleon had incestuous relations with his sister. Poe's knowledge of the continental literary tradition of incest is documented by Anne Dalke, " 'Had I Known Her to Be My Sister. . . .' "

12. Hoffman, *Poe, Poe, Poe, Poe, Poe, Poe, Poe*, p. 243.

13. Because of the confusion over editions, I will cite the book and letter numbers as well as the page.

14. Here, as with other comments on nineteenth-century American literature, I an indebted to the scholarship of Anne Dalke, " 'Had I Known Her to Be My Sister. . . .' " In Chapter 2 she details the reading audience of popular fiction.

15. In his chapter "Incest and American Fiction" in *The Heroic Romantic Ideal*, James D. Wilson has pointed out, "America more closely resembled Germany, which was also at the time a loose collection of city-states lacking the literary, political, or religious cohesiveness characteristic of its more prosperous neighbors. Like their American counterparts, German artists too gave incest harsh treatment: Tieck's *Der blonde Eckbert*, Schiller's *Die Braut von Messina*, and Grillparzer's *Die Abnfrau* all portrayed incest as an unconscious act—as in *Oedipus*—the recognition of which invariably led to dementia and death (p. 139).

16. Patee, "Introduction," *Wieland, or the Transformation*, p. xi. Scholars are at odds as to whether incest actually occurs: Bredahl, "Transformation in *Wieland*"; Fiedler, *Love and Death*; Ziff, "A Reading of *Wieland*; and Wilson, "Incest and American Romantic Fiction, say yes; but Manley, "The Importance of Point of View in Brockden Brown's *Wieland*," says that "obviously" no sexual assault occurs; it is simple homicide.

17. Harry Warfel, "Charles Brockden Brown's German Sources," makes a convincing case that Brown's hesitancy is partly uneasiness with his German sources, most specifically Cajetan Tschink's *Geisterserer*.

18. Renata Wasserman, "The Self, the Mirror, the Other: *The Fall of the House of Usher*," details the specific significance of the "tarn" in terms of the exchange theory of Lévi-Strauss. She argues that just as the tarn will allow no movement of water and therefore turns stagnant, so will human families if they do not overflow into others.

19. Fiedler, *Love and Death*, pp. 415–416. It should be noted that Fiedler is not alone in believing Poe was independent of American cultural tradi-

tion. From Vernon Parrington, *Main Currents in American Thought*, onward, Poe has been viewed as a "private" author who was thus not in the main "current of American thought," but this view is by no means unanimous and, in fact, no longer seems as standard as it once did. In his implicit condemnation of incest Poe is certainly a mainstream American romanticist.

20. Here is D. H. Lawrence, *Selected Literary Criticism*, on Poe's incestuous, vampiric lovers: ". . . the secondary law of all organic life is that each organism only lives through contact with other matter, assimilation, and contact with other life, which means assimilation of new vibrations, non-material. Each individual organism is vivified by intimate contact with fellow organisms . . . . In spiritual love, the contact is purely nervous. The nerves in the lovers are set vibrating in unison like two instruments. The pitch can rise higher and higher. But carry this too far, and the nerves begin to break, to bleed, as it were, and a form of death sets in. . . . It is easy to see why each man kills the things he loves. To *know* a living thing is to kill it. You have to kill a thing to know it satisfactorily. For this reason, the desirous consciousness, the SPIRIT, is a vampire" (pp. 331–335). This view is also reiterated by Allen Tate, "Our Cousin, Mr. Poe."

21. *Alice Doane's Appeal* was published anonymously in 1835 and was subsequently ignored by Hawthorne. He never republished it, or even mentioned it again. Why? Philip Young, *Hawthorne's Secret*, claims this neglect was purposeful, for in this short story Hawthorne came to grips with his own guilt, a guilt that also figures in his stories of the same time—*My Kinsman, Major Molineux, Young Goodman Brown*, and *Roger Malvin's Burial*. Although these stories do not overtly deal with incest, they are closely related in theme, spirit, and especially tone. For more on this argument, see the subsequent note.

22. See Fiedler, *Love and Death*, pp. 229–230; Crews, *The Sins of the Fathers*, p. 37; and Loggins, *The Hawthornes*, p. 279. Recently Erlich, *Family Themes and Hawthorne's Fiction: The Tenacious Web*, and Young, *Hawthorne's Secret: An Un-Told Tale*, have breathed new life into the biographical interpretation by contending that incest not only figured in relations between the Mannings (Margaret, Anstice, and their brother Nicholas) who were maternal ancestors, but also occurred between the author and his sister. Professor Young does not call it "incest"—his unfortunate phrase is "something happened"—but the implication is clear. These two books are especially important, for it is one thing to make intuitive guesses, as do Fiedler and Crews, but it is quite another to provide the connections between biographical fact and literary text.

23. The American sentimental novel has not been as well studied as its English counterpart, but Frank Mott, *Golden Multitudes*, and Herbert Ross Brown, *The Sentimental Novel in America, 1789–1860*, as well as chapter 5 of Dalke, " 'Had I Known . . .' " survey the genre, and the latter concentrates specifically on those novels overtly detailing incestuous configurations.

24. Critics have been kinder to *Pierre* than have readers. From construc-

tive S. Foster Damon, "Pierre the Ambiguous," to deconstructive Eric Sundquist, *Home as Found*, scholars have been able to overlook desultory prose and tedious plotting en route to profundities be they philosophical or psychological. *Pierre* even has the mark of ultimate authority as canonical text: Ralph Willell, ed., *The Merrill Studies in "Pierre"*—a collection of critical essays.

25. There have been a number of incest-centered interpretations of *Pierre* from George Homans, "The Dark Angel," in the 1930s to the affective criticism of the present like Brook Thomas, "The Writer's Procreative Urge in *Pierre*." Recently there has been renewed interest in comparing the use of the Cenci motif in American romanticism: R.L. Carothers, "Melville's 'Cenci,'" and Diane Hoeveler, "La Cenci: The Incest Motif in Hawthorne and Melville."

CONCLUSION

1. An example of how circumspect early twentieth-century authors had become in fictionalizing incest can be seen in Edith Wharton's hesitancy to complete "Beatrice Palmato." As well as we can deduce from her outline and the fragment in the Beineke Library, Wharton initially projected a novel detailing father-daughter incest over two generations. In the first generation Beatrice has such a lasting adolescent liaison with her father that her mother is driven from home; in the second generation Beatrice's daughter starts the same relationship with her father (Beatrice's husband), ending in Beatrice's suicide. In the outline these relationships become clear only after her death as the reader comes to realize exactly what kind of family dynamics could effect such an outcome. But in the fragment that accompanies the outline there is a graphic and sympathetic description of Beatrice's sexual activity with the father. We can only conjecture, as does R. W. B. Lewis, *Edith Wharton* (p. 544), that since the incest is overt, and since no magazine would have ever published it, Wharton may have been experimenting to see if such scenes could be written. That she ultimately put the project aside may tell us much about the standards of decorum in fiction writing and publishing at that time.

2. In America no such literary continuity took place. One has to wait until the 1930s, when Carl Laemmle and his Universal Studios translated these stories onto celluloid. With sequels made throughout the 1940s, Universal delivered these tales to an eager American audience until they became central parts of our myth tradition, staples of American, and now of international popular culture.

3. Ruth Prigozy, in "From Griffith's Girls to Daddy's Girl: The Masks of Innocence in *Tender Is the Night*," traces incestuous father/daughter relationships in the popular culture of the '20s and '30s, concluding that they form a central strain of mid-century culture.

4. One could even argue, as Leslie Fiedler has recently done in "The Profanation of the Child," that this work so defied the sacred topos of the sentimental tradition that modern family life will never quite be the same again. Not only has *Lolita* achieved such importance that there is a reference guide to its criticism done by Samuel Schuman, but Alfred Appel, Jr. has edited *The Annotated Lolita*. To the best of my knowledge this is the only annotated modern novel by any author in the last decade and, more important still, the only annotated novel done while the author was still living.

5. See Appel, *The Annotated Lolita*, pp. 330–333, and Schuman, *Vladimir Nabokov: A Reference Guide*, under "Poe" for the amount of critical attention this connection has received.

6. Nabokov also includes seemingly offhand non sequiturs such as a reference to a weather station on "Pierre Point in Melville Sound" (p. 35), which from the point of view of American literature are not happenstances.

7. To make the doubling more perplexing it might be mentioned that Humbert's double, Quilty, is often accompanied by Vivian Darkbloom—an anagram of Vladimir Nabokov.

8. Patricia Meyer Spacks, "A Chronicle of Women," gives a summary of recent developments and Katherine Dalsimer, *Female Adolescence*, provides a psychoanalysis. For a more historical treatment, see W. Tasker Witham, *The Adolescent in the American Novel*, especially the Appendix, and Barbara A. White, *Growing Up Female*.

9. For an interesting interpretation of the botanical metaphor, see Diana Butler, "*Lolita* Lepidoptera."

10. Alfred Appel, *Nabokov's Dark Cinema*, outlines the *Lolita* scenario, pp. 232–236.

11. "Kubrick" (as interviewed by Gene Philips), p. 32.

12. In 1966 Russell Trainer wrote *The Lolita Complex*, in which he attempted to trace Lolitas in history. What he puts forward is a series of fictional short pieces passed off as case histories interlarded with petty moralizing. That he is unable to substantiate this stereotype in culture is almost as important as the fact that he believes there is a readership who would like to believe the stereotype exists.

Select Bibliography

Adams, Morton S. "Incest: Genetic Considerations." *American Journal of Diseases of Children* 132 (1978), 132:124.

Adams, Morton S., and James V. Neel. "Children of Incest." *Pediatrics* (1967), 18:55–62.

Aggeler, Geoffrey. "Incest and the Artist: Anthony Burgess's *M/F* as Summation." *Modern Fiction Studies* (1972–73), 18:529–543.

Albert, Marvin H. *The Divorce: A Re-Examination.* New York: Simon & Schuster, 1969.

Aldridge, Alfred Owen. "The Meaning of Incest from Hutcheson to Gibbon." *Ethics* (1951), 61:309–313.

Allen, Charlotte V. *Daddy's Girl.* New York: Simon & Schuster, 1980.

Allott, Miriam, ed. *Essays on Shelley.* Totowa, N.J.: Barnes & Noble, 1982.

Anderson, Michael. *Family Structure in Nineteenth Century Lancashire.* Cambridge: Cambridge University Press, 1971.

Appel, Alfred, Jr. *Nabokov's Dark Cinema.* New York: Oxford University Press, 1974.

Appel, Alfred, Jr., ed. *The Annotated Lolita.* New York: McGraw-Hill, 1970.

Armstrong, Louise. "The Crime Nobody Talks About." *Woman's Day,* March 1, 1978, p. 52.

——— *Kiss Daddy Goodnight: A Speak-Out on Incest.* New York: Hawthorne Books, 1978.

Atkins, John. *Sex in Literature: The Erotic Impulse in Literature.* New York: Grove Press, 1970.

Bagley, Christopher. "Incest Behavior and Incest Taboo." *Social Problems* (1969), 16:505–519.

Bagley, John J. *Henry VIII and His Times.* New York: Arco, 1968.

Barnett, Louise R. "American Novelists and the Portrait of Beatrice Cenci." *New England Quarterly* (1980), 53:168–183.

Barthel, Diane L. *Amana: From Pietist Sect to American Community.* Lincoln: University of Nebraska Press, 1984.

Bashi, Joseph. "Effects of Inbreeding on Cognitive Performance." *Nature* (1977), 266:440–442.

Bass, Ellen, and Louise Thornton, eds. *I Never Told Anyone: Writings by Women Suriviors.* New York: Harper & Row, 1983.

Bateson, Fredrick Wilse. *Wordsworth: A Re-interpretation.* 2nd ed. London: Longmans, Green, 1956.

Bateson, Patrick. "Preferences for Cousins in Japanese Quail." *Nature* (1982), 295:236–237.

Battestin, Martin C. "Henry Fielding, Sarah Fielding, and 'dreadful Sin of Incest.'" *Novel: A Forum on Fiction* (1979), 13:6–18.

Bentley, C. F. "The Monster in the Bedroom: Sexual Symbolism in Bram Stoker's *Dracula*." *Literature and Psychology* (1972), 22:27-34.

Bestor, Arthur. *Backwoods Utopias: The Sectarian Origins and the Owenite Phase of Communitarian Socialism in America, 1663–1829.* Philadelphia: University of Pennsylvania Press, 1970.

Bettelheim, Bruno. *The Uses of Enchantment: The Meaning and Importance of Fairy Tales.* 1975; reprint. New York: Vintage, 1977.

Bierman, Joseph S. "*Dracula*: Prolonged Childhood Illness, and the Oval Triad." *American Imago* (1972), 29:186–198.

Bischof, Norbert. "The Biological Foundations of the Incest Taboo." *Social Science Information* (1972), 11:7–36.

Bixler, Ray H. "Incest Avoidance as a Function of Environment and Heredity." *Current Anthropology* (1981), 22:639–654.

―――― "The Incest Controversy." *Psychology Reports* (1981), 49:267-283.

Blackstone, William. *Blackstone's Commentaries on the Law.* 1892; reprint. Bernard C. Gavit, ed. Washington, D.C.: Washington Law Book Co., 1941.

Block, Kenneth. *Human Nature and History: A Response to Sociobiology.* New York: Columbia University Press, 1980.

Bloom, Harold. *The Anxiety of Influence: A Theory of Poetry.* New York: Oxford University Press, 1973.

―――― "War Within Walls." *New York Times Book Review.* May 27, 1984, p. 3.

Bolen, C. A. *The Mysterious Monk, or, The Wizard's Tower.* 3 vols. London: Newman, 1826.

Bolingbroke, Henry Saint-John, Lord. *Collected Works.* 8 vols. London: Johnson, 1809.

Bonventre, Peter, and Marsha Zabarsky. " 'I Married My Sister.' " *Newsweek,* July 2, 1979, p. 36.

Brady, Katherine. *Father's Days: A True Story Of Incest.* New York: Seaview Books, 1979.

Bratt, Carolyn S. "Incest Statutes and the Fundamental Right of Marriage: Is Oedipus Free to Marry?" *Family Law Quarterly* (1984), 18:257–309.

Bredahl, Carl A. Jr. "Transformation in *Wieland.*" *Early American Literature* (1977) 12:177–192.

Brewster, Paul G. *The Incest Theme in Folksong.* FF Communications, vol. 80. Helsinki: Souomalainen Tiedeakatemia, 1972.

Bridges, William E. "Family Patterns and Social Values in America 1825–1875." *American Quarterly* (1965), 17:3–11.

Brody, Jane E. "Personal Health: The Incidence of Incest Is Far More Common Than Most People Realize." *New York Times,* June 13, 1979, p. 8.

Brown, Charles Brockden. *Wieland or the Transformation: An American Tale.* Bicentennial Edition. Kent, Ohio: Kent State University Press, 1977.

Brown, Herbert Ross. *The Sentimental Novel in America 1789–1860.* 1940; reprint. Freeport, N.Y.: Books for Libraries, 1970.

Brown, Nathaniel. *Sexuality and Feminism in Shelley.* Cambridge: Harvard University Press, 1979.

Brown, William Hill. *The Power of Sympathy: or, The Triumph of Nature. Founded in Truth. In Two Volumes.* Boston: Isaiah Thomas, 1789.

Brozan, Nadine. "Helping to Heal the Scars Left by Incest." *New York Times,* January 9, 1984, p. 15.

Bullough, Vernon L. *Sex, Society and History.* New York: Science History Publications, 1976.

—— *Sexual Variance in Society and History.* New York: Wiley, 1976.

—— *Sex and Sanity.* New York: Garland, 1977.

Burnham, Jeffrey T. "Incest Avoidance and Social Evolution." *Mankind.* 10:93–98.

Butler, Diana. "*Lolita* Lepidoptera." *New World Writing* (1960), 16:58–84.

Butler, Sandra. *Conspiracy of Silence: The Trauma of Incest*. San Francisco: New Glide, 1978.

Byron, George Gordon, Lord. *Complete Works*. E. H. Coleridge and Rowland Prothero, eds. 13 vols. London: John Murray, 1922.

Carothers, R. L. "Melville's 'Cenci' ": A Portrait of *Pierre*. *Ball State University Forum* (1969), 10:53–59.

Carruthers, E. A. "The Net of Incest." *Yale Review* (1974), 63:211-227.

Carver, Mrs. *The Horrors of Oakdale Abbey*. London: William Lane, 1797.

Chandler, John W. "The Communitarian Quest for Perfection." In Stuart C. Henry, ed., *A Miscellany of American Christianity*. Durham, N.C.: Duke University Press, 1963.

Chateaubriand, François René de. *Atala and Rene*. Irving Putter, trans. Berkeley, Ca.: University of California Press, 1957.

"Children of Incest." *Newsweek*, October, 9, 1972, p. 58.

Cohen, Yehudi. "The Disappearance of the Incest Taboo." *Human Nature* (1978), 1:72–78.

Colao, Flora, and Tamar Hosansky. *Your Children Should Know: Teach Your Children Strategies that Will Keep Them Safe*. Indianapolis, Ind.: Bobbs-Merrill, 1983.

Coleman, Phyllis. "Incest: A Proper Definition Reveals the Need for a Different Legal Response." *Missouri Law Review* (1984), 49:251–288.

Cory, Donald W., and R. E. L. Masters. *Violations of Taboo: Incest in the Great Literature of the Past and Present*. New York: Julian Press, 1963.

Cowie, Alexander. *The Rise of the American Novel*. New York: American Book Co., 1951.

Crews, Frederick C. *The Sins of the Fathers: Hawthorne's Psychological Themes*. New York: Oxford University Press, 1966.

Crookenden, Ian. *Horible Revenge, or, The Monster of Italy*. London: Harrild, 1808.

Cullen, Stephen. *The Haunted Priory, or, The Fortunes of Rayo*. London: J. Bell, 1794.

—— *Ancient Records, or, The Abbey of Saint Oswythe*. 4 vols. London: William Lane, 1801.

Curties, T. J. Horsley. *St. Botolph's Priory, or, The Sable Mask*. 5 vols. London: Hughes, 1806.

———— *The Watch Tower, or The Sons of Ulthona*. 5 vols. Brentford, England: Norbury, 1804.

Dalke, Anne F. " 'Had I Known Her to be my Sister, My Love Would have been More Regular': Incest in Nineteenth-Century American Fiction." PhD dissertation, University of Pennsylvania, 1982.

Dalsimer, Katherine. *Female Adolescence: Psychoanalytic Reflections on Works of Literature*. New Haven: Yale University Press, 1986.

Damon, S. Foster. "Pierre the Ambiguous." *The Hound and Horn* (1929), 2:115–117.

Darnton, Robert. *The Great Cat Massacre and Other Episodes in French Cultural History*. New York: Basic Books, 1984.

Davenport, Selina. *An Angel's Form and a Devil's Heart*. 4 vols. London: Newman, 1818.

Day, William P. *In the Circles of Fear and Desire: A Study of Gothic Fantasy*. Chicago: University of Chicago Press, 1985.

DeMott, Benjamin. "The Pro-Incest Lobby." *Psychology Today*, March 1980, pp. 11–18.

Deutsch, Helene. *The Psychology of Women: A Psychoanalytic Interpretation*. 2 vols. New York: Grune & Stratton, 1944–45.

Diamond, Arthur S. *The Evolution of Law and Order*. London: Watts, 1951.

Dixon, William H. *Spiritual Wives*. 2 vols. London: Hurst and Blackett, 1868.

Durbach, Errol. "The *Geschwister-Komplex*: Romantic Attitudes to Brother-Sister Incest in Ibsen, Byron and Emily Brontë." *Mosaic: A Journal for the Comparative Study of Literature and Ideas* (1979), 12:61–73.

Durkheim, Emile. *Incest: The Nature and Origin of the Taboo*. 1897; reprint. New York: Lyle Stuart, 1963.

Ellis, Albert. *The Origin and Development of the Incest Taboo*. New York: Lyle Stuart, 1963.

Engels, Friedrich. *The Condition of the Working Class in England*. W. O. Henderson and W. H. Chaloner, trans. and ed. Stanford, Ca.: Stanford University Press, 1968.

Erlich, Gloria C. *Family Themes and Hawthorne's Fiction: The Tenacious Web*. New Brunswick, N.J.: Rutgers University Press, 1984.

—— "Hawthorne and the Mannings." In Joel Myerson, ed., *Studies in the American Renaissance*. Boston: Twayne, 1980.

Farberlow, Norman. *Taboo Topics*. Forward by Gordon Allport. New York: Atherton Press, 1963.

Faulkner, William. *The Sound and the Fury*. New York: Modern Library, 1929.

Fiedler, Leslie. "Giving the Devil His Due." *Journal of Popular Culture* (1979), 12:197–207.

—— *Love and Death in the American Novel*. New York: Stein and Day, 1966.

—— "The Profanation of the Child." *The New Leader*, June 23, 1958, pp. 26–29.

—— *What Was Literature?: Class, Culture and Mass Society*. New York: Simon & Schuster, 1982.

Finkelhor, David. "Sex Among Siblings: A Survey on Prevalence, Variety, and Effects." *Archives of Sexual Behavior* (1980), 9:171–194.

Finkelhor, David. *Sexually Victimized Children*. Riverside, N.J.: Free Press, 1979.

Fisher, Helen E. *The Sex Contract: The Evolution of Human Behavior*. New York: Morrow, 1982.

Flinker, Noam. "Cinyras, Myrrha, and Adonis: Father-Daughter Incest from Ovid to Milton." *Milton Studies* (1980), 14:59–74.

—— "Father-Daughter Incest in *Paradise Lost*." *Milton Quarterly* (1980), 14:116–122.

Forward, Susan, and Craig Buck. *Betrayal of Innocence: Incest and its Devastation*. Los Angeles: J. P. Teacher, 1978.

Foster, Laurence. *Religion and Sexuality: Three American Communal Experiments of the Nineteenth Century*. New York: Oxford University Press, 1981.

Foucault, Michel. *The History of Sexuality*, vol. 1. Trans. Robert Hurley. New York: Pantheon, 1978.

Fox, Joseph, Jr. *Santa Maria, or, The Mysterious Pregnancy*. 3 vols. London: G. Kearsley, 1797.

Fox, Robin. *Kinship and Marriage: An Anthropological Perspective*. 1967; reprint. New York: Cambridge University Press, 1983.

—— *The Red Lamp of Incest*. New York: Dutton, 1980.

Fox, Robin, and Lionel Tiger. *The Imperial Animal*. New York: Holt Rinehart and Winston, 1971.

Freud, Sigmund. *The Complete Letters of Sigmund Freud to Wilhelm Fliess 1887–1904*. Jeffrey Masson, trans. Cambridge: Harvard University Press, 1985.

―――― "On the Universal Tendency to Debasement in the Sphere of Love." *Complete Works*; vol. 11. James Strachey, ed. London: Horgarth Press, 1966.

―――― "The Taboo on Virginity." *Complete Works*; vol. 11. James Strachey, ed. London: Horgarth Press, 1966.

Fry, Carrol L. "Fictional Connections and Sexuality in *Dracula*." *Victorian Newsletter* (1972), 42:20–22.

Gallop, Jane. *The Daughter's Seduction: Feminism and Psychoanalysis*. Ithaca, N.Y.: Cornell University Press, 1982.

Gaskell, P. *The Manufacturing Population of England: Its Moral, Social and Physical Conditions*. 1833; reprint. New York: Arno Press, 1972.

Gaspey, Thomas. *The Mystery, or, Forty Years Ago*. 3 vols. London: Longman, Hurst, Rees, Orme and Brown, 1820.

Geiser, Robert L. *Hidden Victims: The Sexual Abuse of Children*. Boston: Beacon, 1979.

Gibbens, T. C. N. "Sibling and Parent-Child Incest Offenders: A Long-term Follow-up." *British Journal of Criminology* (1978), 18:40–52.

Goetz, William R. "Genealogy and Incest in *Wuthering Heights*." *Studies in the Novel*. (1982), 15:359–376.

Goldfarb, Russell M. "Charles Dickens: Orphans, Incest, and Repression." In Russell M. Goldfarb, ed., *Sexual Repression and Victorian Literature*. Lewisburg, Pa.: Bucknell University Press, 1970.

Goleman, Daniel. "Sexual Fantasies: What are Their Hidden Meanings?" *New York Times*, February, 28, 1984, p. 19.

―――― "Traumatic Beginnings: Most Children Seem Able to Recover." *New York Times*, March 13, 1984, p. 19.

Goodwin, Jean M., Doris Sahd, and Richard Rada. "Incest Hoax: False Accusations, False Denials." *Bulletin of the American Academy of Psychiatry and the Law*. (1978), 6:269–276.

Goody, Jack. "A Comparative Approach to Incest and Adultery." *British Journal of Sociology* (1956), 7:286–305.

Greenberg, Joel. "Incest: Out of Hiding." *Science News*, April 5, 1980, pp. 218–220.

Griffith, Ben J., Jr. "The Removal of Incest from *Laon and Cythna*." *Modern Language Notes* (1955), 70:181–182.

Hackett, Francis. *The Personal History of Henry the Eighth*. New York: Modern Library, 1945.

Hagen, William Henry, Jr. *The Metaphysical Implications of Incest in Romantic Literature*. Ph. D dissertation, University of South Carolina, 1974.

Hagopian, John V. "A Psychological Approach to Shelley's Poetry." *The American Imago* (1965), 12:25–45.

Hagstrum, Jean H. *Sex and Sensibility: Ideal and Erotic Love from Milton to Mozart*. Chicago: University of Chicago Press, 1980.

Hall, Constance, H. *Incest in Faulkner: A Metaphor for the Fall*. Ann Arbor, Mich.: UMI Research Press, 1985.

Hall, Jean. *The Transforming Image: A Study of Shelley's Major Poetry*. Urbana: University of Illinois Press, 1980.

Hamill, Pete. *Flesh and Blood*. New York: Random House, 1977.

Hammel, E. A., C. K. McDaniel, and K. W. Wachter. "Demographic Consequences of Incest Tabus: A Microsimulation Analysis." *Science*, September 7, 1979, pp. 972–977.

Hawthorne, Nathaniel. "Alice Doane's Appeal." In *The Snow-Image and Uncollected Tales*. The Centenary Edition, vol. 11. Columbus: Ohio State University Press, 1974.

Hayter, Alethea. Letter to *Times Literary Supplement*, August 9, 1974, p. 859.

Helme, Elizabeth. *The Farmer of Inglewood Forest*. 4 vols. London: William Lane, 1796.

Herman, Judith Lewis. *Father-Daughter Incest*. Cambridge: Harvard University Press, 1981.

Herman, Judith Lewis, and Lisa Hirschman. "Father-Daughter Incest." *Signs: Journal of Women in Culture and Society* (1977), 2:735–756.

Hirsch, Gordon D. "The Monster Was a Lady: On the Psychology of Mary Shelley's *Frankenstein*." *Hartford Studies in Literature* (1975), 7:116–153.

Hoeveler, Diane L. "La Cenci: The Incest Motif in Hawthorne and Melville." *American Transcendental Quarterly* (1977), 44:247–259.

Hoffman, Daniel. *Poe, Poe, Poe, Poe, Poe, Poe, Poe.* Garden City, N.Y.: Doubleday, 1972.

Hollingshead, John. *Ragged London in 1861.* 1861; reprint. New York: Johnson Reprint, 1973.

Homans, George C. "The Dark Angel: The Tragedy of Herman Melville." *New England Quarterly* (1932) 5:699–730.

Hopkins, Keith. "Brother-Sister Marriage in Roman Egypt." *Comparative Studies in Society and History* (1980), 22:303–354.

Horney, Karen. *Feminine Psychology.* Harold Kelman, ed. New York: Norton, 1967.

—— *The Neurotic Personality of Our Time.* New York: Norton, 1937.

—— *New Ways in Psychoanalysis.* New York: Norton, 1939.

Hutcheson, Francis. *An Inquiry Concerning Beauty and Virtue.* 1725; reprint. New York: Garland, 1971.

—— *A Short Introduction to Moral Philosophy.* Glasgow: Foulis, 1749.

"Incest and 'Vulnerable' Children." *Science News,* October 13, 1979, pp. 244–245.

Irwin, John T. *Doubling and Incest/ Repetition and Revenge: A Speculative Reading of Faulkner.* Baltimore: Johns Hopkins University Press, 1975.

Jamieson, Francis. *The House of Ravenspur.* 4 vols. London: Whittaker, 1822.

Janeway, Elizabeth. "Incest: A Rational Look at the Oldest Taboo." *Ms,* November 1981, p. 61.

Jones, Ernest. *On the Nightmare.* 1931; reprint. New York: Liveright Publication, 1971.

Jones, Fredrick L. "The Revision of *Laon and Cythna.*" *Journal of English and Germanic Philology* (1933), 33:368–371.

"Judge Sentences Brother and Sister for Marrying." *New York Times,* August 2, 1979, p. 12.

Justice, Blair and Rita. *The Broken Taboo: Sex in the Family.* New York: Human Sciences, 1979.

Kael, Pauline. "Review of *Blame It on Rio.*" *New Yorker,* February 20, 1984, p. 115.

Kamin, Leon J. "Inbreeding Depression and I. Q." *Psychological Bulletin* (1980), 87:469–478.

Kaplan, Morton. "Fantasy of Paternity and the *Doppelganger*: Mary Shelley's *Frankenstein.*" In *The Unspoken Motive: A Guide to Psy-*

choanalytic Criticism. Morton Kaplan and Robert Kloss, eds. New York: The Free Press, 1973.

Kay-Shuttleworth, James P. *The Moral and Physical Condition of the Working Classes*. 1832; reprint. Manchester, England: Morten, 1969.

Ketterer, David. *Frankenstein's Creation: The Book, the Monster, and Human Reality*. English Literary Studies Monograph Series, no. 16. Victoria, B. C.: University of Victoria Press, 1979.

Kiely, Robert. *The Romantic Novel in England*. Cambridge: Harvard University Press, 1972.

Kimball, Jean. "James Joyce and Otto Rank: The Incest Motif in *Ulysses*." *James Joyce Quarterly* (1976), 13:366–382.

Kirkwood, L. J. and M. E. Mihaila. "Incest and the Legal System: Inadequacies and Alternatives." *UC-Davis Law Review* (1979), 12:673–699.

Kluckhohn, Clyde. "Recurrent Themes in Myths and Mythmaking." In Henry A. Murray, ed., *Myths and Mythmaking*. New York: George Braziller, 1960.

Koslow, Sally. "Incest: The Ultimate Family Secret." *Glamour*, November 1981, pp. 154–160.

Krantz, Judith. *Princess Daisy*. New York: Bantam, 1980.

Kronhausen, Phyllis and Eberhard. *Erotic Fantasies: A Study of the Sexual Imagination*. New York: Grove Press, 1969.

Kubrick, Stanley. "Kubrick" (as interviewed by Gene Phillips). *Film Comment*. (1971–72), 8:30–35.

Laslett, Peter, ed. *Household and Family in Past Time*. Cambridge: Cambridge University Press, 1972.

Laslett, Peter. *Family Life and Illicit Love in Earlier Generations*. New York: Cambridge University Press, 1977.

Lathom, Francis. *Astonishment!!! A Romance of a Century Ago*. 2 vols. London: Longman and Rees, 1802.

—— *The Mysterious Freebooter, or, The Days of Queen Bess*. 4 vols. London: Lane, Newman, 1806.

Lawrence, D. H. *Selected Literary Criticism*. 1932; reprint. New York: Viking, 1966.

Lefebure, Molly. Letter to *Times Literary Supplement*, November 8, 1974, p. 1261.

—— *Samuel Taylor Coleridge: A Bondage of Opium*. New York: Stein and Day, 1974.

Legman, G. *Rationale of the Dirty Joke: An Analysis of Sexual Humor.* New York: Grove Press, 1971.

Levine, George Lewis. *The Realistic Imagination: English Fiction from "Frankenstein" to "Lady Chatterley".* Chicago: University of Chicago Press, 1981.

——— "Review of Recent *Frankenstein* Criticism." *Wordsworth Circle* (1975), 6:208–212.

Lévi-Strauss, Claude. *The Elementary Structures of Kinship.* Rev. ed. James Bell, John von Sturmer, and Rodney Needham, trans. Boston: Beacon Press, 1969.

Lewis, Matthew G. *The Monk: A Romance.* 3 vols. London: Bell, 1796.

Lewis, R. W. B. *Edith Wharton: A Biography.* New York: Harper & Row, 1975.

Lieberman, William S. *Edvard Munch: Catalog to his Prints.* New York: The Museum of Modern Art, 1957.

Lindzey, Gardner. "Some Remarks Concerning Incest, the Incest Taboo, and Psychoanalytic Theory." *American Psychologist* (1969), 22:1051–1059.

Livingstone, Frank B. "Genetics, Ecology and the Origins of Incest and Exogamy." *Current Anthropology* (1969), 10:45–49.

Locke, John. "Names of Mixed Modes and Relations." In *Essay Concerning Human Understanding.* John Yolton, ed. London: Dent, 1965.

Loggins, Vernon. *The Hawthornes: The Story of Seven Generations of an American Family.* New York: Columbia University Press, 1951.

Lumsden, Charles J., and Edward O. Wilson, *Promethean Fire: Reflections on the Origin of Mind.* Cambridge: Harvard University Press, 1983.

Mackenzie, Anna. *The Irish Guardian, or, Errors of Eccentricity.* 3 vols. London: Longman, Hurst, Rees, and Orme, 1809.

Maisch, Herbert. *Incest.* New York: Stein and Day, 1972.

Malcolm, Janet. *In the Freud Archives.* New York: Knopf, 1984.

Manchester, Anthony H. "The Law of Incest in England and Wales." *Child Abuse and Neglect* (1979), 3:679–682.

Mandeville, Bernard. *The Fable of the Bees.* 2. vols. F. B. Kaye, ed. New York: Oxford University Press, 1924.

——— *A Search into the Nature of Society.* London: Edmund Parker, 1723.

Manley, William. "The Importance of Point of View in Brockden Brown's *Wieland*." *American Literature* (1963), 34:311–321.

Manning, Sylvia. "Incest and the Structure of *Henry Esmond*." *Nineteenth-Century Fiction* (1979), 34:194–213.

Marchand, Leslie A. *Byron: A Biography*. 3 vols. New York: Knopf, 1957.

Marcus, Steven. *The Other Victorians: A Study of Sexuality and Pornography in Mid-Nineteenth Century England*. New York: Basic Books, 1964.

Marks, Judi. "Incest Victims Speak Out." *Teen*, February 1980, p. 26.

Masson, Jeffrey Moussaieff. *The Assault on Truth: Freud's Suppression of the Seduction Theory*. New York: Farrar, Strauss and Giroux, 1984.

Masters, Robert E. L. *Patterns of Incest: A Psycho-Social Study of Incest, Based on Clinical and Historic Data*. New York: Julian Press, 1963.

Masters, William H., and Virginia E. Johnson. "Incest: The Ultimate Sexual Taboo." *Redbook Magazine*, April 1976, pp. 54–58.

Maturin, Charles R. *Melmoth the Wanderer: A Tale*. 4 vols. London: Hurst & Robinson, 1820.

Maugham, W. Somerset. "The Book Bag." In Donald Cory and R. E. L. Masters, eds., *Violation of Taboo: Incest in the Great Literature of the Past and Present*. New York: Julian Press, 1963.

Mayhew, Henry. *London Labour and the London Poor*. 4 vols. 1844; reprint. New York: Dover, 1968.

Mayleas, Davidyne. *Rewedded Bliss: Love, Alimony, Incest, Ex-Spouses and Other Domestic Blessings*. New York: Basic Books, 1977.

Maynard, John. *Charlotte Brontë and Sexuality*. New York: Cambridge University Press, 1984.

McIntyre, Kevin. "Role of Mothers in Father-Daughter Incest: A Feminist Analysis." *Social Work* (1981), 26:462–466.

Meeke, Mary. *Midnight Weddings*. 3 vols. London: William Lane, 1802.

Meiselman, Karin C. *Incest: A Psychological Study of Causes and Effects with Treatment Recommendations*. San Francisco: Jossey-Bass, 1978.

Melchiori, Barbara. "Incest in Shakespeare's Late Plays." *English Miscellany*. (1960), 11:59–74.

Melville, Herman. *Pierre, or the Ambiguities*. Introduction by Laurance Thompson. New York: New American Library, 1964.

Messer, Alfred A. "The 'Phaedra Complex.' " *Archives of General Psychiatry* (1969), 21:213–218.

Michaelis, Johann David. *Commentaries on the Laws of Moses, 1777.* Alexander Smith, trans. 4 vols. London: Rivington, 1814.

Miles, Henry. *Forbidden Fruit: A Study of the Incest Theme in Erotic Literature.* London: Luxor Press, 1973.

Mitchell, Giles. "Incest, Demonism, and Death in *Wuthering Heights.*" *Literature and Psychology* (1973), 23:27–36.

Modleski, Tania. *Loving with a Vengeance: Mass-Produced Fantasies for Women.* New York: Methuen, 1984.

Moore, Thomas V. "Percy Bysshe Shelley: An Introduction to the Study of Character." *Psychological Monographs* (1922), 31:24–29.

Moorman, Mary. Letters to *Times Literary Supplement*, October 4, 1974, p. 1078 and November 15, 1974, p.1288.

Mordell, Albert. *The Erotic Motive in Literature.* New York: Boni and Liveright, 1919.

Mott, Frank L. *Golden Multitudes: The Story of Best Sellers in the United States.* 1947; reprint. New York: Bowker, 1966.

Muldoon, Linda, ed. *Incest: Confronting the Silent Crime.* Arlington, Va.: ERIC Document Reproduction Service, ED 178 826, 1979.

Mullins, Joe, and Ken Potter. "Our Only Crime Was to Fall in Love." *National Enquirer*, July 10, 1979, p. 26.

Muncy, Raymond L. *Sex and Marriage in Utopian Communities; Nineteenth-Century America.* Bloomington: Indiana University Press, 1975.

Murray, Eugene B. " 'Elective Affinity' in *The Revolt of Islam.*" *Journal of English and Germanic Philology* (1968), 67:570–585.

Murray, R. D. "The Evolution and Functional Significance of Incest Avoidance." *Journal of Human Evolution* (March, 1980):173–178.

Nabokov, Vladimir. *Lolita.* New York: G. P. Putnam's Sons, 1955.

Nakashima, Ida I., and Gloria E. Zakus. "Incest: Review and Clinical Experience." *Pediatrics* (1977), 60:696–701.

Noyes, John Humphrey. *Essay on Scientific Propagation, with an Appendix Concerning a Health Report of the Oneida Community*, by Theodore R. Noyes, M.D. 1875; reprint. New York: AMS, 1974.

Oneida Association. *Bible Communism: A Compilation of the Annual Reports and Other Publications of the Oneida Association and Its Branches.* Brooklyn, N.Y.: Office of *The Circular*, 1853.

Otto, Rudolf. *The Idea of the Holy: An Inquiry into the Non-Rational Factor in the Idea of the Divine and its Relation to the Rational.* 1945; reprint. New York: Oxford University Press, 1980.

ient, Steven. *When Fathers Ruled: Family Life in Reformation Europe*. Cambridge: Harvard University Press, 1984.

Parker, Robert A. *A Yankee Saint: John Humphrey Noyes and the Oneida Community*. Philadelphia: Porcupine Press, 1972.

Parrington, Vernon. *Main Currents in American Thought: Romantic Revolution in America 1800–1860*. vol. 2. New York: Harcourt Brace, 1958.

Parsons, Eliza. *Castle of Wolfenback. A German Story*. 2 vols. London: William Lane, 1793.

Parsons, Talcott. "The Incest Taboo in Relation to Social Structure and the Socialization of the Child." *British Journal of Sociology*. (1954), 5:101–105.

Patee, Fred Lewis. "Introduction" to Charles Brockden Brown, *Wieland or The Transformantion Together with Memoirs of Carwin the Biloquist: A Fragment*. New York: Harcourt Brace, 1926.

Patrick, Mrs. *More Ghosts!* 3 vols. London: William Lane, 1798.

Paulson, Morris J. "Incest and Sexual Molestation: Clinical and Legal Issues." *Journal of Clinical Child Psychology* (1978), 7:177–180.

Petter, Henri. *The Early American Novel*. Columbus: Ohio State University Press, 1971.

Poe, Edgar Allen. "The Spectacles." In Thomas O. Mabbott, ed .*Tales and Sketches 1843–1849. Collected Works*. vol. 3. Cambridge: Harvard University Press, 1978.

Pointon Marcia. *Milton and English Art*. Toronto: University of Toronto Press, 1970.

Polidori, John W. *Ernestus Berchtold, or, The Modern Prometheus*. London: Longman, Hurst, Rees, Orme, and Brown, 1819.

Praz, Mario. *The Romantic Agony*. 1933; reprint. New York: Oxford University Press, 1970.

Press, Aric, Holly Morris, and Richard Sandza. "An Epidemic of Incest." *Newsweek*, November 30, 1981, p. 68.

Prigozy, Ruth. "From Griffith's Girls to Daddy's Girl: The Masks of Innocence in *Tender Is the Night*." *Twentieth Century Literature* (1980), 26:189–221.

Radcliffe, Ann. *The Italian, or, The Confessional of the Black Penitents*. 3 vols. London: Cadell and Davies, 1797.

—— *The Romance of the Forest*. 2 vols. London: Hookham and Carpenter, 1791.

Ramey, James W. "Dealing with the Last Taboo." *SIECUS REPORT* (1979), 7:1.

Rank, Otto. *Das Inzest-Motiv in Dichtung und Sage.* Leipzig: Deuticke, 1912.

Rapf, Joanna E. "The Byronic Heroine: Incest and the Creative Process." *Studies in English Literature* (1981), 21:637–645.

Reiman, Donald H. Letters to *Times Literary Supplement.* September 13, 1974, p. 980; November 1, 1974, p. 1231 and December 27, 1974, p. 1464.

Renvoize, Jean. *Incest: A Family Pattern.* London: Routledge & Kegan Paul, 1982.

Richardson, Maurice. "The Psychoanalysis of Ghost Stories." *The Twentieth Century* (1959), 166:419–431.

Rimmer, Robert H. *The X-Rated Videotape Guide.* New York: Arlington House, 1984.

Robinson, Mary. *Vancenza, or, The Dangers of Credulity.* 2 vols. London: Printed for the Authoress, 1792.

Rocke, Regina Maria. *The Castle Chapel: A Romantic Tale.* 3 vols. London: Newman, 1825.

———— *Nocturnal Visit.* 4 vols. London: William Lane, 1800.

Rosenfeld, Alvin A. "Incidence of a History of Incest Among 18 Female Psychiatric Patients." *American Journal of Psychiatry* (1979), 136:791–795.

Roth, Phyllis R. "Suddenly Sexual Women in Bram Stoker's *Dracula.*" *Literature and Psychology* (1977), 27:113–121.

Royce, David, and Anthony A. Watts. "The Crime of Incest." *Northern Kentucky Law Review* (1978), 5:191–206.

Reuben, David R. *Everything You Always Wanted to Know About Sex But Were Afraid to Ask.* New York: Bantam, 1971.

Rush, Florence. *The Best Kept Secret: Sexual Abuse of Children.* New York: McGraw Hill, 1980.

Sandell, Sandra D. "'A Very Poetic Circumstance': Incest and the English Literary Imagination, 1700–1830." Ph.D. dissertation, University of Minnesota, 1981.

Sanford, Linda T. *The Silent Children.* New York: Doubleday, 1980.

Santiago, Luciano P. R. *The Children of Oedipus: Brother-Sister Incest in Psychiatry, Literature, and Mythology.* Roslyn Heights, N.Y.: Libra, 1973.

Sawyer, Susan G. "Lifting the Veil on the Last Taboo." *Family Health*, June 1980, p. 43.

Schore, George R. " 'Incest? Tush!' Jacobean Incest Tragedy and Jacobean England." Ph.D. dissertation, SUNY-Stony Brook, 1983.

Schuman, Samuel. *Vladimir Nabokov: A Reference Guide*. Boston: Hall, 1979.

See, F. G. "Kinship of Metaphor—Incest and Language in Melville's *Pierre*." *Structuralist Review* (1978), 1:55–81.

Seemanova, Eve. "A Study of Children of Incestuous Matings." *Human Heredity* (1971), 21:108–128.

Seligman, Brenda A. "The Incest Taboo as a Social Regulation." *The Sociological Review* (1935), 27:75–93.

———— "The Problem of Incest and Exogamy: A Restatement." *American Anthropologist* (1950), 52:305–316.

Sergeant, Philip W. *The Life of Anne Boleyn*. New York: Appleton, 1924.

Shainess, Natalie. *Sweet Suffering: Woman as Victim*. Indianapolis, Ind.: Bobbs-Merrill, 1984.

Shelley, Mary. *Frankenstein, or, The Modern Prometheus*. 1818; reprint. Afterword by Harold Bloom. New York: New American Library, 1965.

———— *Frankenstein, or, The Modern Prometheus*. 1831; reprint. James Rieger, ed. Indianapolis, Ind.: Bobbs-Merrill, 1974.

———— *Frankenstein, or, The Modern Prometheus*. 1831; reprint. M. K. Joseph, ed. London: Oxford University Press, 1969.

Shelley, Percy Bysshe. *Letters of Percy Bysshe Shelley*. 2 vols. Fredrick Jones, ed. Oxford: Clarendon Press, 1964.

Shepher, Joseph. *Incest: A Biosocial View*. New York: Academic Press, 1983.

Shorter, Edward. *The Making of the Modern Family*. New York: Basic Books, 1975.

Simari, C. Georgia, and David Baskin. *Incest: No Longer a Family Affair*. Arlington, Va.: ERIC Document Reproduction Service, ED 182 616, 1979.

Simenon, George. *Intimate Memoirs: Including Marie-Jo's Book*. New York: Harcourt Brace, 1984.

Siskind, Victor. "Bias in Estimating the Frequency of Incest." *Annals of Human Genetics* (1975), 38:355–359.

Skarda, Patricia L., and Nora Crow Jaffe. *The Evil Image: Two Centuries of Gothic Short Fiction and Poetry.* New York: New American Library, 1981.

Sklar, Ronald B. "The Criminal Law and the Incest Offender: A Case for Decriminalization." *Bulletin of the American Academy of Psychiatry and the Law* (1979), 7:69–77.

Slater, Miriam. "Ecological Factors in the Origins of Incest." *American Anthropologist* (1959), 61:1042–1059.

Slaughter, Carolyn, *Relations.* New York: Mason/Charter, 1976.

Sleath, Eleanor. *The Orphan of the Rhine.* 4 vols. London: Lane, 1798.

Slovenko, Ralph. "Incest." *SIECUS REPORT* (1979), 7:4–5.

Smith, David. "Incest Patterns in Two Victorian Novels." *Literature and Psychology* (1965), 15:135–162.

Smith, Paul E. "The Incest Motif and the Question of Decadence of English Drama, 1603–1632." Ph.D. dissertation, University of Pittsburgh, 1980.

Smith, Susan Harris. "*Frankenstein*: Mary Shelley's Psychic Divisiveness." *Women and Literature* (1977), 5:42–53.

Solomon, Eric. "The Incest Theme in *Wuthering Heights*." *Nineteenth-Century Fiction* (1959), 14:80–83.

Spacks, Patricia Meyer. "A Chronicle of Women." *Hudson Review* (1972), 25:157–170.

Spencer, Joyce. "Father-Daughter Incest: A Clinical View from the Corrections Field." *Child Welfare* (1978), 57:581–590.

Spiers, John. "The Scottish Ballads." *Scrutiny* (1935), 4:35–44.

Spilka, Mark. *Dickens and Kafka: A Mutual Interpretation.* Bloomington: Indiana University Press, 1963.

Stein, Robert. *Incest and Human Love: The Betrayal of the Soul in Psychotherapy.* Baltimore, Md.: Penguin Books, 1974.

Stoker, Bram. *Dracula.* 1897; reprint. New York: Dell, 1973.

Stone, Lawrence. *The Family, Sex, and Marriage in England, 1500–1800.* New York: Harper & Row, 1979.

Stowe, Harriet Beecher. *Lady Byron Vindicated: A History of the Byron Controversy.* Boston: Fields, Osgood, 1870.

Strong, Brian. "Sex and Incest in the Nineteenth Century Family." *Journal of Marriage and the Family* (1973), 35:457–466.

———— "Toward a History of the Experimental Family: Sex and Incest in the Nineteenth-Century Family." *Journal of Marriage and the Family* (1973), 35:457–466.

Sulzberger, A. O., Jr. "Conferees Heard a Controversial View of Incest." *New York Times*, December 3, 1979, p. D9.

Summers, Montague. *The Gothic Quest: A History of the Gothic Novel.* London: Fortune, 1938.

Sundquist, Eric J. *Home as Found: Authority and Genealogy in Nineteenth-Century America.* Baltimore, Md.: Johns Hopkins University Press, 1979.

———— "Incest and Imitation in Cooper's *Home as Found.*" *Nineteenth-Century Fiction* (1977), 32:261–284.

Sykes, Mrs. S. *Margiana, or Widdrington Tower.* 5 vols. London: Lane Newman, 1808.

Tate, Allen. "Our Cousin, Mr. Poe." In Allen Tate, ed., *The Forlorn Demon: Didactic and Critical Essays.* Chicago: Regnery, 1953.

Taylor, Mark. *Shakespeare's Darker Purpose: A Question of Incest.* New York: AMS Press, 1982.

Thomas, Brook. "The Writer's Procreative Urge in *Pierre*: Fictional Freedom or Convoluted Incest?" *Studies in the Novel* (1979), 11:416–430.

Thorslev, Peter. "Incest as Romantic Symbol." *Comparative Literature Studies* (1965), 2:41–58.

Tomlins, Elizabeth S. *Rosalind de Tracy.* 3 vols. London: Dilly, 1798.

Tompkins, Joyce M. S. *The Popular Novel in England, 1770–1800.* London: Constable & Co., 1932.

Tormes, Yvonne M. *Child Victims of Incest.* Denver, Co.: American Humane Society, 1968.

"Touch of Incest." *Time*, July 2, 1979, p. 76.

Tracy, Ann B. *The Gothic Novel 1790–1830.* Lexington: University of Kentucky Press, 1981.

Trainer, Russell. *The Lolita Complex.* New York: Citadel Press, 1966.

Traver, Harold H. "Offender Reaction, Professional Opinion, and Sentencing." *Criminology* (1978), 16:403–419.

Tunley, Roul. "Incest: Facing the Ultimate Taboo." *Reader's Digest*, January 1981, pp. 137–140.

Twitchell, James B. " 'Desire with Loathing Strangely Mix'd': The Dreamwork of *Christabel.*" *Psychoanalytic Review* (1974), 61:33–44.

———— *Dreadful Pleasures: An Anatomy of Modern Horror.* New York: Oxford University Press, 1985.

———— "The Horror of *Frankenstein.*" *Georgia Review* (1981) 37:41–85.

———— "The Incest Theme and the Authenticity of the Percy Version of 'Edward.'" *Western Folklore* (1975), 34:32–35.

———— *The Living Dead: A Study of the Vampire in Romantic Literature.* Durham, N. C.: Duke University Press, 1980.

———— "A Psychoanalysis of the Vampire Myth." *American Imago* (1981), 37: 83–92.

Tylor, E. B. "On the Method of Investigating the Development of Institutions; Applied to Laws of Marriage and Descent." *Journal of the Royal Anthropological Institute* (1888), 18:245–269.

Van den Berghe, Pierre L. "Incest and Exogamy: A Sociobiological Reconsideration." *Ethology and Sociobiology* (April 1980):151–162.

Van den Berghe, Pierre L., and Gene M. Mesher. "Royal Incest and Inclusive Fitness." *American Ethnologist* (1980), 7:300–317.

Wachter, Oralee. *No More Secrets For Me.* Boston: Little Brown, 1983.

Wagenknecht, Edward. *Cavalacade of the American Novel.* New York: Holt, Rinehart, and Winston, 1952.

Wagner, Roy. "Incest and Identity: A Critique and Theory on the Subject of Exogamy and Incest Prohibition." *Man* (1972), 7:601–613.

Walker, George. *Don Raphael.* 3 vols. London: Walker and Hurst, 1803.

Walpole, Horace. *The Castle of Otranto.* London: Lownds, 1765.

Ward, Elizabeth. *Father-Daughter Rape.* Walnut Creek, Ca.: Evergreen Press, 1985.

Warfel, Harry. "Charles Brockden Brown's German Sources." *Modern Language Quarterly.* (1940) 1:357–365.

Wasserman, Renata R. "The Self, the Mirror, the Other: *The Fall of the House of Usher.*" *Poe Studies* (1977), 10:33–35.

Webb, Beatrice. *My Apprenticeship.* London: Longman, Green, 1926.

Weich, M. J. "The Terms 'Mother' and 'Father' as a Defense Against Incest." *Journal of the American Psychoanalytic Association* (1968), 16:783–791.

Weinberg, Samuel K. *Incest Behavior.* Secaucus, N.J.: Citadel Press, 1955.

Weissbury, Michael P. *Dangerous Secrets: Mal-Adaptive Responses to Stress.* New York: Norton, 1983.

Werman, David S. "On the Occurrence of Incest Fantasies." *Psychoanalytic Quarterly* (1977), 46:245–255.

Westermarck, Edward. *The History of Human Marriage.* New York: Macmillan, 1891.

Whigham, Frank. "Sexual and Social Mobility in *The Dutchess of Malfi. PMLA* (1985), 100:167–186.

White, Barbara A. *Growing Up Female: Adolescent Girlhood in American Fiction.* Westport, Ct.: Greenwood Press, 1985.

White, L. A. "The Definition and Prohibition of Incest." *American Anthropologist* (1948), 50:416–435.

Willell, Ralph, ed. *The Merrill Studies in "Pierre."* Columbus, Ohio: Charles E. Merrill, 1971.

Wilson, W. Daniel. "Science, Natural Law, and Unwitting Sibling Incest in Eighteenth-Century Literature." In O. M. Brack, Jr., ed., *Studies in Eighteenth-Century Culture.* vol 13. Madison: University of Wisconsin Press, 1984.

Wilson, Edward O. *On Human Nature.* Cambridge: Harvard University Press, 1978.

—— *Sociobiology: The New Synthesis.* Cambridge, Ma.: Harvard University Press, 1975.

Wilson, James D. "Incest and American Romantic Fiction." *Studies in the Literary Imagination* (1974), 7:31–50. Reprinted as ch. 6 of *The Romantic Heroic Ideal.* Baton Rouge: Louisiana State University Press, 1982.

Wilson, Peter J. *Man, the Promising Primate: The Conditions of Human Evolution.* New Haven: Yale University Press, 1980.

Witham, W. Tasker. *The Adolescent in the American Novel, 1920–1960.* New York: Ungar, 1964.

Wohl, Anthony H. "Sex and the Single Room: Incest Among the Victorian Working Classes." In Anthony H. Wohl, ed., *The Victorian Family: Structure and Stresses.* New York: St. Martin's Press, 1978.

Wood, Barbi, and Jack Geasland, *Twins.* New York: Putnam, 1977.

Woodbury, J., and E. Schwartz. *The Silent Sin: A Case History of Incest.* New York: American Library, 1971.

Wordsworth, Dorothy. *Journals.* Mary Moorman, ed. New York: Oxford University Press, 1971.

Wormhoudt, Arthur. *The Demon Lover: A Psychoanalytic Approach to Literature.* New York: Exposition Press, 1949.

Yorke, Mrs. R. M. P. *Romance of Smyra, or The Prediction Fulfilled!!!.* 4 vols. London: Earle and Hemet, 1801.

Yorukoglu, Atalay, and John P. Kemph. "Children Not Severely Damaged by Incest with Parent." *Journal of the American Academy of Child Psychiatry* (1966), 5:111–124.

Young, Philip. *Hawthorne's Secret: An Un-Told Tale.* Boston: David R. Godine, 1984.

Ziff, Larzer. "A Reading of *Wieland*." *PMLA* (1962), 77:51–57.

Zipes, Jack. *The Trials and Tribulations of Little Red Riding Hood: Versions of the Tale in Sociocultural Context.* South Hadley, Mass.: Bergin and Garvey, 1983.

Index